THE ACTIVIST

THE ACTIVIST

John Marshall, Marbury v. Madison,
and the Myth of Judicial Review

LAWRENCE GOLDSTONE

WALKER & COMPANY

NEW YORK

Published by Walker Publishing Company, Inc., New York

All papers used by Walker & Company are natural, recyclable products made
from wood grown in well-managed forests. The manufacturing processes conform
to the environmental regulations of the country of origin.

All illustrations are from the Library of Congress except page 168, from the collection
of the Supreme Court of the United States, and page 207, from the Free Library of
Philadelphia.

LIBRARY OF CONGRESS CATALOGING-IN-PUBLICATION DATA HAS BEEN APPLIED FOR.

ISBN-10: 0-8027-1488-9
ISBN-13: 978-0-8027-1488-6

Visit Walker & Company's Web site at www.walkerbooks.com

First U.S. edition 2008

1 3 5 7 9 10 8 6 4 2

Typeset by Westchester Book Group
Printed in the United States of America by Quebecor World Fairfield

To Nancy and Emily

Contents

ONE

LAW AND POLITICS

In a 1996 speech at Catholic University titled "A Theory of Constitution Interpretation," Antonin Scalia, associate justice of the United States Supreme Court, noted, "I belong to a school, a small but hardy school, called 'textualists' or 'originalists.'" Describing the meaning of those terms, Justice Scalia observed, "If you are a textualist, you don't care about the intent, and I don't care if the framers of the Constitution had some secret meaning in mind when they adopted its words. I take the words as they were promulgated to the people of the United States, and what is the fairly understood meaning of those words."[1]

To an originalist, then, anything not specifically enunciated in the Constitution cannot be the law.

But Justice Scalia admitted that there is an exception: "The Constitution of the United States nowhere says that the Supreme Court shall be the last word on what the Constitution means. Or that the Supreme Court shall have the authority to disregard statutes enacted by the Congress of the United States on the ground that in its view they do not comport with the Constitution. It doesn't say that anywhere. We made it up."

But the justice is in no way being critical of his brethren for constitutional overreaching. Nor is he denying the right of the Supreme Court to overturn acts of Congress. Quite the contrary. "Now, we made it up very sensibly," Justice Scalia went on, "because what we said was, 'Look, a Constitution is a law, it's a sort of super-law . . . and what the law means is the job of the courts." Since judicial review, the authority to declare acts of Congress and the president unconstitutional, is therefore simply an obvious and universally accepted facet of the Supreme Court's role, it follows that whether or not the Constitution has specifically granted the Court the right of that power is irrelevant.

To buttress his argument, in his speech Justice Scalia began where every other American judge begins, with the most famous and important judicial opinion in United States history, that of Chief Justice John Marshall in the 1803 case of *Marbury v. Madison.*

If there is a seminal case in American jurisprudence, it is *Marbury.* The Supreme Court's unanimous decision in that case, rendered by the chief justice, not only established the right of judicial review but also drastically redefined the notion of separation of powers that had emerged from the Constitutional Convention sixteen years before. The lead entry in almost every constitutional law textbook, Marshall's ruling has spawned an unequaled volume of analysis by legal scholars and historians. Over the years, *Marbury* has seen its impact extend well beyond legal precedent to become a cornerstone of American government itself. In recasting the Court's role in American government, Marshall opened the door for expansion of judicial authority into other areas not anticipated—or intended—by the framers. Thus, in 2000, five government appointees with life tenure, whose fitness to continue in office would never be tested at the ballot box, may well have decided a presidential election.

Marbury itself arose out of a bitter feud between John Adams's Federalists and the Democratic-Republican Party of Thomas Jefferson.* In the election of 1800, after a brutal campaign, Adams, the incumbent, lost the presidency. Federalists lost control of Congress as well. These dual defeats were made all the more indigestible since the new Republican majority had been made possible in no small part by the provision in the Constitution allowing slaves, predominantly in the South, to be counted as three fifths of a person in determining a state's apportionment in Congress, thus allowing slave states a disproportion of electoral votes.†

---

* "John Adams's Federalists" is something of a misnomer, since there were large numbers of Federalists under the spiritual leadership of Alexander Hamilton, often called "High Federalists," who detested Adams almost as much as Jefferson and plotted actively for his defeat. Under the circumstances, that Adams did as well as he did was amazing.
† Without the electoral bulk that slave states achieved through the 3/5 compromise, Adams would have been re-elected, 63–61.

Although Adams had been decisively beaten, through a quirk in the constitutional provision for choosing a president in which electors cast votes for president and vice president without stipulating which vote was for which office, the Electoral College deadlocked and it fell to the House of Representatives to choose the winner.* Late in January 1801, facing the likelihood that Jefferson would ultimately prevail, Adams appointed his secretary of state, John Marshall, to be chief justice of the Supreme Court, replacing the recently retired Oliver Ellsworth. Marshall was confirmed on February 4 but agreed also to remain on as secretary of state until Adams's term ended.[2] Although he was a Virginian like Jefferson—they were, in fact, cousins— Marshall was an ardent Federalist who loathed Jefferson personally. (The sentiment was heartily reciprocated.) Marshall could thus be counted on to use the Court wherever possible to curb the new president's power.

The battle for electors dragged on, and not until February 17, after thirty-six votes in the House, did Thomas Jefferson finally receive enough votes to be confirmed as the third president of the United States. The final ballot came only fifteen days before the scheduled inauguration on March 4.

Although they had been turned out of two branches of the government, Federalists had no intention of melting quietly away. In their last weeks in the lame-duck Congress, Federalist legislators had voted to create seven new federal circuit courts, to be manned by nineteen new judges. Hundreds of administrative officers and minor judgeships were also added to the federal court system. Among these were an undefined number of justices of the peace for the new national capital in the District of Columbia, each of whom would serve a five-year term.† Packing the judiciary with loyal party members, Federalists felt, was the only way to ensure that at least one branch of government remained beyond the reach of Jefferson and his rabble. Jefferson grumbled that the Federalists "have retired into the judiciary as a strong hold."[3]

On March 2, his next-to-last day in office, as part of a flurry of eleventh-hour activity, Adams nominated forty-two justices of the peace for the capital

---

* It was not Adams who finished second, but rather Jefferson's vice presidential candidate, Aaron Burr.

† The District of Columbia was originally a ten-mile-square city with sections on either side of the Potomac. In 1801, the Maryland side was designated Washington County ("Washington, D.C.") and the Virginia side Alexandria County (which was called "Alexandria, D.C."), and citizens of each county were allowed to vote in the appropriate state. In 1846, Alexandria County reverted to Virginia, and Washington was all that remained of the District.

district. This was an absurd number of judges for a city that was still largely swamp and whose population was only a few thousand. These nominations, one of which was for a Federalist functionary named William Marbury, were ratified by the Senate the following day. According to law, in addition to ratification, the official commissions had to be "signed, sealed, and delivered" before taking effect. Adams and Marshall sat up by candlelight in the President's House, as the White House was then called, until the early hours of inauguration day affixing both their signatures and the seal of the United States to each of the documents, thus earning the appointments the sobriquet "Midnight Judges." Then, at four in the morning, Adams left town so as not to be forced to attend Jefferson's swearing-in.

All that remained was for Secretary of State Marshall to deliver the commissions to the new judges. Through carelessness or oversight—Marshall later wrote to his brother James that "the extreme hurry of the time" and the absence of the chief clerk were responsible—many of the commissions lay undelivered when Marshall had to hurry off to the special session of Congress in which he was to swear in President-elect Jefferson. Among those who did not receive his signed and sealed commission was William Marbury.

After assuming the presidency, Jefferson discovered Marshall's blunder and ordered that none of the overlooked commissions be delivered. Then Jefferson proceeded to void the appointments.*

Undeterred, Marbury did everything he could to obtain his commission. He wrote letters, petitioned officials of the new administration, and eventually worked his way to a personal meeting with James Madison, whom Jefferson had appointed to replace Marshall in the cabinet. The new secretary of state would not be moved. There was no way, Marbury was told, that he would receive his warrant.†

Finally, in December 1801, Marbury (joined by three others)‡ sued to gain his judgeship, asking for a writ of *mandamus* (literally "we order"), which directs a public agency or governmental body to perform an act required by law when it has neglected or refused to do so. Instead of opting for

---

* Jefferson eventually relented and accepted all but seventeen of Adams's appointments.
† Marbury, who was from Baltimore, was an especially attractive target. A fervent Adams supporter, he made no secret that he favored a change in the way presidential electors were selected in Maryland. If Marbury had had his way, it might have tipped the balance of the election and returned Adams to the White House for a second term.

the recently empaneled federal circuit court in the District of Columbia, the four chose to take their suit directly to the Supreme Court. Marbury and his cohorts doubtless assumed that by placing the case before a political ally—and the same man whose negligence had created the grounds for the action in the first place—their claim would receive a sympathetic hearing.[5] For the basis of their claim, the four plaintiffs cited Section 13 of the Judiciary Act of 1789, the legislation by which the First Congress had laid out a detailed plan for the judicial branch of the federal government.[6] Because they chose this particular piece of legislation and this particular court in which to press their claim, William Marbury and his three co-litigants set off a constitutional crisis that has reverberated for more than two centuries.

Chief Justice Marshall did not, in fact, welcome Marbury's decision to seek redress from his court. He knew all too well that if he sided with his fellow Federalist and ordered Marbury's commission to be delivered, Jefferson would simply refuse, and Marshall had no means to compel him to comply.[*] The Court's authority would therefore be weakened, thus defeating the Federalist scheme to maintain its power through the judiciary. If he denied Marbury's claim, he would be using a Federalist bastion to strengthen Jefferson's power to make arbitrary rulings, an equally unpalatable alternative.

The case was not decided for fifteen months. That Marshall found a way through the thicket changed American history.[7] With inspired misdirection, he began his opinion with a complete validation of Marbury's claim. Yes, Marbury had been properly appointed; yes, he was entitled to receive his commission; yes, Secretary of State Madison had been obligated to deliver that commission; and no, neither the president nor his secretary of state had had a right to void the appointment.

Unfortunately, however, Marshall went on, Marbury had originated his suit before the Supreme Court under Section 13 of the Judiciary Act. Although the wording is ambiguous, Section 13 seems to grant the Supreme Court only appellate jurisdiction in issuing writs of *mandamus*. From here, what Marshall should have done—and what any subsequent court would have done—was return the case to the lower court with appropriate jurisdiction.[8]

---

[*] Two decades later, another Marshall antagonist, Andrew Jackson, would state famously, "The chief justice has made his ruling. Now let him enforce it."

But instead of allowing the case to be heard in circuit court, where he would have no control over the outcome, Marshall chose to hear *Marbury* anyway, a ploy that allowed him to shift the argument from the validity of Marbury's suit to the validity of Section 13. Section 13, he then ruled, was in contradiction to Article III of the Constitution, which had not expressly granted original jurisdiction to the Supreme Court in such cases. And, since the Judiciary Act was now in conflict with the Constitution, at least according to Marshall, one of the two had to be set aside.

Not surprisingly, in his ruling of February 24, 1803, the chief justice declared Section 13 of the Judiciary Act unconstitutional and Marbury's suit, although he was in the right, was dismissed because he no longer had a valid statute on which to support his petition. Marshall had thus succeeded in denouncing Jefferson for violating Marbury's civil rights without being forced to issue a writ of *mandamus*, which Jefferson would certainly have ignored.

Now Jefferson was in a bind. If he did nothing, he was tacitly granting power to the Federalist Supreme Court to oversee the constitutionality of legislative acts, a repugnant alternative. The only way to avoid setting such a precedent was to deliver commissions to Marbury and the others, thereby undermining his authority throughout the Union.

Jefferson chose to continue to refuse the commissions, and the power of judicial review was born. With his ruling, John Marshall forever expanded the role of the federal judiciary in American life. He went on to serve for thirty-two more years, going down in history as "the second father of the Constitution—the man who made the Court supreme."[9]

After *Marbury*, the Supreme Court became not merely the instrument to determine questions of "Law and Equity," as specified in Article III, Section 2 of the Constitution, but also the final authority on the meaning and application of the Constitution itself. The right to interpret the law, to say "what the Constitution means," passed from the legislature to the judiciary. This was no accident or unintended byproduct—in his *Marbury* opinion, Chief Justice Marshall announced his intention of claiming that very role.[10] Although the Supreme Court would not again strike down a federal statute for another fifty-four years, in another inflammatory case—*Dred Scott v. Sandford*—the power of constitutional oversight is now one of the Supreme Court's most potent weapons.

After *Marbury*, justices' constitutional philosophy became every bit as important as their knowledge of statutes. At first, this meant that Marshall's Federalist views, which emphasized strong central authority and separation of powers, were pitted against Jefferson's, which favored decentralization and popular sovereignty. The terms "strict construction" and "broad construction," therefore, were—and are still—not so much philosophies in and of themselves, but rather political positions determined by whether or not one's viewpoint was at the time dominant in the Court.

Stanley Elkins and Eric McKitrick, in their wise and profound *Age of Federalism*, asserted that strict construction is "the resort of persons under ideological strain." Strict constructionists prefer to "renounce a range of positive opportunities for action in return for a principle which will inhibit government from undertaking a range of things one does not approve of." Rather than view the Constitution as an instrument of progress, they prefer to use the document "as a protection against those designs of others which have come to be seen as usurping and corrupting."[11] Under the Marshall court, then, Federalists who favored expanding the power of the judiciary were accused of broad construction by the strict-construction Republicans who wanted to restrain it. As the Republicans slowly began to supplant Federalists in the judiciary, those terms would reverse. Throughout American history, the terms have continued to skate about, depending on whether liberals or conservatives (two other often variable terms) have held the reins of power.

Without Marshall's bloodless coup in *Marbury*, then, terms such as "originalism," "textualism," "strict construction," "broad construction," and "original intent" might have merely remained fodder for legal theorists, the subject of poorly attended graduate school seminars. With *Marbury*, however, these terms and the points of view that they represent spilled over into mainstream politics and became one of the most hotly contested issues of government. The uneasy balance between legal application and political application was—and, after two centuries, still is—at the root of the debate over strict construction and broad construction. At its crux, the clash of philosophies pivots on whether or not the framers of the Constitution intended to grant final authority to the one branch of government that is not subject to popular will and whose members, once appointed, serve without oversight for the rest of their lives.

In this, Justice Scalia's argument is very powerful. The Constitution proclaims itself the "supreme law of the land," and so the text of that document is, to use the justice's term, "a super-law." And who more than those who represent the pinnacle of legal knowledge and achievement, the justices of the Supreme Court, should be entrusted to administer and evaluate this law?

Once again, however, the argument teeters on whether or not the Court and the sitting justices are seen as judicial or political beings. Justice Scalia would certainly assert himself to be the former, one who therefore exercises judgment objectively—or as objectively as possible—basing decisions only on law and precedent, removed from the grime of power politics. In this, the justice would get no argument from virtually every other justice, law school professor, and legal scholar, regardless of location on the conservative/liberal continuum. After all, responsibility to "say what the law means" certainly implies the elimination of point of view or partisanship. Justice Scalia quite rightly decries any judge who rules on a case simply based on his or her opinion of what the law should be, in other words, makes up law on the fly to suit personal taste. It is the very essence of originalism to avoid such tortured subjectivity. If this is true, it would seem to make perfect sense that the Constitution would implicitly and inarguably grant the power of interpretation to the Court.

But the Constitution is, after all, not only America's supreme legal instrument, but also its preeminent political document. It is used not only to determine questions of justice, but also of power. It provides not only rules whereby one party can prevail over another in a court of law, but also at the ballot box, and ultimately the councils of government. Thus the question of whether or not the Supreme Court has the right to inject itself into the political process becomes intertwined with its post-*Marbury* role of applying the law.

It is not uncommon for one person or group of persons—originalists, for example—to decide that their understanding of the text is objectively true while their adversaries are merely "interpreting" or "extrapolating." At that point, originalism ceases to be a legal term and becomes a political one. If Supreme Court justices, regardless of ideology, cannot help but function as political beings—to "legislate from the bench"—it would seem inconceivable that the framers, who took such enormous pains to create a government based in elections and on mutual accountability, would have granted the overarching power to define the Constitution to an unelected, unaccountable body.

Yet Americans are regularly told, not only by most of those who study government, but also by journalists and commentators, that the executive and legislative are the two "political" branches of government, thereby implying that the judicial branch is somehow above politics. This definition obviates the need for political control, thus allowing the judiciary to function without significant checks in a checks-and-balances system.*

Vital, then, is to disentangle the political and the judicial qualities of both the Constitution and the Court, both in the present and in historical context. A determination of to what extent *Marbury v. Madison* was a judicial act and to what extent political will provide great insight into what extent originalism is a judicial doctrine and to what extent political.

Tracing the evolution of the Court and the judicial branch from their formation at the Constitutional Convention in 1787, then proceeding through the events leading up to the case, examining the outcome and Marshall's opinion—and doing so through a textualist's eye, subjecting *Marbury* to the test Justice Scalia advocates for other questions before the Court—is the best way in which to reach such a determination. Only if tangible evidence exists that Convention delegates, ratification delegates, senators and representatives who passed judiciary legislation, and even other justices, saw the courts as textualists do, will it be possible to determine whether or not, as Justice Scalia says, judicial review is a self-evident aspect of the Supreme Court's power.

So, with *Marbury* goes textualism. Either it is a philosophy on how to view the law, or it is simply a different sort of rationalization that allows its proponents to grab for political power.

---

* Impeachment being a difficult, unwieldy, and therefore rare alternative.

PART I

CREATING A JUDICIARY

TWO

CONVENTION: A FEW GOOD MEN

F ROM MAY 25 TO SEPTEMBER 17, 1787, a federal convention met in secret on the ground floor of the State House in Philadelphia with the aim of refashioning the Articles of Confederation by which the fledgling United States had been governed since 1781.[1] Congress had petitioned all thirteen states to send representatives to this meeting, and eventually fifty-five men from twelve states did take part, only Rhode Island refusing to participate. While a few of the men who attended, most notably James Madison, saw the convention as an opportunity to scrap the Articles entirely and start from scratch, most had assumed that the Philadelphia conclave would be just another in a string of feeble attempts at reform. As a result, many of the delegates exhibited a marked lack of enthusiasm and contributed next to nothing during the four months. Attendance, even among the committed, could generously be described as spotty, and no more than ten of the fifty-five were present for all of the sessions.* A small percentage of delegates dominated the debates; although thirty-nine of them eventually signed the Constitution, in a very real sense fewer than twenty could truly be called "framers."† Perhaps the less zealous members did not realize the role that history had staked out

---

* Madison attended every day, but the two delegates from New Hampshire did not arrive until late July. Two of the three delegates from New York walked out in early July and the third, Alexander Hamilton, was absent for more than half of the meetings. With voting by state, for much of the convention, that left only ten states available to pass on the most important issues facing the new nation. In addition, George Wythe, a highly respected delegate from Virginia, left almost immediately, and John Dickinson of Delaware was absent for much of the Convention. Most of the other delegates came and went regularly.

† Some of the supporters were not present for the signing but subsequently supported ratification in their home states.

for them, since most expected to retain both the form of the existing government and the power and prerogative of the individual states. Figuring out how to give a central government more power without sacrificing any themselves did not promise to be a gratifying exercise.

The men who came to Philadelphia were an appropriate group to create a document that would be "the supreme law of the land." Of the fifty-five, fully thirty-five have been described as "lawyers" or having "some legal training."[2] The percentage is higher still in the group that did most of the talking. Of those roughly seventeen, thirteen had substantial legal training or experience. Even so, pragmatic trial lawyers like South Carolina's John Rutledge or Luther Martin of Maryland had little in common with legal theorists like Madison.

Under the Articles of Confederation, the government of the United States consisted of only one branch, the legislative, with only a single house of Congress. There was no executive and no national judiciary;[3] general agreement existed that if the government was to be strengthened, both would be required. Deciding how to establish each of these new departments and what powers to give them, however, was a thornier matter.

With the executive, the chief stumbling block was a lack of consensus among the delegates on even the fundamental definition of a head of state. Should the executive be one man or three? How long should he serve? Should he be eligible for reelection? How should he be elected? What powers should he exercise? What should be the limitations on those powers? Should he be called "Your Excellency"? All of these were brought to the floor, discussed, voted on, then scrapped, only to have the process begin again. More than sixty separate votes were ultimately required to complete Article II of the Constitution. The delegates were forced to spend such time and energy working through these permutations because, although the need for some form of head of state was unquestioned, no institution was in place that might serve as a model. State executives, where they existed, would not do.[4] These offices were deemed either too parochial or too arbitrary to fit into a checks-and-balances system. There was no alternative for the delegates but to grind it out.

A national judiciary faced a different set of obstacles. Although the need for some form of national *court* was apparent, many delegates opposed a national court *system*. Each state already had a functioning legal apparatus whose power and responsibility would necessarily be diminished as those of a national judiciary were enhanced. The delegates, therefore, were reluctant to grant any national court too broad a scope. Moreover, state courts were seen by many as tools of the rich, the instrument by which creditors enforced their claims on debtors—often struggling farmers—and helped centralize first economic and then political power.[5] Placing a high court in the national capital or lower courts in state population centers (where federal courts were likely to sit) would further disenfranchise and disillusion the common man.

Federal courts offered other troubling scenarios. Ceding local or state control over the judiciary to a national court that might not contain a single member from one's own state promised to raise a significant howl. As the powers granted a national court increased, the fear that federal judges would act despotically toward individual state governments increased as well. South Carolinians or Virginians justifiably wondered whether a supreme court would undercut the rights of slaveholders, while New Englanders feared an active judiciary limiting rights to commerce. Add to that the projected cost of a federal court system to a virtually bankrupt nation, and it is not difficult to understand why the delegates in Philadelphia were inclined to tread lightly in empowering the national judiciary.

As a result, after the delegates agreed on a national tribunal—a "supreme court"—vast disagreement remained on whether the new government should include a national court system at all. An alternative was to empower state courts to simply expand their jurisdictions and hear federal cases, with the Supreme Court exercising appellate power over their decisions. Yet in some cases, such as maritime claims or those involving ambassadors or other foreign officials, many delegates were not willing to entrust jurisdiction to state courts. Because of all this uncertainty, details of the actual structure of the court system seemed far less urgent—and less advisable—to define than those of the legislature or the executive.

Thus, compared to the protracted negotiations over the other two branches, the makeup of the judiciary was hardly debated. Even the descriptions in the Virginia Plan and New Jersey Plan* were remarkably similar.

---

* The Virginia Plan, presented on May 28 by Edmund Randolph but written almost entirely by James Madison, has also been called the "large states plan," in that apportionment in the legislature was by population and therefore favored the more populous states. The New Jersey Plan, written and presented by William Paterson on June 15, has also been called the "small states plan," in that apportionment in the legislature was by state, as then existed under the Articles of Confederation, and therefore favored the less populous states. Charles Pinckney of South Carolina and Alexander Hamilton of New York also presented detailed plans of government, but neither was debated by the delegates.

Madison's resolution in the Virginia Plan began: "that a National Judiciary be established to consist of one or more supreme tribunals, and of inferior tribunals to be chosen by the National Legislature, to hold their offices during good behaviour; and to receive punctually at stated times fixed compensation for their services, in which no increase or diminution shall be made so as to affect the persons actually in office at the time of such increase or diminution."[6] The only changes William Paterson made in the New Jersey Plan, submitted later, were to eliminate the provision for "inferior tribunals" and stipulate that judges be appointed by the executive rather than the legislature.[7]

As to powers, there was significant overlap as well. Madison gave the inferior federal tribunals original jurisdiction and the Supreme Court appellate jurisdiction over all federal cases. Paterson favored having federal cases originate in state courts, heard by state judges (who, in these cases, would be required to adhere to federal law), with the Supreme Court again holding appellate jurisdiction. Both plans provided the Supreme Court with final authority over "all piracies & felonies on the high seas," "captures from an enemy," and "the collection of the National revenue." Paterson granted the Supreme Court original jurisdiction over impeachments of "National officers," while Madison kept original jurisdiction in the "inferior tribunals." Whereas Paterson gave the Supreme Court jurisdiction over "acts for regulation of trade," Madison proposed a sweeping power under which the Supreme Court could rule over "questions which may involve the national peace and harmony." Neither plan specified the size or composition of the Supreme Court, nor did either address—or anticipate—granting the Court the power to nullify laws passed by Congress.

Debate on what was to become Article III, Section 1, which laid out the structure of the national court system, was cursory. The only two issues of contention, both of which were raised before Paterson submitted the New Jersey Plan, had been a minor disagreement as to whether the legislative or the executive branch should appoint judges, and whether or not to create "inferior tribunals."* The first was settled without debate in favor of the executive, and the second was not settled at all.

John Rutledge, the ardent proponent of states' rights from South Carolina, insisted, as did Paterson, that state courts should hear federal cases

---

* This latter argument was to resurface in the ratifying debates.

first and they should "decide . . . the right of appeal to the supreme national tribunal." Creating distinct lower federal courts would be "an unnecessary encroachment on the jurisdiction of the States and create unnecessary obstacles to their adoption of the new system."[8]

But Madison replied that without lower federal courts "dispersed throughout the Republic," which could render final judgments, "appeals would be multiplied to a most oppressive degree." Madison saw risk precisely where Rutledge saw virtue—that state courts would interpret federal law as they saw fit. He added, "An effective Judiciary establishment commensurate to the legislative authority, was essential. A Government without a proper Executive & Judiciary would be the mere trunk of a body, without arms or legs to act or move."[9]

In the end, the delegates decided to allow for "such inferior Courts as Congress may from time to time ordain and establish." This was less compromise than abdication. With any number of incendiary issues to resolve, they seemed reluctant to add the judiciary to the mix, especially when

James Madison

vagueness appeared to solve the immediate problem nicely. It was a decision that would have serious ramifications in the months ahead.

An additional debate ensued over what would become Article III, Section 2, which laid out the power of the federal courts, but even here the delegates eventually chose to keep the wording broad and the definitions general.[10] The sense of the Convention that the Supreme Court should be primarily an appellate body, having only original jurisdiction in cases "affecting Ambassadors, other public Ministers and Consuls, and those in which a State shall be Party," was accepted without significant debate.

Although neither Section 1 nor Section 2 mentions judicial review, most legal scholars have agreed with Justice Scalia that the formal power of a supreme court to overturn acts of the legislature or executive orders was tacitly accepted by the delegates as an obvious and understood power of the federal courts.[11] This assertion is generally supported in two ways. First, a number of the delegates made statements in the Convention that seem to indicate either that they favored judicial review or that they considered it implicit in the judicial function.[12] Second, various state provisions seem to indicate that judicial review, as an enunciation of separation of powers, was already an integral part of state government and could therefore logically be expected to be extended to any national system.

Indeed, with twenty-first-century eyes, separation of powers seems to have become a generally accepted notion by 1787. The Virginia Declaration of Rights, for example, in Article V, stated quite plainly:

> The legislative and executive powers of the State should be separate and distinct from the judiciary; and that the members of the two first may be restrained from oppression, by feeling and participating the burdens of the people, they should, at fixed periods, be reduced to a private station, return into that body from which they were originally taken, and the vacancies be supplied by frequent, certain, and regular elections, in which all, or any part of the former members, to be again eligible, or ineligible, as the laws shall direct.[13]

Nonetheless, not at all clear is whether Virginians meant that the courts could negate laws passed by the legislature, for plainly stated in Article VII (which is understandably quoted less frequently by partisans of judicial review) is that "All power of suspending laws, or the execution of laws, by any authority, without consent of the representatives of the people, is injurious to their rights, and ought not to be exercised."[14]

The Massachusetts constitution also contained provisions that seem to both allow and restrict judicial review, although the latter is more firmly asserted than the former. Article XXX gave a somewhat ambiguous blessing to judicial oversight. "In the government of this commonwealth, the legislative department shall never exercise the executive and judicial powers, or either of them: the executive shall never exercise the legislative and judicial powers, or either of them: the judicial shall never exercise the legislative and executive powers, or either of them: to the end it may be a government of laws and not of men."[15] But Article XX explicitly stated, "The power of suspending the laws, or the execution of the laws, ought never to be exercised but by the legislature, or by authority derived from it, to be exercised in such particular cases only as the legislature shall expressly provide for."[16] Both Virginia and Massachusetts specifically recommended that judges hold office for as long as they exercised "good behavior," which also meant that they would never be answerable to the people at the ballot box. It seems likely, therefore, that the legislators of each state would have been leery of granting lifetime appointees the uncontrolled power to review laws they themselves had passed.

Certainly, many of the delegates to the Philadelphia Convention arrived envisioning a role for the judiciary in enforcing a separation of powers. Still, given the confusion even in those states where some form of judicial oversight was present, the exact role that the judiciary might play in providing a check on the legislature was by no means clear.

While judicial oversight was mentioned by a number of delegates in the course of the debates, "judicial review" in the modern sense was never discussed at all at the Convention. The power of the judiciary to overturn an act of the legislature that it considered in violation of the Constitution was raised almost exclusively with regard to the court's participation in a "council of revision," in which the Supreme Court, with the executive, would essentially sign off on every congressional act.[17] But granting the Court a limited veto power over Congress is not at all the same thing as ceding it final authority to "say what the Constitution means." Vetoes can, after all, be overridden by the same body that passed the law; whereas, once declared unconstitutional, a law can only be reinstated by amendment. The judiciary's role in the legislative process was deliberated extensively (judicial checks on the executive did not come up at all), and from these discussions it is indeed

possible to get a sense of whether or not the delegates favored the far different review power as later enunciated in *Marbury*.[18]

Judicial veto was divided into two distinct questions. The first, which occupied the preponderance of the debate, was based in section 8 of the Virginia Plan, which proposed that the Executive and "a convenient number of
the National Judiciary" comprise a council of revision "with authority to examine every act of the National Legislature before it shall [become law]." If
the council rejected the law, and it could do so on any grounds it chose, the
legislation would be returned to Congress.[19]

This council of revision, then, was to have the same role as is currently enjoyed exclusively by the president in striking down legislative acts. The Virginia Plan provision had not specified whether the council's veto power was to
be limited simply to laws that ran counter to the Constitution, or whether it
should have a much broader application, including any law deemed "unjust,"
and each interpretation had a number of powerful adherents. In either case,
however, a veto might ultimately be merely a holding action against the legislature in which, as is the case today, a super-majority could then reinstate the
measure.

The second question, which was never extensively discussed, applied
specifically to the judiciary and was confined simply to whether or not a
court had the right to refuse to enforce a law that it considered counter to
the Constitution. While the distinction between "refuse to enforce" and
"strike down" seems trivial, it was far weightier in 1787, when the judicial
system was not hierarchical and it was by no means assured that even the
Supreme Court's refusal to enforce an act of the legislature would have anything but local impact.

The Virginia Plan proposal for a council of revision first came to the floor
on June 4. Elbridge Gerry, a maverick from Massachusetts, opened the debate by questioning whether the judiciary should be part of such a council.
The national courts, he asserted, "will have a sufficient check agst. encroachments on their own department by their exposition of the laws, which involved a power of deciding on their Constitutionality." Gerry's remarks are
invariably cited as proof that delegates favored judicial review, sometimes
but not always with the admission that Gerry himself refused to sign the
Constitution.

To show how sweeping this power could be, Gerry added, "In some States the Judges have actually set aside laws as being agst. [state] Constitutions." Instead, Gerry proposed that "the National Executive shall have a right to negative [sic; the word meant "negate" or "veto" at the time] any Legislative act which shall not be afterwards passed by parts of each branch of the national Legislature." What is significant in this motion is that in saying "any Legislative act," Gerry seems to have proposed that the national executive be empowered to strike down state as well as federal laws.

Rufus King seconded Gerry's motion. Madison, who had after all written the Virginia Plan and strongly favored a council of revision, maintained in his notes that King claimed "that the Judges ought to be able to expound the law as it should come before them, free from the bias of having participated in its formation," thus indicating that King favored judicial review as well. Robert Yates of New York, however, who also took notes on the proceedings until he left in early July, reported in his journal that "Mr. King was against the interference of the judicial [as] they may be biased in the interpretation," which has a different meaning entirely. King, according to Yates, "therefore [proposed] to give the executive a complete negative."[20]

As Gerry and King tried to limit the judiciary's role in the council, James Wilson tried to push the power of shared control over the legislature still further.* He was "for varying the proposition in such a manner as to give the Executive & Judiciary jointly an absolute negative." Another of the delegates cited as favoring judicial review, Wilson was here looking for a much broader power, a means by which the federal government could maintain control over the states, not a separation of powers within the federal government itself. He was joined by Hamilton in a motion to amend Gerry's motion. "There was no danger they thought of such a power being too much exercised," Madison noted, as Hamilton pointed out that "the King of G. B. had not exerted his negative since the Revolution."

After Gerry insisted that a veto without recourse was too extreme, Benjamin Franklin noted that in Pennsylvania, "the negative of the Governor was constantly made use of to extort money. No good law whatever could be passed without a private bargain with him. An increase of his salary, or

---

* Unlike businessmen Gerry and King, Wilson was a lawyer himself and always envisioned a larger role for judges than many of his colleagues. He would eventually serve on the Supreme Court.

some donation, was always made a condition; till at last it became the regular practice, to have orders in his favor on the Treasury, presented along with the bills to be signed, so that he might actually receive the former before he should sign the latter." He favored including the judiciary in the oversight function, since "if the Executive was to have a Council, such a power would be less objectionable."

Although no one had discussed the notion of granting judges an absolute veto over legislative action, which, in the end, is the essence of judicial review, the notion of one branch being able to frustrate the other two was clearly anathema to many of the delegates. Roger Sherman agreed with Gerry and Franklin, noting that he was "agst. enabling any one man to stop the will of the whole." Gunning Bedford of Delaware pronounced himself against any check on the legislature at all. He thought it "sufficient to mark out in the Constitution the boundaries to the Legislative Authority, which would give all the requisite security to the rights of the other departments. The Representatives of the People were the best judges of what was for their interest, and ought to be under no external controul whatever." Even George Mason IV, who was later to frame a description of judicial review that would be very close to Marshall's, presented an impassioned denunciation of granting a power without check. Raising the dread specter of hereditary monarchy, Mason insisted that "he never could agree to give up all the rights of the people to a single Magistrate."[21]

Voting at the Convention, as in the Confederation Congress, was by state, each of which was determined by a majority of its delegates. The motion to grant an absolute veto was defeated, 10 states to 0. While this vote specifically applied only to Gerry's first motion, and thus to the executive alone, the idea of absolute veto, even in regard to a council of revision, had been thoroughly discredited and did not come up again. Apparent, then, is that this debate, which contained so many of the statements later cited by those who claimed that judicial review was an understood part of the judicial function, in fact proves just the opposite. The delegates seemed to perceive separation of powers as more of a game of rock–paper–scissors, with no one branch able to act with impunity against the other two.

After the insertion of a clause providing the power to override a veto if two thirds of each house approved, Gerry's second motion to provide a veto power to the executive alone passed 8–2, only Connecticut and Maryland against.[22] Although proponents tried again the following day to reconsider the decision to exclude the judiciary from the veto process, in which Madison gave a long, impassioned speech defending his council of revision, the measure failed, 8–3.

The question was not dead, however. On July 21, Wilson tried again, proposing once more "that the supreme Natl Judiciary should be associated with the Executive in the Revisionary power." Wilson added that although "this proposition had been before made, and failed," he was so certain of its worth that he "thought it incumbent on him to make another effort."[23]

Once again, as he soon made clear, Wilson was proposing not judicial review, but the ability to strike down laws on a completely subjective basis *even if they conformed to the Constitution.* "The Judiciary ought to have an opportunity of remonstrating agst. projected encroachments on the people as well as on themselves," he went on. "It had been said that the Judges, as expositors of the Laws would have an opportunity of defending their constitutional rights . . . *but this power of the Judges did not go far enough.* Laws may be unjust, may be unwise, may be dangerous, may be destructive; and *yet may not be so unconstitutional as to justify the Judges in refusing to give them effect.*"* Give the judiciary a share in the "reversionary power," Wilson exclaimed, and they will "counteract . . . by the weight of their opinions the improper views of the Legislature." Madison, desperate to save his council of revision, seconded Wilson's motion.

Nathaniel Gorham, who, like Gerry, King, and Caleb Strong, his fellow delegates from Massachusetts, opposed a council of revision, "did not see the advantage of employing the Judges in this way." "Judges," he asserted, "are not to be presumed to possess any peculiar knowledge of the mere policy of public measures." He thought "it would be best to let the Executive alone be responsible, and at most to authorize him to call on Judges for their opinions." Oliver Ellsworth, a judge himself, spoke next and felt that with their "systematic and accurate knowledge of the Laws . . . the aid of the Judges will give more wisdom & firmness to the Executive."

Madison continued to press for the council of revision as "useful to the Community at large as an additional check agst. a pursuit of those unwise & unjust measures which constituted so great a portion of our calamities," and Mason continued to voice his support of a council that "would give

---

* Italics added.

a confidence to the Executive, which he would not otherwise have, and without which the Revisionary power would be of little avail."

Wilson's proposal blurred the distinction between the courts deciding on the constitutional fitness of a law and giving judges a kind of executive power over the legislature. Elbridge Gerry once gain protested that the veto was a balancing mechanism in which judges should play no part. He "conceived of the Revisionary power as merely to secure the Executive department agst. legislative encroachment. The Executive therefore who will best know and be ready to defend his rights ought alone to have the defence of them." Judges should not be given veto power because this would "establish an improper coalition between the Executive & Judiciary departments . . . making Statesmen of the Judges and setting them up as the guardians of the Rights of the people. He relied for his part on the Representatives of the people as the guardians of their Rights & interests." These are hardly the sentiments of a man who wanted the judicial branch to become the ultimate arbiter on constitutionality.

Caleb Strong, another Massachusetts delegate, who would play a major rule in defining the judicial branch, agreed that "the power of making ought to be kept distinct from that of expounding the laws" and added that "judges in exercising the function of expositors might be influenced by the part they had taken in framing the laws."

Gouverneur Morris agreed that "the public liberty was in greater danger from Legislative usurpations than from any other source," and while it was necessary certainly to provide a check on the legislature, "the question is in what hands it should be lodged." The executive, Morris asserted, "appointed for 6 years, and impeachable whilst in office," would not alone "be a very effectual check." The alternative, however, which Morris preferred, was not to leave the power in the hands of the courts, but merely that the executive "be reinforced by the Judiciary department." To support his argument, he turned to England, where "Judges had a great share in ye Legislation. They are consulted in difficult & doubtful cases. They may be & some of them are members of the Legislature. They are or may be members of the privy Council, and can there advise the Executive as they will do with us if the motion succeeds."

But even a combination of the executive and the courts might not be enough. "The interest of our Executive is so inconsiderable & so transitory, and his means of defending it so feeble, that there is the justest ground to fear his want of firmness in resisting encroachments." Morris feared that "the auxiliary firmness and weight of the Judiciary would not supply the deficiency." A council of revision "is indeed a great means of diminishing the evil, yet it is found to be unable to prevent it altogether."

The July 21 debates are often parsed selectively to demonstrate tacit acceptance of judicial review among the delegates. When read in their entirety, however, they once more lead to just the opposite conclusion. The delegates were certainly casting about in an attempt to assign the proper role for both the executive and the judiciary in preventing the legislature from usurping power. But a widespread fear of unbridled judicial authority dominated their thinking as well. Transferring unchecked authority to the Supreme Court to interpret the Constitution—judicial review, at least in the sense referred to by Justice Scalia—did not seem to be on anyone's mind. Notable by its absence was a single specific proposal that approximated the judicial role that Marshall later staked out in *Marbury*.

The closest proposal to Marshall's subsequent formulation came from two non-signers. The first, ironically, was Luther Martin of Maryland, who was to become Marshall's bitter ideological enemy.[24] Ever the opponent of centralized authority, Martin considered "the association of the Judges with the Executive as a dangerous innovation; as well as one which could not produce the particular advantage expected from it. A knowledge of Mankind, and of Legislative affairs cannot be presumed to belong in a higher degree to the Judges than to the Legislature." Martin, a ferocious Anti-Federalist, then enunciated the very position that the Federalist Marshall would seventeen years later. "As to the Constitutionality of laws," Martin insisted, "that point will come before the Judges in their proper official character. In this character they have a negative on the laws."[25]

Madison, who could rarely bring himself to agree with Martin on the time of day, disagreed with him again here, even though Martin had taken the very position that Madison would later espouse in his efforts to get the Constitution ratified. Combining the executive and judiciary in a council of revision, Madison insisted, was in no way a "violation of the maxim which requires the great departments of power to be kept separate & distinct." In fact, Madison asserted, a council of revision would strengthen separation of powers. To support this counterintuitive position, Madison used the same argument of human nature as had Martin. "If a Constitutional discrimination of the departments on paper were a sufficient security to each agst.

encroachments of the others," he observed, "all further provisions would indeed be superfluous. But experience had taught us a distrust of that security; and that it is necessary to introduce such a balance of powers and interests, as will guarantee the provisions on paper. Instead therefore of contenting ourselves with laying down the Theory in the Constitution that each department ought to be separate & distinct, it was proposed to add a defensive power to each which should maintain the Theory in practice." Madison concluded that creating a council of revision with the executive and judiciary "did not blend the departments together."[26]

When Madison had taken his seat, George Mason, who, like Luther Martin, refused to sign the Constitution on September 17, rose and, after noting that "defence of the Executive was not the sole object of the Revisionary power," proceeded to present the most direct case for judicial review that would be expressed in the entire four months.

"Notwithstanding the precautions taken, in the Constitution," Mason observed, "it would still so much resemble that of the individual States, that it must be expected frequently to pass unjust and pernicious laws." Mason refuted Martin's assertion that allowing the judiciary to overturn laws passed by Congress would amount to "a double negative, since in their expository capacity of Judges they would have one negative." Mason asserted that judges "could impede in one case only, the operation of laws. They could declare an unconstitutional law void." If an "oppressive or pernicious law" was not unconstitutional, judges would be "under the necessity . . . to give it a free course." Mason lamented this limitation on judicial oversight and hoped "further use to be made of the Judges, of giving aid in preventing every improper law."

James Wilson once more defended a council of revision. "The separation of the departments," he insisted, "does not require that they should have separate objects but that they should act separately though on the same objects. It is necessary that the two branches of the Legislature should be separate and distinct, yet they are both to act precisely on the same object."

But Elbridge Gerry was having none of it. He would "rather give the Executive an absolute negative for its own defense than thus to blend together the Judiciary & Executive departments. It will bind them together in an offensive and defensive alliance agst. the Legislature, and render the latter unwilling to enter into a contest with them."

Gouverneur Morris, who, unlike Gerry, Mason, and Luther Martin, endorsed the Constitution (and wrote the final draft), then presented a philosophy of separation of powers that is never quoted by advocates of judicial
review. Morris was surprised that any provision securing the effectual separation of the branches of government should be considered an improper mixture of them, and offered an example: "Suppose that the three powers, were to
be vested in three persons, by compact among themselves; that one was to
have the power of making, another of executing, and a third of judging, the
laws." Morris asserted that nothing could be more natural than two parties in
a tripartite agreement acting together to prevent domination by a third. "If
three neighbours," he noted, "had three distinct farms, a right in each to defend his farm agst. his neighbours, tended to blend the farms together."

Nathaniel Gorham of Massachusetts noted that "all agree that a check
on the Legislature is necessary," but he was firmly against "admitting the
Judges to share in it." Gorham was also speaking in the context of a council
of revision. Absent is any affirmation of the right of judges to overturn legislative acts on their own.

After John Rutledge, one of the most successful trial lawyers in the nation,
"thought the Judges of all men the most unfit to be concerned in the revisionary Council. The Judges ought never to give their opinion on a law till it
comes before them," Wilson's motion for a revisionary council failed, although by an extremely close vote, 4–3, with Massachusetts, one of the two
states generally cited as having incorporated judicial review into its own government, providing the margin of defeat. Immediately afterward, the vote to
establish a qualified executive veto, requiring two thirds of each house of the
legislature to override, passed unanimously. If the delegates wished to discuss
a judicial role in the voiding of a law, this was the place to do it, but no delegate raised the issue.

In the end, whether the delegates accepted judicial review as a principle
cannot be discerned from the debates. Their discussions concerned not so
much the power of the judiciary as the balance of power between the legislative and the executive. Lacking specific data to demonstrate that the delegates in Philadelphia considered judicial review an obvious and accepted
power of the Supreme Court, no textualist can rightly extrapolate such an
awesome and virtually unchecked power from Article III. Even if the power
to "expound on the law" is taken to mean that a court might refuse to
enforce a law that it deemed contrary to the Constitution, it would be a

mistake to assume that, for the delegates, it meant the same thing as "striking it down." Many of the very same delegates who asserted the right of exposition for the courts were equally firm on the need to prevent the judiciary from establishing preeminent power over the legislature. And, since the primary aim of a council of revision seemed to be to prevent one branch, the legislature, from encroaching on the power of another, the executive, it is unlikely that the delegates had then favored a principle that would allow the judiciary to encroach on the power of the legislature.

If anything, the evidence that judicial review was specifically omitted from Article III has more weight. As one scholar put it, "the Framers did not mean for the Supreme Court to have the authority to void acts of Congress."[27]

At the close of debate on September 8, the Convention appointed a committee whose task was to "revise the stile of and arrange the articles which had been agreed to by the House." Although the delegates elected an elite group—Madison, Gouverneur Morris, Alexander Hamilton, William Samuel Johnson of Connecticut, and Rufus King—to complete this final draft, the committee immediately delegated the task to Morris, considered the most accomplished writer among them. Four days later, Morris's draft was circulated to the delegates.

He did not disappoint, producing a document that has not only endured as a profound testament to democracy and self-rule, but also one whose flowing and dynamic prose has echoed for more than two centuries. Perhaps the most famous passage in the entire document is the first: "We the people of the United States." Powerful and succinct, nothing captures the very spirit of the Constitution and the roots of its legitimacy more than those seven words.

But in his zeal to create an elegant product, Morris had altered the words of the working document that the Committee of Style had been given as the basis for their work. The Committee of Detail, which created the prototype Constitution in July and early August, had drafted the preamble as, "We the People of the States of New-Hampshire, Massachusetts, Rhode-Island and Providence Plantations, Connecticut, New-York, New-Jersey, Pennsylvania, Delaware, Maryland, Virginia, North-Carolina, South-Carolina, and Georgia, do ordain, declare and establish the following Constitution for the Government of Ourselves and our Posterity."[28] This

wording was accepted without dissent or debate by the delegates and remained when the draft was given to the Committee of Style. The preamble
that emerged in Morris's version was the elegantly crafted "We the People
of the United States, in Order to form a more perfect Union, establish Justice, insure domestic Tranquillity, provide for the common defence, promote the general Welfare, and secure the Blessings of Liberty to ourselves
and our Posterity, do ordain and establish this Constitution for the United
States of America."[29] This new wording was also accepted by the delegates
without dissent or debate.

Morris, of course, was one of the more intense nationalists in Philadelphia, but whether he changed the prologue for political as well as stylistic
reasons will never be known.[30] The political impact, however, was unmistakable. As became clear during the Pennsylvania ratifying convention two
months later, removing the names of the individual states had altered the
very source of legitimacy for the new government, or at least the perception
of it. Rather than drawing legitimacy from states, as had been true under

Gouverneur Morris

the Articles of Confederation, the national government would now draw legitimacy directly from the people, bypassing state governments entirely.

In the Pennsylvania ratifying convention, James Wilson asserted that the United States "is not a government founded upon compact [between states]; it is founded upon the power of the people. They express in their name and their authority, 'We the People do ordain and establish,' &c., from their ratification, and their ratification alone it is to take its constitutional authenticity . . . I know very well all the common-place rant of State sovereignties, and that government is founded in original compact. If that position was examined, it will be found not to accede very well with the true principle of free government. It does not suit the language or genius of the system before us. I think it does not accord with experience, so far as I have been able to obtain information from history."*

Morris's changes would almost certainly not have gone unchallenged if Luther Martin of Maryland had not left the convention in late August. In early 1788, he published a tract, tersely titled "The Genuine Information, delivered to the Legislature of the State of Maryland, relative to the Proceedings of the General Convention, held at Philadelphia, in 1787, by Luther Martin, Esq., Attorney-General of Maryland, and one of the Delegates in the said Convention," in which he detailed his objections to the new Constitution clause by clause. Martin never said or wrote something in one sentence when thirty would do, and Genuine Information is a typically long-winded and rambling treatise. Incurable lack of focus was one reason that Martin has been diminished by both peers and historians (incurable drunkenness was another), but volubility should not deter from a first-rate, incisive intellect and an ability to analyze issues more clearly than he wrote or spoke about them.

Martin saw quite clearly that the United States under the new Constitution

> was not in reality a *federal* but a *national* government, not founded on the principles of the *preservation*, but the *abolition* or *consolidation* of all *State governments* . . . we appeared *totally to have forgot* the business for which we were sent, and the situation of the country for which we were preparing

---

* As the proceedings of the Convention had been kept secret, Wilson was free to pretend that "We the people," rather than "We the people of the states," had been an intentional choice.

our system—that we had not been sent to form a government over the *inhabitants* of America, considered as *individuals* . . . the *system of government* we were *entrusted* to prepare, was a government over *these thirteen States*; but that in our proceedings, we adopted principles which would be right and proper, *only* on the supposition that there were *no State governments at all*, but that *all the inhabitants* of this *extensive continent* were in their *individual capacity, without government*, and in a *state of nature*.[31]

Another defender of states' rights who would certainly have challenged Morris's preamble had he been present in Philadelphia was Patrick Henry. In the Virginia ratifying convention, he also left no doubt that the essential nature of the United States would change if the Constitution was adopted. "That this is a consolidated government is demonstrably clear," Henry said, "and the danger of such a government is, to my mind, very striking. I have the highest veneration for those gentlemen; but, sir, give me leave to demand, What right had they to say, *We, the people*? My political curiosity, exclusive of my anxious solicitude for the public welfare, leads me to ask, Who authorized them to speak the language of, *We, the people*, instead of, *We, the states*? States are the characteristics and the soul of a confederation. If the states be not the agents of this compact, it must be one great, consolidated, national government, of the people of all the states."[32]

The source of legitimacy would be fiercely debated throughout the ratification process and beyond. In once again leaving ambiguous what those who would come later needed made specific, the Convention delegates encouraged the very rifts that a new Constitution was meant to close. On the broad scale, by an unwillingness to describe unequivocally from whence the new government would draw legitimacy, the delegates might certainly be said to have enabled the future Civil War. As to judicial review, Marshall would use the preamble, or at least what he considered to be its understood meaning, as a prime justification for postulating the implicit power of the Supreme Court to interpret the Constitution.

THREE

To the States: The Struggle
to Ratify Begins

Almost from the moment the Constitutional Convention adjourned on September 17, the struggle for ratification began and, with it, the first exercise in constitutional interpretation. The ratification process, therefore, might well be thought of as a sort of "re-convention," albeit spread among the thirteen states that were to decide whether or not they wished to live under this new set of laws. Since records of the Convention itself had been kept secret, members of state conventions would be forced to decide what the delegates had meant in producing the finished document, no simple task since much of the wording was ambiguous.

According to Article VII of the new Constitution, "Ratification of the Conventions of nine States, shall be sufficient for the Establishment of this Constitution between the States so ratifying the Same." The simple act of requiring approval of only nine rather than all thirteen states, as would have been mandatory under the Articles of Confederation, signaled how radical a departure would be this new system. Proponents—dubbed "Federalists"— saw the Constitution as strengthening a fragmented nation whose government had been rendered impotent by the limitations of the Articles, while opponents—"Anti-Federalists"—were convinced that granting a centralized authority broad, undefined, and possibly uncontrollable powers was the first step on an inexorable road to tyranny.

Most Americans fell between these two extremes. Despite dissatisfaction with the status quo, they found the risks inherent in switching to a sweeping and untried new Constitution more than a little troubling. As no government had ever existed that could provide insight on how constitutional democracy might work, it fell to theorists and zealots on either side to persuade the undecided to either take or eschew a leap of faith.

Inertia being the powerful force that it is, those in favor of the Constitution faced the more daunting challenge. In a number of state legislatures, that a ratifying convention would even be authorized was in no way certain, and Federalists occasionally resorted to some decidedly undemocratic means to move the process along. Two members of the Pennsylvania state legislature known to oppose the Constitution were dragged bodily through the streets and deposited on the floor of the assembly to provide a quorum so that those in favor could vote to approve a ratifying convention. In New Hampshire, opponents were allegedly plied with drink at lunch in order that they not be able to appear at an afternoon convention session and vote against the plan.[1]

To assuage the fears of the populace—or stoke them—Federalists and Anti-Federalists engaged in a massive campaign of either education or disinformation, depending on to which point of view one subscribed: Pamphleteering, public meetings, and debates, both in and out of government facilities, proliferated throughout the thirteen states. By January 9, 1788, five states—Delaware, Pennsylvania, Georgia, Connecticut, and New Jersey—had ratified the Constitution.[2] In none of these states did delegates explicitly assert a power of judicial review in their votes to approve the plan. Massachusetts, where ratification had been in doubt, followed in February after Federalists convinced the vain and pompous John Hancock, an erstwhile opponent, that he was in line to be Washington's vice president, or even president if Washington declined to serve. Once again, judicial review, already an ambiguous concept in the Commonwealth, was not enunciated as a power mandated in the document.

Ratification was expected in South Carolina, but resistance to the Constitution seemed insurmountable in New Hampshire, Maryland, Rhode Island, and perhaps North Carolina. That left New York and Virginia as the keys to the new government—both were thought to be needed to get to the nine-state minimum—and hostility to the plan in both states was intense. To the delight of Federalists, Maryland ratified with unexpected ease on April 28 and South Carolina followed on May 23, leaving Federalists technically only one state short.

In fact, however, Maryland's surprising turnabout in no way lessened the need for both New York and Virginia to join the Union. If anything, their mutual ratification became only more vital. Even if New Hampshire, Rhode Island, and North Carolina all eventually decided to ratify, the loss of either New York or Virginia would cleave the nation in two, and into thirds if both declined to join. Without New York, land routes from New England to the remainder of the country would be cut; if Virginia opted for independence, Georgia and the Carolinas would be severed from the North.* Virginia also happened to be the home of not just Washington, but Madison, Jefferson, James Monroe, and a host of other national figures.[3]

As approval of the plan became more likely, therefore, Federalist intensity in both New York and Virginia increased. In each state, the Anti-Federalist forces were led by a powerful governor, George Clinton of New York and Virginia's redoubtable Patrick Henry. In order to defeat ratification, Clintonians would have to best Alexander Hamilton, and Henry, a powerhouse but more of a one-man show, needed to outmaneuver the wily James Madison. With the stakes so high and the players so august, debate on every aspect of constitutional interpretation would be thorough indeed. Thus, the explicit powers of the judiciary could be expected to be placed under the closest scrutiny and, if judicial review was tacitly assumed to be an implicit constitutional power, debates in these two states would likely make that understanding clear.

Anti-Federalists in Virginia and New York had the opportunity to present a united front and thereby increase their chances to scuttle the plan. Yet, while there was some communication between Anti-Federalists in the two states, because of the egos involved—most notably Henry's—a coordinated strategy never materialized. As a result, the ratification struggle took very different forms: in Virginia, the battle was fought face to face during debate in the ratification convention; in New York, the issues were hashed out by dueling pamphleteers.

Some similarities nonetheless existed. In both New York and Virginia, opponents of the Constitution were aware that mere squeamishness toward change would be insufficient to ensure rejection of the plan. Ratification by eight states had created momentum for the experiment, and dissatisfaction

---

* In 1788, Virginia included most of what is present-day Kentucky, so the blockade would extend to the Mississippi, then owned by Spain.

with the Articles of Confederation was sufficiently deep and widespread to stem any enthusiasm for a return to fractured government. In order to triumph, Anti-Federalists would need to identify solid issues around which fear of centralized authority might coalesce. Even if outright rejection could not be attained, they might at least succeed in inducing sufficient dissatisfaction with the Philadelphia product to require a second national convention.

Many Anti-Federalists were confident they would win such a rematch. They had been blindsided in Philadelphia. At a convention called merely to reform the Articles of Confederation, Madison and his fellow nationalists had come much more prepared than their opponents. In the opening days, before many of the delegates had even arrived, Madison presented a detailed plan to overhaul the government that had been more or less accepted as a preliminary working draft. If a second convention were to be called, Anti-Federalists would not make the same mistake: they would come prepared to thwart any similar attempt to unduly centralize power.

In both Massachusetts and South Carolina, proposals to amend or alter the Constitution had been attached to their ratification reports, but these amendments had not been made conditional to ratification. Conditional ratification—a vote to ratify that was only valid if the amendments were accepted by the other states—seemed the perfect vehicle to slow Federalist momentum. If enough states submitted amendments in this fashion, the process would become so unwieldy as to descend into chaos. From there, Anti-Federalists could press a call for the second convention, something Federalists were desperate to avoid.

Two issues that Anti-Federalists seized on as particularly amenable to amendment were related to the legal system: The first was the lack of provisions in the Constitution to specifically protect individual liberties—a bill of rights. The second was the lack of detail about a national court system that might easily turn tyrannical.

A bill of rights had been specifically omitted from the plan that had emerged from Philadelphia because the delegates believed that individual liberties were implicit in the Constitution they drafted. Even if not, individual liberty was the province of the states which, after all, retained all powers not specifically assigned to the national government. A major force for omitting a bill of rights had been Madison, who was quoted in the Virginia ratifying convention: "As to a solemn declaration of our essential rights, he thought it unnecessary and dangerous—unnecessary, because it was evident that the general government had no power but what was given it, and that the delegation alone warranted the exercise of power; dangerous, because an enumeration which is not complete is not safe."[4]

As to the court system, the very issues that had caused the delegates in Philadelphia to tread gingerly—cost, necessity of travel to get to federal court, out-of-state judges unsympathetic to local needs, potential for judicial despotism—were exploited by Anti-Federalists. Thus, in both New York and Virginia, these two judicial issues promised to be pivotal in determining whether or not the Constitution would be accepted without conditional amendments.

Before ratification votes could be held in either New York or Virginia, however, on June 21, 1788, to the surprise of everyone, including most of the delegates to its own ratifying convention, New Hampshire approved the Constitution.[5] Although a sufficient number of states had now ratified for the Constitution to take effect, New Hampshire's approval had actually made matters even more tenuous.

With the Constitution now officially the basis of government for the states in which it had been ratified, the United States had effectively been transformed into two overlapping nations. The first consisted only of the nine ratifying states; the second, those nine plus the four remaining states—Virginia, New York, Rhode Island, and North Carolina—which continued to operate, at least for the moment, under the Articles of Confederation. While there was no guarantee that the holdouts would agree to be ruled under the Constitution, most Americans—had they known of New Hampshire's ratification—would doubtless have seen this overlap as an anomaly, a nation temporarily in transition from one set of laws to another. After all, as things stood, if there really were to be two separate political entities, George Washington would no longer be a citizen of one of them.

Word of New Hampshire's ratification did not travel quickly, however, and Virginians, in the third week of a bitterly debated ratifying convention, continued to operate under the assumption that only eight states were in the fold and, further, that ratification was unlikely in any of the remaining four states if Virginia refused.[6] Proud Virginia therefore saw itself in exactly the place it thought appropriate—the fate of the nation resting on its decision.

At that moment, the decision was far from certain. That there would be some opposition in the Old Dominion was no surprise, but the ferocity of the Anti-Federalist attack against the Constitution had knocked Federalists on their heels. As the vote to choose delegates to the ratifying convention had drawn near, Federalists realized that their opponents actually held the advantage. The situation had been sufficiently critical for James Madison to abandon his plans to manage the transition to the Constitution from Congress in New York and return to Virginia to get himself elected as a delegate from Orange County.

Federalists planned a coordinated counterattack. Aside from Madison, Federalists could also draw on the talents of Edmund Pendleton, future Supreme Court associate justice Bushrod Washington, legal theorist George Wythe, former governor Edmund Randolph (who had been brought over to the Federalist cause), and a young and successful lawyer with a spotless war record named John Marshall.

John Marshall was born in 1755 in a log cabin in the tiny community of Germantown in Fauquier County,[7] "one of the frontier counties of Virginia," as Marshall himself described it, the first of what would eventually be fifteen children.[8] But Marshall's was no Lincolnesque childhood. His father, Thomas, was a surveyor, a respected local official, and he held a commission in the Virginia militia. Descended from Welsh artisans who had immigrated to Virginia two or three generations before, Thomas Marshall had been born in 1730 and raised near the Atlantic coast in Westmoreland County, where he began a lifelong friendship with his neighbor George Washington. Although he had little formal education, the elder Marshall was a ravenous reader with an unquenchable thirst for self-improvement, traits he passed on to his children.

Like his cousin Peter Jefferson, Thomas Marshall had "married up."[9] Marshall's mother, Mary, was directly descended from William Randolph of Turkey Island and Mary Isham of Bermuda Hundred, local aristocrats whose families had been in the colony since the 1630s and who were sometimes referred to as the "Adam and Eve of Virginia."[10] They had nine children and thirty-seven grandchildren—one son married Pocahontas's great-granddaughter—and their descendants included not only Marshall's mother but also Thomas Jefferson, Robert E. Lee, and, of course, Edmund Randolph.

Although he improved his social standing somewhat by marriage, Thomas Marshall, unlike Peter Jefferson, was never accepted into genteel, aristocratic Virginia society. His wife's mother, another Mary, had been an outcast, involved in numerous scandals and all but disowned by her family.* Thomas Marshall, although he was a man of incorruptible character and reputation, inherited, unlike others of the clan, only a small piece of property and could not compete in the plantation economy that had dominated the Virginia tidewater. He sold his land and, with Washington's help, became a land agent for Lord Fairfax, the colony's largest landholder. He moved to Germantown two years before John was born, surveyed the surrounding area, and eventually became sheriff, first magistrate, the county's delegate to the House of Burgesses, and tax collector.†

John Marshall spent his boyhood steeped in the contrast between the hard-driven, log-cabin frontier spirit of the pioneers around him and the intellectually curious household in which he resided. According to Marshall himself, his father gave him "an early taste for history and poetry," and by twelve he "had transcribed Pope's Essay on Man, and some of his Moral Essays."[11] John Marshall was unique among his peers. "The young men within my reach were entirely uncultivated; and the time I passed with them was devoted to hardy athletic exercises."[12] Hardy athletics obviously agreed with him. Marshall developed into a fast and tireless runner—he eventually earned the sobriquet "Silverheels"—and could reportedly jump a remarkable (and quite possibly apocryphal) six feet in the air.[13]

Other than one year when was he fourteen and was sent away to study privately with an area clergyman, Marshall was educated entirely in his home.[14] As his family grew, they moved several times, relocating ever westward, until they had crossed into what is now Kentucky, but always on the vast Fairfax estates. With each move, the Marshall family acquired more land and attained more affluent living conditions than the one before. To further both his ambition and his drive for learning, Thomas Marshall

---

* When she was just in her teens, she ran off with a slave overseer, married him secretly, and had a child. The family went and got her, killing her husband in the process. A few years later, she married a local minister, John Marshall's grandfather, again in violation of her family's wishes. The family shunned her and, as a result, Marshall almost never discussed his link to the Randolphs. She ultimately went mad and died insane (Jean Smith, Marshall, p. 25).
† The latter position was particularly lucrative, since a tax collector was entitled to keep a portion of the taxes he collected.

constantly acquired books for the family library, first borrowing volumes from Lord Fairfax, then, as he became more prosperous, purchasing them on his own. Thus the Marshall family was always surrounded by classics—Livy, Horace, Pope, Dryden, Milton, and Shakespeare.[15] John and his siblings, also educated exclusively in the Marshall home, all became intellectually sophisticated and accomplished.* Among Thomas Marshall's purchases in 1772 was the first American edition of *Commentaries on the Laws of England* by William Blackstone, a set of volumes that immediately engaged the attention of his eldest son.

As John Marshall entered his late teens, "the controversy between Great Britain and her colonies had assumed so serious an aspect as almost to monopolize the attention of the old and the young."[16] Thomas Marshall was already an officer in the Virginia militia, and his eldest son soon volunteered as well. At age nineteen, he was appointed lieutenant and second in command of a company of about fifty men, and then, in 1775, assigned to a larger regional battalion when Virginia organized its defenses. Both father and son had distinguished war records. Thomas Marshall was on the line at Brandywine, in 1777, in a holding action that was credited with preventing Cornwallis from overtaking and decimating Washington's main army, and John fought in a number of minor battles in the early months of the war.[17]

John Marshall spent the winter of 1777–78 with Washington at Valley Forge, where he shared a cabin with James Monroe, and it became one of the defining episodes of his life. With acute shortages of food, clothing, and blankets, and disease rampant, one man in six of Washington's seventeen-thousand-man army died, although not a shot was fired in four months. Marshall's loyalty to Washington became unbreakable in those frozen months. He also became a source of comfort and encouragement to his men.† One of his colleagues later reported, "He was an excellent companion and idolized by the soldiers and his brother officers, whose gloomy hours were enlivened by his inexhaustible fund of anecdote."[18]

As 1779 drew to a close, the three-year enlistments of many of the soldiers in Marshall's battalion were up. He was ordered home by the Virginia

---

* Marshall's younger brother James eventually married the daughter of Philadelphia financier Robert Morris.
† Reported equally is that Marshall's intense antipathy for Jefferson was formed by the latter's failure to join his fellows at Valley Forge, although Marshall probably did not need Valley Forge for an excuse.

legislature on extended furlough to await new conscriptions and, as he put it, "availed myself of this inactive interval for attending a course of law lectures given by Mr. [George] Wythe."[19] By July 1780, the legislature had still not acted in raising new troops and Marshall obtained a license to practice law.*

Marshall intended to begin his practice immediately, but, with the war on, most of the courts were closed. In September 1780, the Virginia legislature had still not assigned Marshall a new command, so he left for Philadelphia to rejoin the army, traveling on foot as much as thirty miles a day. He was not in Philadelphia long before he was sent back to Virginia with Baron von Steuben to help raise troops to repulse Cornwallis, who had taken Charleston and was heading north. Marshall helped persuade 1,500 men to enlist, only to learn that financially strapped Virginia, under Governor Thomas Jefferson, refused to appropriate the funds to buy shoes and uniforms.† The lack of official support disgusted him and, in February 1781, after more than five years in the army, Marshall resigned his commission to begin his law practice.

His reasons for resigning when the war was at a critical juncture have been a matter of some speculation. Marshall himself said "as we had more officers than soldiers," he thought he might "without violating the duty I owed my country, pay some attention to my future prospects."[20] The war had caused certainly great deprivation to his family, as it had to most Virginians, and he no doubt felt an obligation to try to earn some money. Also, during the 1780 furlough he had fallen in love with fourteen-year-old Mary Willis Ambler, known as "Polly," the daughter of the Virginia state treasurer, but well-bred young women didn't marry paupers. One biographer indicated, however, that Marshall's departure might have been a result of falling out with Steuben.[21] Whatever the reason, eight months later, when Washington defeated Cornwallis at Yorktown, Marshall was some fifty miles away, preparing to set up his law practice in Richmond.

---

* Congress had no power to raise troops. That was left to the individual states, whose efforts and willingness to spend money could be less than enthusiastic. Lack of manpower was a source of constant consternation to Washington.

† His cousin's war record as Virginia's governor was a major factor in Marshall's estrangement, although there is no evidence that Marshall ever denounced Jefferson publicly for his failure to serve in the army.

John Marshall around 1782

Marshall was made for the law—he once wrote "from infancy I was destined for the bar."[22] He was analytical, logical, and drawn to detail. He enjoyed nothing more than digesting a complex argument to find any minute crack that he might then exploit to demolish the entire edifice. Equally important to his success was an easy delivery, booming laugh, infectious wit, and love of wine and good fellowship. With this fierce and ruthless intellect camouflaged by a shambling, slovenly dressed, loose-limbed *joie de vivre*, Marshall remained popular with most opponents throughout his life, even while taking the most partisan positions.*

Regardless of how much Marshall was ready for the law, the courts had not reopened, and so the law was not yet ready for Marshall. His courtship of

---

* Not all his opponents, of course. Jefferson detested him and Andrew Jackson would have gleefully slit his throat. Still, for a man so often in the path of the storm, Marshall was remarkably well liked.

Polly Ambler, however, provided him entrée into Virginia society, where his quirky backwoods manner, war record, and obvious intelligence came to the attention of political leaders. He was persuaded to run for election for a seat in the Virginia House of Delegates from Fauquier County, and in 1782, still only twenty-seven years old, successfully completed his first foray into politics.[23]

Marshall's initial session as a delegate lasted thirty-eight days. The House of Delegates was a disorganized, inefficient hash, "not a body to inspire respect."[24] Legislative sessions often descended quickly into personal invective and chaos. Little, if anything, ever got done. Observing the anarchy around him, his years as a soldier caused his instinctive Federalism—his desire for orderly, efficient government—to ripen. "The general tendency of state politics convinced me that no safe and permanent remedy [for the suffering in the army] could be found but in a more efficient and better organized general government."[25] From there, Marshall developed not only a belief in a strong national government, but also in a constitution to control it, and an unconditional zeal to guarantee the right to property. But unlike Hamilton and many other northern Federalists, Marshall's views were always tempered by frontier pragmatism, replacing absolutism with efforts to find workable middle ground.

There was a sharp division in Virginia between those, like Marshall and, at the time, James Madison, who favored a strong national government, and others, like Jefferson and Patrick Henry, who decried centralized authority. Virginia, not without justification, already saw itself as the political and spiritual center of the nation, and those who stressed state autonomy enjoyed great popularity. The Richmond area in particular strongly opposed ceding authority to a central government, and it is a testament to Marshall's popularity that voters continued to elect him.

Marshall soon became an influential member of what one biographer termed "the establishment faction" of the Virginia Assembly.[26] Concurrent with his legislative service, Marshall, with the help of Edmund Randolph, established a law practice and also became an intermediary for investors who had bought land warrants from the commonwealth and wished to convert them into surveyed acreage.

Later in 1782, with his future father-in-law's help, Marshall was elected by joint ballot of the Senate and House of Delegates to be one of eight members of the Virginia council of state, a quasi-executive advisory committee. The position held great prestige but minimal power. Soon afterward, in January 1783, as the Treaty of Paris was being negotiated to end the war, Marshall married Polly Ambler.

During his tenure on the council of state, Marshall participated in a constitutional controversy that provided a window into his future decision in *Marbury*. Virginia's governor, Benjamin Harrison, had asked the council for an opinion as to whether, under a recently passed law, a particular magistrate could be removed for alleged misdeeds while on the bench. Although it was not mandated to take action itself, the council, as part of its statutory duties, was charged with determining whether these misdeeds had actually taken place.

Judges tended to be from the gentry, and removing one for malfeasance promised to be controversial. So, rather than ruling on the behavior of the judge, Marshall instead persuaded the council to look into whether the law violated Virginia's constitution. The council's report then pronounced unconstitutional the act of the legislature that had authorized the council to evaluate judicial conduct. The language of the opinion presages that which Marshall would employ two decades later. "The [Council] are of the opinion that the Law authorizing the Executive to enquire into the Conduct of a Magistrate . . . is repugnant to the Act of Government, contrary to the fundamental principles of our constitution."[27]

The relative power of a constitution and the legislature it defined had been debated for decades, not just in the United States, but also in Europe, and this debate goes directly to the question of separation of powers, in which judicial review is grounded.

If the constitution was deemed superior to laws enacted by legislature, judged to be the sort of "super law" Justice Scalia describes, any legislation counter to the constitution must give way. Although opinion on this question was by no means unanimous, most scholars, both then and now, agree that a constitution should take precedence over laws enacted under its provisions.

The question remains as to which arm of government should be entitled to determine when the legislature has overstepped its bounds, and then to adjudicate conflicts. To Justice Scalia, the answer is simple—the courts. But the great William Blackstone, spiritual godfather of conservative judges throughout the English-speaking world, and a man whom Marshall revered, had rejected judicial activism and specifically declared that the courts should not be granted this power. Only the legislature can overturn a legislative act.

"Because the legislature," Blackstone wrote in a passage with which Marshall was familiar, "being in truth the sovereign power, is always of equal, always of absolute authority . . . Acts of parliament that are impossible to be performed, are of no validity, and if there arise out of them any absurd consequences, contradictory to reason, they are, with those collateral consequences, void. If parliament will positively enact an unreasonable thing, there is no power in the ordinary forms of the constitution vested with authority to control it. The judges are not at liberty to reject it, *for that were to set the judicial power above that of the legislature, which would be subversive to all government.*"[28] Thus, to Blackstone, separation of powers, the ultimate guarantor of liberty, *demanded* that the courts have no power to overturn legislative acts.

But Blackstone added an exception, when a cause before the bar arose from an unforeseen consequence of a legislative act. In that circumstance, he felt judges were entitled to ignore the act. As he put it, "But where some collateral matter arises out of the general words, and happens to be unreasonable; there the judges are in decency to conclude that this consequence was not foreseen by the parliament, and therefore they are at liberty to expound the statute by equity, and only *quoad hoc* [to this extent] disregard it."[29] This passage, while in no way an endorsement of judicial review, does provide justification— potentially quite broad justification—for a court to refuse to enforce a statute in specific cases.

Still, in his conclusion, Blackstone left little doubt where his overall sentiments lay. "There is no court that has power to defeat the intent of the legislature, when couched in such evident and express words, as leave no doubt whether it was the intent of the legislature or no."[30]

Oddly, Marshall, in the issue before the council, would have found more support in Montesquieu,[31] who would become the favored philosopher of Jefferson and the hated Republicans. As Montesquieu asserted that the executive should act as a control on the legislature, the Virginia council, being technically an executive body, was within its rights in nullifying the offending statute.

But, like Blackstone, Montesquieu also rejected both judicial review and an active judiciary. "National judges are no more than the mouth that pronounces the words of the law, mere passive beings, incapable of moderating either its force or rigor."[32] Again as had Blackstone, Montesquieu also postulated that the legislature must sometimes act as a check on itself. "That part, therefore, of the legislative body, which we have just now observed to be a necessary tribunal on another occasion, is also a necessary tribunal in this; it belongs to its supreme authority to moderate the law in favor of the law itself, by mitigating the sentence."[33]

Montesquieu's and Blackstone's exceptions notwithstanding, in advising the governor that the law was void, Marshall was staking out new and uniquely American territory. The council's ruling was "the first recorded instance in the United States of an act of a legislature being annulled because it conflicted with the constitution."[34] Governor Harrison was loath to set such precedent and attempted to persuade the council to reconsider and rule on the judge's fitness anyway, but the council stood its ground.

As was to become common in his long and storied career, by seizing on a narrow question and using it as a lever to advance his philosophical agenda, Marshall created a storm in the surrounding political arena. In this case, the controversy over separation of powers, which Marshall had been instrumental in creating, reverberated in the Virginia legislature for the next two years.

At first, the Virginia assembly accepted the ruling of the council, or at least refused to overturn it, suggesting "that the supremacy of the constitution was a concept well understood in Virginia."[35] The concept could not have been that well understood, however. Two years later, after Marshall had resigned from the Executive Council, the council agreed to rule on the fitness of another judge. One of the members, Spencer Roane, resigned in protest.* Clearly, separation of powers was a construct that evoked a good deal more acrimony than agreement. Still, during Marshall's tenure on the council, he succeeded in transforming himself from a promising upstart to a man whose views held great significance within the government.[36]

Also during his time on the council, Marshall began an intimate business relationship with James Monroe, who would eventually become a political adversary and close ally of Jefferson. Monroe had solicited Marshall to oversee land warrants in Kentucky. At one point, Marshall wrote, likely tongue

---

* Roane's agreement with Marshall's position is ironic. After Jefferson's election to the presidency, Spencer Roane was the man Jefferson wanted to nominate to be chief justice of the Supreme Court after he had succeeded in removing the sitting chief justice, John Marshall.

in cheek, "I have been maneuvering amazingly to turn your warrants into cash; if I succeed, I shall think myself a first rate speculator."[37]

Marshall's reason for leaving the council seems to have been financial. His law practice was still not bringing in the money he had hoped for, so he freed himself from political obligations to become a full-time lawyer. Once again, with his father-in-law's connections, Marshall quickly turned his practice around and, when financially stable, turned his attention once more to politics. In 1784, he was again elected to the House of Delegates.

While in the house, where he served on the Committee for Courts and Justice, Marshall championed a bill to establish a series of circuit courts to replace the existing system in which magistrates sat in one district only, often as minor potentates. Circuit riding was to become a dominant and pivotal issue with regard to the federal court system, and Marshall would become deeply embroiled in the question as a member of the Supreme Court.

Frustration at the Byzantine practices of the Virginia legislature again got the better of Marshall, and after only one term, he left the House of Delegates to resume his now lucrative law practice. He had permanently settled in Richmond with Polly, who had borne the first of his children, although he was also given a country home by Polly's father. He became active in local government in the capital, serving on the volunteer fire brigade, the city council, and as a magistrate.[38]

Thus, in early 1787, when Shays's Rebellion in Massachusetts sent a chill through the nation and spurred the call for a constitutional convention to meet in Philadelphia in May, Marshall for a third time stood for election to the House of Delegates, this time from his adopted Richmond instead of Fauquier County. Now a well-known and popular figure in the capital, he was elected easily. Marshall was present when, at the conclusion of the Philadelphia Convention, the House of Delegates was charged with deciding whether Virginia should call a ratifying convention.

While the calling of the ratifying convention itself was never much in doubt, the rules under which it would operate were very much so. Federalists wanted a simple up or down vote on the product that had emerged from Philadelphia. Led by Henry, opponents proposed allowing a ratifying convention *only* if Virginia could first propose amendments conditional to acceptance of the Constitution. The number of amendments promised to be extensive and they would, if not kill the Constitution outright, at least necessitate calling the second convention that was at the core of the Anti-Federalist strategy.

Marshall proposed leaving the question of amendments to the delegates to the ratifying convention itself, which would allow the meeting to proceed without any preconditions or limitations on debate. The motion passed unanimously, and Marshall was rewarded by his subsequent election as a delegate to the ratifying convention itself.

Thus, when Marshall arrived at the ratifying convention in June, while he had not yet attained the status of a Madison or a Henry, he was poised for a leap to prominence. The Virginia ratifying convention was his first foray into national politics and, as a delegate, he was now among 170 of the state's most prominent and influential citizens.

FOUR

MAKING A NEW NATION:
RATIFICATION IN VIRGINIA

MORE EVANGELIST THAN THEORIST, Patrick Henry was one of history's most breathtaking orators, a titanic figure who could sway multitudes by force of personality alone. He could speak for hours at a stretch to a packed auditorium without a single person noticing the time pass. From the Virginia ratifying convention's opening day on June 2, 1788, Virginians lined up to hear what has been described as "the most eloquent performance in the annals of forensic virtuosity."[1] Henry roared; he whispered; he used logic and sarcasm; he probed for every tiny opening in which he could instill fear of the abyss into which ratification of the Constitution would send his state and his country. Henry was so voluble that, early in the proceedings, the shorthand stenographer assigned to keep records of the convention could not keep up with him. Midway through a typically electrifying speech, this on the inevitable despotism of the president, the secretary merely inserted, "Here Mr. Henry strongly and pathetically expatiated on the probability of the President's enslaving America, and the horrid consequences that must result."[2]

If Henry had a weakness, it was an inability or an unwillingness to keep to the point. He cast his argument like a great net, trawling to see what opportunities might be ensnared by his rhetoric. If Henry was to be defeated, it would be by precision and guile, not bare-knuckles floor argument.

James Madison, in the Federalist camp, was unmatched for precision and guile. But as summer approached, Madison was not in Virginia. He had remained in New York to spearhead the newly ratified Constitution through Congress. However, after friends warned him that Henry had succeeded in fomenting widespread opposition to the Constitution, Madison was forced to alter his plans. In late April 1788, Madison reluctantly left New York and returned home. He quickly submitted his name as a convention delegate from his native Orange County and was easily elected.

Although they may have been equals as politicians, Madison could not have been more different from Henry in style. Where Henry was large and voluble, Madison was tiny and quiet, as methodical and meticulous as Henry was spontaneous. Madison had helped carry the day in Philadelphia by arriving more prepared for the constitutional debates than any other delegate. He now repeated that technique in Virginia—he had studied every article, every clause of the new Constitution, in terms of both how to attack and how to defend it, and had the additional advantage of being one of only a handful of delegates who had been present for every session in Philadelphia, so he could speak knowingly to the nuances of the debates.

At the ratifying convention's outset, to blunt Henry's rhetorical legerdemain, Madison secured a rule that the debates would be clause-by-clause. In such a dissection of the Constitution, Madison could shine, offering detailed

Patrick Henry

explanations in defense of the plan. But while structurally the clause-by-clause rule was adhered to, Henry refused to be penned in. (At one point, he entered a motion to scrap the format, but it was dismissed. Henry responded by simply ignoring it.) Ranging far in his denunciations, Henry made little attempt to parse specifics or to dissect the positions of his opponents. Instead, he railed against the new Constitution as an instrument of tyranny. Although, under the thunder, Henry's main thrust was to decry a loss of state sovereignty, his dire warnings of a despotic central government run by non-Virginians denying individual rights and liberties struck a responsive chord in Anti-Federalist Virginia.*

For the first few days, defense of the Constitution fell to Edmund Randolph (who had refused to sign it in Philadelphia, but had since converted to supporter) and Edmund Pendleton. Finally, on the afternoon of June 6, Madison, beset by illness, spoke for the first time. The contrast with Henry's theatrics could not have been more striking. The secretary recorded that Madison "spoke so low that his exordium could not be heard distinctly."[3]

But Madison's reserve masked a tenacity equal to Henry's. While each man had impressive adherents,† the debates ultimately reduced to a head-on duel, the orator against the philosopher, emotion against reason. Time after time, Henry rose to respond to Madison or Madison to Henry. In one stretch, Madison took the floor thirty-five times in four days, quietly, methodically countering each of Henry's charges.

By June 19, after almost three weeks of argument, the outcome was so much in doubt that each side thought it held a small edge. On that day, and for the remainder of the convention, the debates would focus on Article III, the judiciary.

Pendleton opened the debate by claiming that the vagueness with which Article III had been drawn was actually a virtue. "The first clause contains an arrangement of the courts—one supreme, and such inferior as Congress may ordain and establish. This seems to me to be proper. Congress must be the judges, and may find reasons to change and vary them as experience shall dictate. It is, therefore, not only improper, but exceedingly inconvenient, to

---

* He worked at every fear, especially those of slave owners. "They'll take your niggers," he said famously.
† Henry's adherents were less a supporting cast than simply others who coincidentally shared his position. George Mason, for example, who could have matched Madison in classical rhetoric and logic, never coordinated with the diva, Henry, and in the end it cost them dearly.

fix the arrangement in the Constitution itself, and not leave it to laws which may be changed according to circumstances."[4]

Pendleton then defined the jurisdiction of the Supreme Court in a manner that would have great significance fifteen years hence. "The next clause settles the original jurisdiction of the Supreme Court, confining it to two cases—that of ambassadors, ministers, and consuls, and those in which a state shall be a party. It excludes its original jurisdiction in all other cases . . . Congress may go further by their laws, so as to exclude its original jurisdiction, by limiting the cases wherein it shall be exercised. . . . Yet the legislature cannot extend its original jurisdiction, which is limited to these cases only."[5]

Pendleton offered the narrow interpretation of Article III, Section 2, since the next sentence states: "In all the other Cases before mentioned, the supreme Court shall have appellate Jurisdiction, both as to Law and Fact, with such Exceptions, and under such Regulations as the Congress shall make." For Pendleton, "exceptions" were confined to appellate jurisdiction, although, since he had not been a delegate in Philadelphia, he was merely stating an opinion. In fact, there had been no agreement at all at the Convention as to whether or not Congress might extend the Supreme Court's original jurisdiction.[6] But not once in his extended enunciation of the Supreme Court's responsibilities did he mention the power to annul an act of Congress.

The remainder of the June 19 session was dominated by George Mason, who argued that a national judiciary would *a priori* tend to despotism by overpowering the states and removing the courts from the people. The proceedings were then adjourned.

The next day, June 20, Madison opened with a lengthy speech discussing each of the areas of jurisdiction, both original and appellate, of the proposed Supreme Court. In more than two hours, he never mentioned Edmund Pendleton's assertion that Congress was prohibited from altering the rules of the Court's original jurisdiction, nor did he mention the power of the judiciary to refuse to enforce a law on the grounds of unconstitutionality. Indeed, to this point in the proceedings, the immense power of judicial review had not come up.

After Henry once again took the floor to rail against the unspeakable horrors that would inevitably spring from a national judiciary—the ruination of state courts, the abolition of trial by jury, crippling lawsuits by foreigners—Pendleton attempted without much success to rebut him. George Mason spoke briefly in counter-rebuttal. Then John Marshall was granted the floor.

"Mr. Chairman," Marshall began, "this part of the plan before us is a great improvement on that system from which we are now departing."[7] He spoke for the better part of two hours. Employing the same Socratic techniques he would later use on the bench, Marshall refuted each of Henry's and Mason's assertions, first by restating them, then by subjecting their arguments to a series of withering rhetorical questions, rendering each of the points a *reductio ad absurdum*.

Marshall began with Mason's charge that "the federal courts will not determine the causes which may come before them with the same fairness and impartiality with which other courts decide." To that, he replied,

> What is it that makes us trust our judges? Their independence in office, and manner of appointment. Are not the judges of the federal court chosen with as much wisdom as the judges of the state governments? Are they not equally, if not more, independent? If so, shall we not conclude that they will decide with equal impartiality and candor? If there be as much wisdom and knowledge in the United States as in a particular state, shall we conclude that the wisdom and knowledge will not be equally exercised in the selection of judges?[8]

To answer Henry's charge that a fair trial could never be assured in a national court, Marshall replied, "Is there not the utmost reason to conclude that judges, wisely appointed, and independent in their office, will never countenance any unfair trial?"[9]

Marshall then turned his attention to the inflammatory issue of judicial expansion. Henry, and particularly Mason, had continually made the point that, because Article III was so vague on how many national courts could be created, a federal judiciary would ultimately overwhelm state courts. Marshall turned the issue on its head. Citing another of Henry's objections, that a national court would be so remote for many citizens as to make justice unattainable, Marshall asserted, "But I did not conceive that the power of increasing the number of courts could be objected to by any gentleman, as it would remove the inconvenience of being dragged to the centre of the United States. I own that the power of creating a number of courts is, in my estimation, so far from being a defect, that it seems necessary to the perfection of this system."[10]

Then Marshall came to judicial review.

Mason had insisted that Article III gave federal courts unlimited jurisdiction. As a result, state courts would eventually be rendered impotent, since, as the laws of the United States were superior, federal courts could simply extend their reach to any case they so chose.[11] Marshall's reply went straight to the question of who says what the law is:

> With respect to its cognizance in all cases arising under the Constitution and the laws of the United States, [Mason] says that, the laws of the United States being paramount to the laws of the particular states, there is no case but what this will extend to. Has the government of the United States power to make laws on every subject? Does he understand it so? Can they make laws affecting the mode of transferring property, or contracts, or claims, between citizens of the same state? Can they go beyond the delegated powers? If they were to make a law not warranted by any of the powers enumerated, it would be considered by the judges as an infringement of the Constitution which they are to guard. They would not consider such a law as coming under their jurisdiction. They would declare it void.[12]

A bit later in his speech, Marshall added, "To what quarter will you look for protection from an infringement on the Constitution, if you will not give the power to the judiciary? There is no other body that can afford such a protection."[13]

Neither Henry nor Mason responded to Marshall's declaration. Certainly, Mason had asserted this very position on judicial review at the Convention. No one in the Federalist camp commented either. Judicial review, after one ephemeral appearance, was buried in the avalanche of rhetoric.

Except for one brief comment, Marshall did not speak for the remainder of the convention. For the final week of debate, the battle was between Madison and Henry. Would the inclusion of amendments be a condition of Virginia's ratification? Henry, whose main argument was the necessity of state sovereignty, had the emotions of patriotic Virginians to play upon. But Madison had practicalities on his side. If the Constitution was rejected, how then would the United States be governed? What did Henry propose as an alternative? The status quo? Keep the Articles of Confederation? That was suitable to no one.

The prospect of continuing under a failed system finally persuaded undecided delegates to vote Madison's way. On Wednesday, June 25, 1788, two votes were taken. The first, a motion by Henry to make the inclusion of amendments conditional to Virginia's ratification, failed, 88 votes to 80. The second, to ratify the Constitution, but also include amendments as nonbinding suggestions for revision, passed, 89–79. A list of twenty proposed amendments to be attached to Virginia's certification to Congress was agreed to two days later.

Unbeknownst to the delegates, Virginia had not created a new union, but simply joined one that had been in existence for less than a week. In mid-July, word finally arrived in Richmond that New Hampshire had already ratified the Constitution.

FIVE

Uniting a New Nation: Ratification in New York

CONGRESS, STILL MEETING under the Articles of Confederation in New York, received word of New Hampshire's ratification earlier, on Wednesday, July 2. That same day, Congress issued a directive "that the ratifications of the constitution of the United States transmitted to Congress be referred to a committee to examine the same and report an Act to Congress for putting the said constitution into operation in pursuance of the resolutions of the late federal Convention."[1] In the vote to authorize the committee, only one congressman voted against, New York's Abraham Yates.[2] With only one other member of its delegation present, New York's vote was thus left as "divided." Although word of Virginia's ratification had yet to arrive, the state's three delegates all voted "aye." Of the other two holdouts, North Carolina was not present and the Rhode Island delegates, who were in the chamber, were marked "excused."[3] Thus, the states that had yet to ratify were already being forced to grapple with a nation that had chosen to move on, either with them or without them.

While in North Carolina and Rhode Island sentiment remained firmly against the Constitution, seventy-five miles up the Hudson River from the congressional chamber, at the New York ratifying convention in Poughkeepsie, the battle for ratification was raging. The convention was an exercise in high drama as the brilliant, mercurial (and outnumbered) Alexander Hamilton tried to wrest victory from the leader of the Anti-Federalists, Governor George Clinton.[4] Although the New York ratifying convention lasted longer than that in any other state—June 17 to July 28—what makes the struggle for ratification in New York so memorable was not the slugfest in Poughkeepsie, but rather the ethereal debate in New York City that had occurred in the months before the convention convened. Remarkably, not only did the participants never meet, they never even knew each other's identities, as the debate was conducted entirely through pamphlets published in rival newspapers. Yet nowhere was the contest between those who would opt for the Constitution and those who would reject it conducted with more intensity, more intelligence, or more lasting impact than between these pamphleteers. They left America with perhaps its most enduring legacy of constitutional theory and analysis.

New York was an unlikely scene for a philosophical discourse over government. Other than Rhode Island, which had not even sent a delegation to Philadelphia, New York's three Constitutional Convention delegates had exhibited less enthusiasm for the proceedings than those of any other state. Two of the men—Robert Yates, a New York judge and Abraham Yates's younger brother, and the politician Robert Lansing Jr., to whom Yates was related by marriage—shared an ardent opposition to abdicating state authority to a central government. Yates and Lansing were appointed to go to Philadelphia in large part to ensure that New York's third delegate, the archnationalist Hamilton, did not try to hijack the Convention and overstep the bounds of the mandate to merely reform the Articles of Confederation.

In early July, when it became clear that the Convention intended to replace the Articles with a much more powerful central government, Yates and Lansing left, writing in a letter to Clinton that "for so important a trust as the adopting of measures which tended to deprive the state government of its most essential rights of sovereignty, and to place it in a dependent situation, could not have been confided by implication," and "our powers could not involve the subversion of a Constitution which, being immediately derived from the people, could only be abolished by their express consent."[5]

Hamilton, after giving a six-hour speech in June during which he advocated, among other measures, the elimination of the states as political entities and an executive that sounded suspiciously like a monarch, left even before Lansing and Yates and eventually missed nearly two months of the Convention. When Hamilton returned to stay, at the end of August, he thought it wrong that any state's vote should be cast by only one delegate and New York abstained on all questions until the Convention rose. Still, although it fell far short of his ideals, Hamilton became an enthusiastic supporter of a plan that he saw as a vast improvement on the status quo.

On October 18, 1787, less than a month after the text of the Constitution was published in the *Pennsylvania Packet,* an article appeared in the *New York Journal* signed by "Brutus." It was addressed "To the Citizens of the State of New-York," and began "When the public is called to investigate and decide upon a question in which not only the present members of the community are deeply interested, but upon which the happiness and misery of generations yet unborn is in great measure suspended, the benevolent mind cannot help feeling itself peculiarly interested in the result."[6]

After noting "We have felt the feebleness of the ties by which these United-States are held together, and the want of sufficient energy in our present confederation, to manage, in some instances, our general concerns," Brutus went on to observe, "if the constitution, offered to your acceptance, be a wise one, calculated to preserve the invaluable blessings of liberty, to secure the inestimable rights of mankind, and promote human happiness, then, if you accept it, you will lay a lasting foundation of happiness for millions yet unborn; generations to come will rise up and call you blessed."[7] Then, for the remainder of the essay and in fifteen additional essays that stretched into April of the following year, Brutus persuasively and elegantly detailed why the new Constitution would achieve none of those aims, but rather would centralize power and overwhelm state governments, which would, in turn, "lead to the subversion of liberty," and threaten "to establish a despotism, or, what is worse, a tyrannic aristocracy."[8]

Brutus had chosen his pseudonym with care. Although now popularly associated exclusively with the man who committed the ultimate betrayal of Julius Caesar (in the name of saving the republic from tyranny), late-eighteenth-century readers were also well aware of the earlier Lucius Junius Brutus who, in the sixth century B.C., led a successful revolt against the last Roman king, Tarquin the Proud, and became one of the founders of the Roman republic. As was the custom at the time, the New York "Brutus" did not reveal his true identity.[9]

Nine days after Brutus's essay appeared in the *Journal,* another essay was published in a rival newspaper, the *New York Independent Journal,* this one addressed "To the People of the State of New York," and signed by "Publius." That this essay was in response to Brutus there could be no doubt. Publius Valerius was an eminent statesman of the Roman republic, whose fame and power crested after Lucius Junius Brutus died in battle trying to prevent Tarquin from retaking his throne. So popular was Publius Valerius with the citizenry of Rome that he was granted the additional honorific, "Publicola," which according to Plutarch meant "people-cherisher."

Publius would write eighty-five essays, the last of which would appear in May 1788, all of them extolling the virtues of the new Constitution.[10] Just after the final essay appeared, the entire body of work was published as a two-volume set titled *The Federalist*. The essays were translated into French soon after—just in time for the revolution—and eventually into almost every other language. *The Federalist* has been in print ever since.

The *Federalist* essays have been called the "most important work in political science that has ever been written, or is likely ever to be written, in the United States."[11] While the essays are certainly brilliant dissertations on both political theory and the permutations and ramifications of the new Constitution, they were written to persuade, to advocate for ratification, not to even-handedly discuss or dissect Constitutional issues.[12]

Like Brutus, Publius did not reveal his identity and, even as editions of *The Federalist* began to be read throughout Europe in the 1790s and early 1800s, the author's anonymity was maintained. Finally, in July 1804, as his duel with Aaron Burr drew near, Alexander Hamilton, in putting his affairs in order, included a brief note that revealed that the *Federalist* essays had been written on his initiative and that Publius was in fact three men—himself, James Madison, and John Jay. Jay had written five of the essays, and Madison and Hamilton had split the rest.[13]

That the Publius essays had abruptly ended although ratification in New York was still very much in doubt had been a cause of consternation to Federalists. Why had Publius put down his pen just as the most crucial time was upon them? The timing of the termination was not explained until the identity of the authors was revealed. Hamilton and Jay had to be off to Poughkeepsie as delegates to the very New York ratifying convention they had been trying to influence; and, most importantly, Madison had been forced to leave the state and return to Virginia in an attempt to thwart Patrick Henry.

Publius's first essay, written by Hamilton, began in the same manner as his opponent's. "You are called upon to deliberate on a new Constitution for the United States of America," he wrote. "The subject speaks its own importance; comprehending in its consequences nothing less than the existence of the UNION, the safety and welfare of the parts of which it is composed, the fate of an empire in many respects the most interesting in the world."[14] Publius agreed with Brutus that arriving at the correct decision was vital. "It

Alexander Hamilton

seems to have been reserved to the people of this country, by their conduct and example, to decide the important question, whether societies of men are really capable or not of establishing good government from reflection and choice." Publius further agreed that the stakes involved all humanity, present and future. "The crisis at which we are arrived may with propriety be regarded as the era in which that decision is to be made; and a wrong election of the part we shall act may, in this view, deserve to be considered as the general misfortune of mankind."[15]

While Publius spent significant time on every aspect of the plan, as well as the philosophic underpinnings of democratic government in general, Brutus targeted only those aspects that were most threatening and would therefore rouse the most Anti-Federalist sentiment. As such, he devoted fully five of his sixteen essays to the branch of government that had been defined the most vaguely in the Constitution: the judiciary.

On January 31, 1788, Brutus's eleventh paper opened, "The nature and extent of the judicial power of the United States, proposed to be granted by this constitution, claims our particular attention." Although Anti-Federalists were both at the time and subsequently accused of fear-mongering, Brutus 11 proved to be eerily prescient of the post-*Marbury* judiciary. Noting that the judiciary under the new Constitution would "be placed in a situation altogether unprecedented in a free country," Brutus explained that judges "are to be rendered totally independent, both of the people and the legislature, both with respect to their offices and salaries," which turned out to be exactly the constitutional necessity that Chief Justice Marshall would insist upon in the *Marbury* opinion.[16] The effect, Brutus would warn in his fifteenth essay, was "that the supreme court under this constitution would be exalted above all other power in the government, and subject to no control."[17]

Article III, to Brutus, "vests the courts with authority to give the constitution a legal construction, or to explain it according to the rules laid down for construing a law," which will necessarily involve "a certain degree of latitude of explanation." Supreme Court justices will therefore "give the sense of every article of the constitution, that may from time to time come before them. And in their decisions they will not confine themselves to any fixed or established rules, but will determine, according to what appears to them, the reason and spirit of the constitution."[18] Where were the checks and balances, he wondered, when "the opinions of the supreme court, whatever they may be, will have the force of law; because there is no power provided in the constitution, that can correct their errors, or control their adjudications. From this court there is no appeal." He added later, "And I conceive the legislature themselves, cannot set aside a judgment of this court, because they are authorised by the constitution to decide in the last resort."[19] Thus, to Brutus, judicial review, as conceived by Marshall in the Virginia debates, was nothing more than usurpation of a power that rightly belonged in the other branches.

Brutus ignored the power to amend the Constitution, since the amendment process was intentionally made so difficult both to initiate and complete. Amendments to rectify judicial usurpation were likely to be rare. The upshot to Brutus was that for Supreme Court justices, exercise of this virtually uncontrolled power "will enable them to mould the government, into almost any shape they please," and "will operate to a total subversion of the state judiciaries, if not, to the legislative authority of the states."[20]

Brutus 15 was published on March 20, 1788. Publius, this time in the person of Hamilton, did not take up the judiciary until May in Federalist 78; but in his opening paragraph, he once again made plain that he was writing as a response. After noting that "the propriety of the [judicial] institution in the abstract is not disputed; the only questions which have been raised being relative to the manner of constituting it, and to its extent," Hamilton wrote, "to these points, therefore, our observations shall be confined."[21]

Although he listed three general areas of dispute, he dismissed the first, "the mode of appointing judges," in a single sentence as "the same with that of appointing the officers of the Union in general," which he had already discussed at length. The second question, "tenure by which they are to hold their places," and the third, "the partition of the judiciary authority between different courts, and their relations to each other," were discussed at length.

Hamilton, to reassure the people of New York, described the judiciary far differently than John Marshall would in the Virginia ratifying convention. Referring to Montesquieu, Publius noted "that the judiciary is beyond comparison the weakest of the three departments of power; that it can never attack with success either of the other two; and that all possible care is requisite to enable it to defend itself against their attacks."[22]

But weakness was not impotence. Later, in Federalist 78, Hamilton at last took up the subject of judicial oversight and was unambiguous in his opinion. "No legislative act, therefore, contrary to the Constitution, can be valid," he asserts bluntly. Then, lest anyone assume that he was taking Blackstone's view, Hamilton added:

If it be said that the legislative body are themselves the constitutional judges of their own powers, and that the construction they put upon them is conclusive upon the other departments, it may be answered, that this cannot be the natural presumption, where it is not to be collected from any particular provisions in the Constitution. It is not otherwise to be supposed, that the Constitution could intend to enable the representatives of the people to substitute their *will* to that of their constituents. It is far more rational to suppose, that the courts were designed to be an intermediate body between the people and the legislature, in order, among other things, to keep the latter within the limits assigned to their authority. The interpretation of the laws is the proper and peculiar province of the courts. A constitution is, in fact, and must be regarded by the judges, as a fundamental law. It therefore belongs to them to ascertain its meaning, as well as the meaning of any particular act proceeding from the legislative body.

If there should happen to be an irreconcilable variance between the two, that which has the superior obligation and validity ought, of course, to be preferred; or, in other words, the Constitution ought to be preferred to the statute, the intention of the people to the intention of their agents.[23]

This is the single most powerful enunciation of the power that Marshall would later claim for the Supreme Court to appear anywhere in any record of the constitutional period. And yet it remains only Hamilton's opinion. Hamilton had not even been present in the Convention when the Supreme Court's powers, as defined in the Committee of Detail, were hashed out.

To a major degree, the Brutus/Publius debate, as well as many of the other ideological tussles during ratification, turned strict construction on its head. Federalists, who intended that the Constitution be applied with a degree of breadth not specifically delineated in the text, often donned the mantle of strict construction to assure the general population that the new central government would not go too far; Anti-Federalists, who intended to limit the powers of government to the narrowest possible interpretations of the wording of each article, argued from broad constructionism to demonstrate that it would.

In Federalist 78, as Brutus warned, Hamilton returned to the Federalists' broad construction roots to grant to the Supreme Court a power that was not in any way made explicit in the Constitution. His reasoning, however, was clear. The courts, he was trying to convince skeptical New Yorkers, represented "the people," and judicial nullification gave "the people"—us—power over the legislature—them. Hamilton dispelled any doubt regarding this point in the next paragraph of Federalist 78.

Nor does this conclusion by any means suppose a superiority of the judicial to the legislative power. It only supposes that the power of the people is superior to both; and that where the will of the legislature, declared in its statutes, stands in opposition to that of the people, declared in the Constitution, the judges ought to be governed by the latter rather than the former. They ought to regulate their decisions by the fundamental laws, rather than by those which are not fundamental.[24]

However, just when it seemed clear that the Hamiltonian vision of judicial review would be just as Marshall would later insist it was, Hamilton added a qualification. This passage is not cited nearly as often as the ones preceding, although it should be.

> It can be of no weight to say that the courts, on the pretense of a repug-nancy, may substitute their own pleasure to the constitutional intentions of the legislature. . . . The courts must declare the sense of the law; and if they should be disposed to exercise WILL instead of JUDGMENT, the conse-quence would equally be the substitution of their pleasure to that of the legislative body.[25]

For all their lofty intellectualism, as the New York convention began on June 17, 1788, the Publius essays appeared to have been an exercise in futil-ity. The Clintonians enjoyed a seemingly insurmountable advantage. With Rhode Island, North Carolina, and New Hampshire safely on their side (or so they thought) and Virginia expected to reject the plan as well, Clintoni-ans seemed satisfied to go through the motions of debate, then simply vote the Constitution down.

In the first weeks, everything seemed to go according to plan. To open the proceedings, Federalist Robert Livingston gave a long, impassioned speech about the benefits of the new Constitution, culminating in a motion to forgo the question of amendments until the document itself had been through a clause-by-clause discussion. Believing the Constitution doomed in any case, Anti-Federalists acquiesced to Livingston's motion.

The convention droned on, with long speeches and little action. Dele-gates evoked everyone from Montesquieu to Falstaff, while Hamilton tried desperately to persuade less doctrinaire Anti-Federalists of the benefits of the Constitution to their state, their country, and their wallets.

During the course of debate, amendments were regularly proposed in vi-olation of the earlier agreement, nine alone to Article III. All were aimed at limiting judicial power, but none addressed the possibility of the Supreme Court nullifying an act of Congress.

When word arrived on June 24 that New Hampshire had ratified without amendments, Clintonians were stunned, but were also aware that without Vir-ginia and New York there could effectively be no United States. When, how-ever, word arrived of Virginia's ratification on July 2, Anti-Federalists were thrown into disarray and Hamilton had the opening he had been praying for.

Sessions were abbreviated from July 4 to 7, canceled entirely on the eighth and ninth, and cut short on the tenth. Then, on July 11, the change of fortunes was epitomized by John Jay's motion at the opening of the session "that the Constitution under consideration ought to be *ratified* by this Convention."[26] In response, after four days of acrimonious debate in which Anti-Federalists, once so certain of victory, were forced to accept the inevitability of defeat, Melancthon Smith could only propose that ratification be conditional.

Hamilton took control. Using a combination of reason, persuasion, and threat (at one point he indicated that Federalist New York City might secede from the state if the Constitution were rejected), he wooed Clintonians. The governor desperately tried to hold his bloc together. George Clinton, however, while a wily politician, lacked both the charisma and the oratorical skills of Patrick Henry. One by one, his followers defected.

On July 19, Robert Lansing renewed the motion to ratify conditional to a bill of rights being attached, which passed. Hamilton responded by reading a letter from Madison expressing doubt whether conditional ratification would be accepted by Congress. Samuel Jones, an erstwhile Anti-Federalist, then made a counter-motion four days later to eliminate the words "on condition" and substitute "in full confidence."[27] Jones's motion passed, 31–29. Three days later, the entire package, including suggested amendments, was approved, 30–27.

Governor Clinton appended a letter that stated "Several articles . . . appear so exceptionable to a majority of us, that nothing but the fullest confidence of obtaining a revision of them by a general convention, and an invincible reluctance to separating from our sister states, could have prevailed upon a sufficient number to ratify it, without stipulating for previous amendments."[28] He circulated his letter to other states, calling for other outraged legislatures to petition for a second convention. His sentiments were nonbinding, however; and, in any case, the fact that his own state had ratified unconditionally undermined his call and left Clinton railing against the wind.

SIX

TRANSITION: CONGRESS IS TRANSFORMED AND SO IS MADISON

WITH THE AGREEMENT OF VIRGINIA AND NEW YORK, eleven states had joined the Union. In all, more than one hundred amendments had been offered, twenty by Virginia and thirty-two by New York, not one of them conditional to ratification.[1] While some represented parochial state interests and others concerned the mechanics of government or separation of powers, most were directed at the lack of definition with respect to the legal system, either as regards the broad powers granted the federal judiciary or the absence of guarantees of individual liberties. With Federalists and most of the erstwhile framers on record as opposing amendments, at least until the bugs were out of the new government, the Constitution, exactly as it had emerged from the Philadelphia Convention, would likely remain the supreme law of the land when the newly elected Congress convened. The notion of including a bill of rights at that point seemed simply one more of George Clinton's or Patrick Henry's failed attempts to derail ratification and force a second convention.

North Carolina and Rhode Island continued to resist ratification, but the business of forming a new government was initiated without them. The first order of business was for Congress, still meeting under the Articles of Confederation in New York, to prepare for the transition, thereby setting in motion the machinery of its own demise. The two holdout states remained part of this, the final Confederation Congress, and were thus allowed to participate in proceedings that, unless they relented, would force them to leave the Union.

Congress had taken the first step on July 2, 1788, when it had appointed the five-man committee to handle the transition. The following week, the committee recommended that on the first Wednesday in December, the states that ratified would appoint presidential electors as specified in Article II; on the first Wednesday in January, the electors would meet and select a chief executive; and on the first Wednesday in February, the first Constitutional Congress of the United States would convene and swear in its first president. On July 14, 1788, Madison reported Virginia's ratification, and on July 28, the committee proposed putting back by one month each the dates for the appointing of electors, casting of ballots, and convening the new government, making March 4, 1789, the day that the Constitution would become the nation's governing document. Not until September 13 did Congress vote unanimously to approve those dates and thus set in motion the process of choosing not only presidential electors, but representatives and senators for the new bicameral Congress. Representatives would be elected by popular vote, by district in six states—including Virginia—and on an at-large basis in five. Senators would be selected by state legislatures.

In Virginia, Patrick Henry, still smoldering after being bested by Madison at the ratifying convention, was determined to even the score, and the grudge he bore may well have been responsible for the Bill of Rights.

Displaying an apparent generosity of spirit that shocked even his friends, Henry supported Madison to be a part of Virginia's delegation to the final Confederation Congress. Madison was duly elected by his peers and set off for New York in early July to personally report Virginia's ratification and to help preside over the change to the new form of government that he had been so indispensable in creating.

The minute Madison was out of the state, Henry set to work, determined that none of the members of Virginia's new congressional delegation in either house would be named Madison.

Madison, as expected, was immediately nominated by the Virginia legislature to fill one of the Senate seats. Calling in favors, bullying, threatening, flattering, and cajoling—in short, behaving in character—Henry succeeded in blocking his nemesis and instead secured the appointment to the Senate of Richard Henry Lee and William Grayson, both of whom had solid Anti-Federalist credentials. In the words of a biographer, "To humiliate Madison, Henry managed his rejection by the Assembly for a seat in the Senate, referring to him as one unworthy of the confidence of the people."[2] At that point, if Madison was to be a member of the First Congress, he would need to be elected as a representative from a congressional district.

While at first glance it seemed a certainty that Madison would have no trouble securing a congressional seat from his Orange County home district, Henry was not done. The Virginia legislators were also charged with drawing district boundaries, and Henry persuaded them to sufficiently distort Madison's district to take in a large Anti-Federalist contingent that rendered the eventual result uncertain. "In an attempt to exclude Madison from the House of Representatives as well, Henry, a master of the '*gerrymander*' long before that term had been invented, placed Orange County (Madison's home area) in a congressional district otherwise composed of counties considered heavily anti-federal."[3]

To further nettle his antagonist, Henry persuaded the popular young Anti-Federalist James Monroe to stand against Madison. By late autumn, while Madison remained in New York, Monroe gained substantial support in a district where fear of centralized authority was strong. Exactly what Madison was actually up to in the capital was unclear, since, after September 13, except for sporadic activity, Congress had been inactive. From October 10 until official adjournment on March 2, the lame-duck legislature ceased conducting business altogether, only one or two congressmen attending any particular session in order that the government not be seen as having disbanded. Still, as winter approached, Madison feared to leave Congress, as "it will have an electioneering appearance which I always despised and wish to shun."[4] It was a rare political blunder by one of the most astute politicians in American history.

In early December 1788, Madison finally grasped that his political future was in dire jeopardy and that he should return home without delay. Madison left New York so quickly that he did not even take the time to write to his father and tell him of his departure.[5] He arrived in Alexandria on December 17 and traveled on to Orange County two days later. As soon as he arrived, he understood that he had been outmaneuvered by Henry. In the political vacuum that had been created by his absence, Monroe had made immense headway by backing a strong bill of rights. Furthermore, Madison's opposition to amendments, as reported by Henry's minions, seemed to be a matter of record.

Within two weeks, Madison, with typical dexterity, had made a pragmatic switch. On January 2, 1789, he received a letter from a supporter, George Nicholas, confirming to him that Henry "and his tools" had circulated the notion that Madison was opposed to all amendments. Nicholas urged him to counter. "It gives me pleasure," Nicholas wrote, "to find by your letter of the 29th of Dec that you have returned home and intend to make your sentiments known to the inhabitants of your district."[6] That same day, Madison wrote to a local minister, George Eve.

"Being informed that reports prevail not only that I am opposed to any amendments whatever to the new federal constitution, but that I have ceased to be a friend of the rights of Conscience," Madison began, obviously referring to Henry's calumny, ". . . but having been induced to offer my services to this district as its representative in the federal legislature, considerations of a public nature make it proper that . . . my principles and views be rightly understood."

Madison continued, "Whilst [the Constitution] remained unratified, and it was necessary to unite the states in some one plan, I opposed all previous alterations as calculated to throw the States into dangerous contentions, and to furnish the secret enemies of the Union with an opportunity of promoting its dissolution. Circumstances are now changed. The Constitution is established on the ratifications of eleven States and a very great majority of the people of America, and amendments, if pursued with a proper moderation and in a proper mode, will be not only safe, but may serve the double purpose of satisfying the minds of well meaning opponents, and of providing additional guards in favour of liberty. Under this change of circumstances, it is my sincere opinion that the Constitution ought to be revised, and that the first Congress meeting under it, ought to prepare and recommend . . . the most satisfactory provisions for all essential rights."[7] Within those essential rights, Madison stressed those that relate to "right of Conscience": in other words, freedom of speech, religion, and association. In what was billed to Eve as a clarification, Madison had in fact staked out completely new ground and reversed a position that, until his return from New York, he had insisted was correct.

Now a supporter of the amendment process, Madison took the offensive. Always sickly, he nonetheless rode on horseback throughout the district, often in freezing January weather, assuring potential constituents of his commitment to individual liberty. He debated Monroe wherever possible, using the occasions to stress his commitment to amendments to cut the ground from under his opponent. In what must have been an unpleasant irony to Patrick Henry, not only did Madison and Monroe become friends that January, but Madison began to be seen as a champion of the very issues that Henry had for the previous eighteen months claimed as his own. When the election took place on February 2, Madison won by 366 votes.

The House of Representatives did not achieve a quorum until April 1, 1789, three weeks after Madison arrived, the Senate not until April 6. Even with the required twelve senators in the chamber, only eight of the eleven states were initially represented. Ironically, one of the states with neither senator present was Congress's home state of New York, whose legislature had yet to appoint either member of the upper house.* With both houses of Congress at that point officially in session, much of their collective first day was spent in joint session, tabulating the electoral votes for president and vice president and preparing communications to the victors. George Washington was confirmed as the first president, receiving all 69 electoral votes, with the new vice president, John Adams, coming in second with 34.[8]

The next day, April 7, the senators confined their business to the appointment of two committees. One consisted of five senators—Oliver Ellsworth of Connecticut, William Maclay of Pennsylvania,[9] Richard Bassett of Delaware, Richard Henry Lee of Virginia, and Caleb Strong of Massachusetts—who were charged with preparing rules of procedure, coordinating with the House of Representatives on rules for conference committees, and considering the manner of appointing chaplains. The second committee, which consisted of the same five men plus Paine Wingate of New Hampshire, William Paterson of New Jersey, and William Few of Georgia, was appointed "to bring in a bill for organizing the Judiciary of the United States."[10]

The committee to create a judicial branch, then, had one senator from each of the eight states represented. When Charles Carroll of Maryland and Ralph Izard of South Carolina arrived the following Monday, they were immediately added to the committee so that each state present would continue to be represented. Five of the ten members, therefore, charged with creating the judicial branch of the government—Ellsworth, Bassett, Strong, Paterson,

---

* New York would remain unrepresented until Rufus King presented his credentials on July 25. Philip Schuyler joined the Senate two days later.

and Few—had been delegates to the Constitutional Convention that had largely abdicated this responsibility. Moreover, the committee roster was noteworthy for the surprising paucity of legal scholarship among the members. Of the ten, only Ellsworth, Paterson, and Strong were sophisticated legal theoreticians, and so these three former delegates immediately took control of the committee.[11]

The committee began its work immediately, but left negligible written records of its deliberations. Within three weeks, however, the committee appears to have come to some general agreement as to the outlines of a bill.[12] Two weeks after that, on May 11, Maclay reported that the committee had appointed a subcommittee—consisting, naturally, of Ellsworth, Paterson, and Strong—to draft a finished bill. "I do not like it in any part," Maclay wrote.[13]

The Anti-Federalist Maclay's distaste is not surprising. All three men were staunch northern Federalists. Ellsworth had been one of the key delegates at the Constitutional Convention, with a hand not only in fashioning the Connecticut Compromise, which provided for by-state vote in the Senate, but also in a compromise at the end of August 1787 with the South Carolina rice planters whereby Northern merchants gained assurance of the free flow of commerce in return for extending the slave trade for twenty years. He had returned to Connecticut to lead the battle for ratification. Paterson had arrived in Philadelphia as a leading Anti-Federalist and had authored the small states' New Jersey Plan. With the adoption of the Connecticut Compromise, however, he had switched allegiance and become a fervent proponent of the new Constitution and brawny central government. Strong had spoken little at the convention but made no secret of his agreement with the other two on all major Federalist tenets.

Much to Maclay's chagrin, the three separated themselves from their seven colleagues and proceeded to work privately to draft a judiciary bill, functioning much as had the Committee of Detail in Philadelphia, of which Ellsworth had been a member. Although Ellsworth and Strong wrote letters to colleagues in their respective states to ask for opinions on certain procedural issues with which they were wrestling, none of the three included other committee members in their deliberations. One month later, on June 12, the draft was complete and the full committee met to consider the product. Although there was at least tentative general agreement, the caustic Maclay found the draft bill "long and somewhat confused."[14]

The first sections of the draft bill, in Paterson's handwriting, were largely concerned with the organization of the judicial branch.[15] Paterson delineated the number of Supreme Court justices (six), when the Court would meet (semi-annually), and what constituted a quorum (four).

The federal judiciary would be divided into three layers. Directly under the Supreme Court would be a tier of three circuit courts (eastern, middle, and southern), and, under the circuit courts, thirteen federal district courts. This organization demonstrates that the three Federalists were certainly cognizant of philosophical strife and tried to walk a middle ground. While they stopped short of the Anti-Federalist notion of using state courts as inferior federal courts, they did create a sufficient number of district courts to "bring the judiciary to the people." The mid-layer circuit courts would be

William Paterson

staffed not with their own judges but rather with a district court judge and two Supreme Court justices, who would ride circuit twice a year in between sessions of the high court.[16]

Circuit-riding was not new, of course, but rather an established feature of the British court system. Judges regularly ventured from Westminster into the countryside to dispense justice, thereby, according to Sir Matthew Hale in his *History of the Common Law*, ensuring "a consonancy, congruity, and uniformity" in the administration of the law.[17] By emulating this system and manning the circuit courts with existing judges, the bill could also help obviate another pressing problem with Anti-Federalists. Funding for all those new judges promised to be a strain on an already overburdened treasury, to say nothing of the uproar that would certainly emanate from many quarters of the citizenry at the prospect of diverting scarce resources to a court system that many did not want in the first place. Using Supreme Court and district court judges as circuit court judges would at least help keep the expenditures down.

But circuit-riding in what was largely a frontier nation like the United States would prove to be quite a different phenomenon than that in settled, domesticated England. "In the early decades of the Supreme Court's history, riding circuit for its justices meant bouncing thousands of miles over rutted, dirt roads in stagecoach, on horseback, and in stick gigs to bring the federal judiciary system to the American communities strewn along the Eastern seaboard."[18] As the nation expanded, the situation would only get worse. Further exacerbating the disagreeability of circuit-riding was that the justices were not young men and, with lifetime tenure, were not likely to get younger. Circuit-riding was to engender a series of problems of its own and contribute in no small way to the crisis that was to threaten the Republic twelve years later.

Also included in the bill was Section 13, which included innocent-enough phrasing, or so it seemed at the time:

> The Supreme Court shall also have appellate jurisdiction from the circuit
> courts and courts of the several states, in the cases hereinafter specially
> provided for; and shall have power to issue writs of prohibition to the dis-
> trict courts, when proceeding as courts of admiralty and maritime juris-
> diction, and writs of *mandamus*, in cases warranted by the principles and

usages of law, to any courts appointed, or persons holding office, under the authority of the United States.

The draft judiciary bill was first debated in the Senate on Monday, June 22, and Anti-Federalists immediately tried to minimize the jurisdiction of federal courts. Richard Henry Lee proposed "That the jurisdiction of the Federal courts should be confined to cases of admiralty and maritime jurisdiction."[19] Federalists countered. "Elsworth [sic] answered them, and the ball was kept up until past three o'clock."[20] The Anti-Federalist Maclay on this occasion supported Ellsworth, whom he loathed:

> I rose and begged to make a remark or two. The effect of the motion was to exclude the Federal jurisdiction from each of the States except in admiralty and maritime cases. But the Constitution expressly extended it to all cases, in law and equity, under the Constitution and laws of the United States; treaties made or to be made, etc. We already had existing treaties, and were about making many laws. These must be executed by the Federal judiciary. The arguments which had been used would apply well if amendment to the Constitution were under consideration, but certainly were inapplicable here.[21]

Wrangling over the bill continued for the remainder of the week, into the next and eventually to July, Maclay more than once characterizing a speech as "harangue." "The lawyers were in a rage for speaking," he said at one point.[22] Debate once again centered on jurisdiction—just how many cases would come to federal court rather than being decided in state court. Lee and his cohorts, insisting that federal courts should hear almost no cases, moved to limit the number of district courts and eliminate circuit courts entirely. Ellsworth, of course, opposed both motions, although he was careful to couch his arguments in the need for a national judiciary rather than discuss the tendency of a national judiciary to overpower the states. In all the debates, however, careful attention was paid by both sides to ensure that the final version conformed to the Constitution. Hundreds of minor changes were proposed and dozens were made. In endless hours of parsing and revision, however, no one, it appears—not one of all those "lawyers" Maclay complained about—thought to question whether the expansion of the Supreme Court's original jurisdiction in Section 13 violated the Constitution.

The bill, after additional changes in language (but again none in the salient phrase of Section 13) finally passed the Senate on July 17 by a vote of 14–6, Maclay and Lee being among the losers. Maclay, although he supported Ellsworth on some constitutional questions, left no question as to his sentiments for the man or the bill. "This vile bill is a child of his, and he defends it with the care of a parent, even with wrath and anger. He kindled, as he always does, when it is meddled with."[23] The bill was then passed on to the House three days later.

With such a vital bill finally reaching its chamber, members of the House might have been expected to begin at once to debate the organization of the judiciary. Instead, they did not take up the bill for more than five weeks. Robert Morris, growing impatient with the delay, wrote angrily to a friend in early August that the House "had been amusing themselves with proposing Amendments to the Constitution."[24]

Those amendments—which would become the Bill of Rights—were, of course, the product of James Madison's conversion from Federalist to proto-Republican.[25]

By the time Madison took his seat in Congress on March 14, 1789, he was a man transformed. Not only would he refuse to recant his conversion to a bill of rights to amend the Constitution, he would become its most passionate and effective champion. By the time the First Congress adjourned two years later, James Madison had abandoned virtually all the theories with which he had arrived in Philadelphia in May 1787 and replaced them with Jeffersonian decentralization.

Madison's metamorphosis was one of the great turnabouts in political history. He became as passionate, as scholarly, as reasoned, and as ruthless a Republican as he had previously been as a Federalist. In the process, he went from friend and intimate of Alexander Hamilton to bitter enemy.[26] Although it would have been unthinkable at the Philadelphia Convention or the Virginia ratifying convention, in the great battle to come between the Federalist ideal of a powerful central government—with judiciary to match—and Republican determination to dilute both, Madison would be the defendant in the case that would determine the winner. Even more unthinkable, Madison would misread the results of that case, thinking himself the winner when, in actuality, he had been the loser.

Although Robert Morris had not been completely fair in his denunciation—the House dealt with myriad other bills during that five weeks—Madison had certainly attempted to coerce his fellow representatives into enacting what had become his pet measure.

On June 8, Madison had presented rambling draft amendments to the House. His notion was to incorporate the amendments by revising the text of the document that had emerged from Philadelphia and had just endured the ratification process.[27] Although critical organization and revenue business had been dominating the early sessions, Madison asked that the legislators put these aside and immediately discuss his proposal. Madison blithely assured his colleagues that the amendments could be approved that very same day.[28] There was immediate protest. Not everyone was pleased with the idea of amendments at all, and even supporters believed that Madison's notion of completing the business so quickly was ludicrous. One representative pointed out that amending the Constitution before a judiciary had been created to enforce its provisions seemed to have things backwards.[29] After a number of long speeches objecting to the waste of a day, Madison pointed out that if the speeches had been on the question at hand "we might have rose and resumed the consideration of other business before this time."[30]

Madison's measure was effectively tabled, but he reintroduced his amendments on July 21, the day after the judiciary bill had been transmitted from the Senate. "Mr. Madison begged the House to indulge him in further consideration of amendments to the constitution, and, as there appeared in some degree, a moment of leisure, he would move to go to a Committee of the whole on the subject, conformably to the order of the 8th of last month."[31] "Moment of leisure" was something of an overstatement, but by this time the House had disposed of enough pressing legislation—although it had tabled the judiciary bill—that Madison was successful in initiating debate on the amendments. Ultimately the matter was referred to an eleven-man committee, of which Madison was a member.

The following week, the committee presented its report. Some Anti-Federalists, dissatisfied with Madison's emphasis on civil liberties, had suc-ceeded in adding a number of amendments that would have watered down the power of the central government with respect to the states. In the in-terim, debate on the judiciary bill had again been postponed so that the House could finalize other legislation on government organization. Al-though the committee had also pared down Madison's language, feeling on the floor remained extreme and the amendments were recommitted. Finally, on August 13, after even further machinations, discussion began. The House did little else for the following ten days (thus prompting Robert Morris's complaint).[32]

During the discussion, Madison realized that Anti-Federalists were at-tempting to hijack the amendment process to alter the very fundamentals of government that the Constitution had created. "But while I approve of these amendments [his own] I should oppose the consideration at this time of such as are likely to change the principles of government."[33]

On Saturday, August 22, the House voted to approve twelve amend-ments to the Constitution, to be appended as a supplement.[34] At the next session, on August 24, the House sent the amendments on to the Senate. During that same session, discussion of the judiciary bill was finally begun.

Fresh from the acrimony over amendments, bickering about the courts began instantly. Anti-Federalists once again proposed countless alterations, everything from reducing the number of Supreme Court justices to chang-ing the definition of a quorum to limiting district courts to admiralty cases to eliminating district courts entirely to not empaneling a Supreme Court and, finally, to simply eliminating the legislation entirely. Virtually every clause that either granted the new national judiciary what was seen as sweeping power or provided advantage to the federal courts over those of the states was attacked.[35] In defense, Federalists were reduced to mouthing the same assurances as they had in the ratifying conventions. After that un-productive beginning, the judiciary bill was tabled for another five days.

When debate resumed on Saturday, August 29, the discussion was more focused.[36] Although objections still came in many forms, most, at their core, centered on the potential of federal district courts to usurp jurisdiction that Anti-Federalists were convinced rightly belonged to the states. Except for certain specific types of cases, opponents of the bill were, in effect, attempt-ing to eliminate a national court system entirely. As Egbert Benson of New

York noted, "If the House decided in favor of the present question, it would involve a total abandonment of the judicial power, excepting those cases the honorable gentlemen mean to provide for, namely, the Courts of Admiralty and the Supreme Courts."[37] In any case, jurisdiction of the federal system was being defined as narrowly as possible. Some of the proposals to limit breadth were substantive, many were trivial. William L. Smith of South Carolina was so exhaustive in his objections that Madison replied, "He was inclined to amend every part of the bill, so as to remove the gentleman's jealousy, providing it could be done consistently with the constitution."[38]

With such scrutiny cast on the question of jurisdiction, one might well expect any clause that expanded the power of the national courts—Section 13, for example—to come under attack. But it was never mentioned.

Debate continued on Monday, and the measure was tabled until September 9. Finally, on September 17, the judiciary bill passed, by a vote of 36–17. Although no complete record of the debates exists—the House reporter often simply wrote "discussion ensued," or "after desultory discussion"—neither is there any indication that the "mandamus" sentence of Section 13 was questioned. Had Congress had any notion of the importance that this one simple phrase would take on, debate would have been fierce.

That a seemingly innocuous clause turned out to be pivotal is not surprising. What is surprising is that such a flagrant violation of a short and seemingly straightforward Article III escaped the notice of two Houses of Congress during six weeks of furious and often petty debate in which no fewer than eight key delegates to the Philadelphia Convention took part.[39] Did it never occur to one of them to protest this unbridled expansion of the Supreme Court's original jurisdiction or to chastise fellow delegates Ellsworth, Paterson, and Strong for perverting the document that had been so tortuously and painfully produced?

Nor is it credible that such a significant expansion of the Supreme Court's power simply slipped by everyone. Thus, clearly, either Congress, including all those Philadelphia delegates, thought Section 13 an appropriate expression of legislative power, or they read the clause as not expanding original jurisdiction and not conflicting with the prohibitions of Article III, Section 2. Supporting these latter scenarios is that Ellsworth and Paterson, the bill's key authors, were both intimate with the proceedings in Philadelphia as well as being first-rate legal scholars. Both would sit on the Supreme Court, Ellsworth as the third chief justice and Paterson as a key associate, and it seems extremely unlikely that these men would knowingly draft a law that violated a Constitution they had been so instrumental in drafting.

The bill authorizing amendments was returned from the Senate to the House on September 24, passed, and sent to President Washington for sig-nature. The same day, the judiciary bill was sent to the president as well.

The combination of *tabula rasa* and an effective one-party system made the first Congress perhaps the most productive in American history. They chose a site for the national capital, set tariffs to raise revenue, and passed a plethora of laws to organize the new government. The two most far-reaching actions, however, were in plugging the holes in the legal system. The Bill of Rights, of course, is still with us today; and the judiciary act, although tossed about, stayed in force for a century.[40]

PART II

"The Weakest of the Three"

SEVEN

A LONG AND FRUSTRATING RIDE: JAY
TAKES THE REINS

R EORGANIZATION OF THE GOVERNMENT was very much done on the fly. In April 1789, with the Articles of Confederation defunct, the nation was technically operating under a legal system limited to the specific—and broadly drawn—provisions of the new Constitution. Until the Senate and the House agreed in what manner to provide weight and definition to Article III and passed it on to President Washington for signature, the only judicial posts certain to be filled were some small but indeterminate number of justices to the Supreme Court.*

Still, constitutional vagueness notwithstanding, there was no doubt that chief justice—for there was sure to be one of those—would be a plum job. More than thirty of the fifty delegates to the Convention had been lawyers, and members of the legal profession dominated the new Congress. Not surprisingly, applications for appointment as the highest judicial officer in the land were received almost as soon as the new government was formed. James Wilson, for example, as early as April 21, 1789, wrote an obsequious and almost laughably transparent note to President Washington announcing his fitness, availability, and, most of all, his eagerness for the post.

Aware that lobbying for a position that was supposed to be non-political and impartial might be considered unseemly, Wilson wrote, "A delicacy arising from your situation and character as well as my own has hitherto prevented me from mentioning to your Excellency a subject of much importance to me. Perhaps I should not even now have broken silence but

---

* Washington himself was powerless to jump-start the process, as Article III, Section 1 had specifically left the design of the judiciary to Congress.

for one consideration. A regard to the dignity of the Government over which you preside will naturally lead you to take care that its honours be in no event exposed to affected indifference or contempt. For this reason, you may well expect that before you nominate any gentleman to an employ-ment (especially one of high trust) you should have it in your power to pre-clude him, in case of disappointment, from pretending that the nomination was made without his knowledge or consent. Under this view, I commit myself to your Excellency without reserve and inform you that my aim rises to the important office of Chief Justice of the United States. But how shall I proceed? Shall I enumerate reasons in justification of my high pretensions? . . . Your Excellency must relieve me of this dilemma. You must think and act properly on the occasion, without my saying anything on ei-ther side of the question."[1]

Wilson should have been a fitting and obvious choice, but Washington was faced with considerations that far outweighed the judicial credentials of the first chief justice. For one thing, Wilson's close association with Robert Morris—he had for some time been Morris's lawyer—could have presented a risk that Morris would by association gain control of a branch of the gov-ernment. Morris, although generally a loyal Federalist, reserved his main loyalty for himself, and thus appointing Wilson to head the Court might well have been out of the question on that ground alone.

Wilson was far from the only supplicant. John Rutledge of South Car-olina wanted the job desperately. Cleverer than Wilson, Rutledge persuaded friends to bombard Washington with pleas to appoint him rather than make the entreaties personally. Robert Livingston of New York also made little se-cret that he actively sought the appointment. Alexander Hamilton was ru-mored to be interested, although running the nation's finances as head of the treasury was said to hold greater appeal. Any number of lesser lights coveted the position as well, many of them longtime friends or associates of the president.

Washington, whose own political deftness is often underrated, held him-self above the fray. He maintained publicly and in letters to associates that the judiciary was a branch of government unlike the other two, and that the Supreme Court therefore had to remain free of any taint of partisanship. Ap-pointments to the bench were to be made on the strength of qualification alone. "Impressed with a conviction that the true administration of justice is the firmest pillar of good government," he wrote to Edmund Randolph,

"I have considered the first arrangement of the judicial department as essential to the happiness of our country and the stability of its political system. Hence the selection of the fittest characters to expound the laws and dispense justice has been an invariable subject of my anxious concern."[2]

Washington was even more nimble with Livingston, whom he had no intention of appointing.* Aware that Livingston enjoyed wide popular support, Washington wrote, "When I accepted of the important trust committed to my charge by my country, I plainly foresaw that the part of my duty that obliged me to nominate persons to office would, in many instances, be the most irksome and unpleasing . . . I was fully determined to keep myself free from every engagement that could embarrass me in discharging this part of my administration. I have therefore declined giving any decisive answer to the numerous applications which have been made to me."[3]

While Washington might be able to deflect the ambitions of applicants whom he did not want, finding the man he did want was an operation that required great delicacy. Precisely because the Constitution had been so vague and a federal judiciary was to be such an unknown, the political risks of putting the wrong man in the job were acute. His lofty public remonstrations notwithstanding, the Supreme Court was from the first considered by virtually everyone to be a political body, as much an instrument of policy as an arbiter of federal law. Washington could ill afford a chief justice who would use the Court to stake out his own power base, as Rutledge was almost certain to do, or provide one by proxy, as might Wilson. The president also had to be at least fairly certain that the Court would be an extension of Federalist principles and not an independent body that struck off on its own to thwart the new administration's key objectives.

Since treaties, for example, fell under the purview of Congress and, by extension, the judiciary, the new Supreme Court might certainly soon be faced with cases arising from outstanding debts owed by American citizens to British creditors. Although payment of these debts had been guaranteed in the Treaty of Paris, there was widespread sentiment in parts of the nation to simply ignore British claims. Courts in many states, particularly in the South, had refused to enforce collection, regardless of anything the treaty might have said, but Washington was determined that these obligations be

---

* Livingston had committed the politically fatal error of arousing the enmity of Hamilton during the power struggle for control of New York's Federalist Party.

paid. Default would provide the Crown with justification to also disregard the treaty and maintain forts and garrisons in the Northwest, choking off expansion and trade, to say nothing of providing an ever-present threat of invasion to population centers on the Atlantic seaboard. If Washington was going to be able to compel state courts to adhere to the treaty, a strong federal court system was the most workable option, and the court system, especially in such an ephemeral environment, would likely be a reflection of the man chosen to head it.*

So Washington was faced with finding a man sufficiently strong to do the job, one on whom he could count politically, but also of sufficient prestige and perceived independence not to be seen as simply a tool of the president or Congress. Wilson was not that man, nor was Rutledge, nor Livingston, nor any other of the proffered candidates. Hamilton, temperamentally perfect and a powerhouse, was far too divisive. There was, however, a candidate who seemed perfect and, fortuitously, turned out not only to be available but, in a conversation with the president in August 1789, had indicated that he wanted the job.

Of impeccable character and credentials, John Jay had been president of the Continental Congress, minister to Spain, secretary for foreign affairs in the Confederation, a member of the quartet charged with negotiating peace with England, co-author of the Federalist papers (although few knew that at the time), and a resolute Federalist nonetheless acceptable to George Clinton as well as to Alexander Hamilton. Best of all, Jay, also mentioned as a candidate for secretary of state, was an intimate of Washington's and shared the president's view that properly adjudicating British claims against Americans would perhaps be the Court's most vital initial function.

There were, however, two drawbacks to Jay's appointment. The first was that, although he had served two years as chief justice of the New York Supreme Court, "his practice as a lawyer had been of short duration."[4] In fact, Jay had not appeared in a courtroom in more than a decade, and his legal credentials were not especially impressive. For him, judicial sensibilities were subordinate to political exigency, which, ironically, made him all the more appealing to Washington.

---

* Another argument against Rutledge was that, as a loyal Carolinian, he might well have supported negating claims by British creditors. His antipathy to the North a matter of record, he would feel little concern about the presence of British forts in the Northwest.

The second problem was political: during an attempt to negotiate a treaty with Spain in 1785, Jay had aroused the enmity of the Southern states when he had shown himself willing to bargain away navigation rights to the Mississippi for access to some of the more desirable Spanish ports in the Caribbean. When he had presented the deal—in which he had specifically violated his mandate not to surrender rights to the great river—he had been shouted down in Congress and accused of treachery and deceit. A Jay appointment, Washington knew, would signal a tilting to Northern commercial interests—as a Rutledge appointment would do the opposite—and might well set up renewed protests from settlers in the Southwest.

But complaints from backcountry South Carolinians and Virginians were not about to dissuade Washington, and so, on September 24, the day he signed the Judiciary Act of 1789 into law, Washington sent the nomination of John Jay as first chief justice of the Supreme Court to Congress. On the same day, he submitted nominations for the five men who would be Jay's associates. Rutledge and Wilson were both given consolation prizes, as were

John Jay

two other aspirants to Jay's job, both distinguished judges, William Cushing of Massachusetts and Robert H. Harrison of Maryland. The fifth associate was Washington's close friend and fellow Virginian John Blair, a noted legal theorist and chief justice of the Virginia Court of Appeals, who had been a delegate to the Constitutional Convention but had never spoken or served on any of the committees. The geographical spread of the appointees was no accident—in addition to the obvious advantage of a Supreme Court that was representative of the diversity of the nation it served, the circuit-riding provision of the Judiciary Act created an almost mandatory requirement that at least one justice live in each of the three delineated circuits. This first complement would allow Jay and Cushing to cover New England, Wilson and Harrison the middle states, and Rutledge and Blair the South, although Blair would be the only justice who would not ride circuit in his home state.[*]

The Senate quickly confirmed all six appointments, and the first step in creating a federal judiciary would have been complete except that four days later, Justice Harrison resigned, preferring to remain in Maryland, where he had just been appointed chancellor. Whether or not the circuit-riding requirement contributed to his decision, the speedy resignation of a justice to take what seemed a far less important state office did not portend well for the prestige of the Court. Washington chose not to immediately fill Harrison's seat and did not do so until the following year, when he appointed James Iredell of North Carolina.[5] Rutledge was a bigger problem. Furious at being passed over for chief justice, he simply refused to travel to the North—which he had detested dating back to his days in the Stamp Act Congress in New York in 1765—but nor would he resign his seat. Although he would ride circuit in the Carolinas and Georgia, he would never once appear for a meeting of the full Court in either New York or Philadelphia, until finally he resigned his seat in 1791 to become chief justice in his home state.[6]

Four months passed until the Court actually met on February 1, 1790, as mandated in the Judiciary Act. The Court had no dedicated chambers, so

---

[*] North Carolina was not yet in the Union—it joined November 21, 1789—and so the southern circuit consisted only of South Carolina and sparsely populated Georgia. Washington was loath to appoint two justices from one state, and naming a justice from Georgia over one from either Maryland or Virginia was equally out of the question.

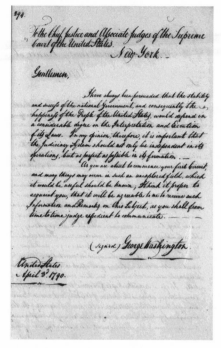

George Washington's letter to John Jay and his Supreme Court associates

the initial meeting was held in the second-floor courtroom of the Exchange Building at the foot of Broad Street in New York City.[7] The ground floor, ordinarily a public market, was closed for the day to provide proper decorum for the occasion.

The first session of the Supreme Court of the United States was ushered in with great fanfare, but while the courtroom was filled with dignitaries, the bench was not. Only three justices—Jay, Wilson, and Cushing—had showed up for the opening session, although each was bedecked in a black silk robe highlighted in what one observer called "party colors."* Lacking a quorum or any business to do, it lasted less than ten minutes, Jay then adjourning until the next day when William Blair arrived.

While the second day of the session was more productive than the first— a good deal of administrative business was attended to, including the granting of credentials to a number of lawyers to plead before the Court—the

---

* Most likely red or, in Jay's case, salmon.

docket remained empty, and so Jay adjourned this meeting quickly as well. Two days later, the first session of the Supreme Court was closed, after which the justices—those who had bothered to show up—were feted at a grand banquet at Fraunces Tavern. From there, Jay and the associates left to ride circuit.

Although the actual travel was tedious, the chief justice's first circuit experience belied how controversial the semi-annual judicial caravans would become. Whether it be New York, New Haven, Boston, or Portsmouth, New Hampshire, Jay was met by enthusiastic members of the legal community and local dignitaries, lodged at convivial inns, and treated with the adulation that accompanied his personification of another major step in the new republic's maturation. And while only a handful of cases were brought before the new federal circuit courts, the mere existence of such courts in cities across the nation had fulfilled the founders' desire to bring justice to the people.

The second session of the Court convened in August 1790, this time with five justices present, lacking Rutledge but including the newly appointed Iredell. Although the docket was once again bare, the first hint of acrimony was injected into the proceedings when Justice Iredell demanded a reconsideration of the circuit-riding rules.

While Jay and Cushing, in the northern circuit, traveled between well-settled cities on generally good roads and stayed in comfortable inns, the southern circuit was often little more than wilderness. As the Supreme Court Historical Society described, "After jolting in a stagecoach many hours daily over savage roads of ruts and rocks or helping lift the stagecoach from quagmires of mud, the Justices passed restless nights in crowded way stations. Battered and exhausted by the rigors of travel, Justices often arrived at the circuit courts too late or too sick to hold a session."[8] Iredell also pointed out that just getting to his circuit from New York involved extensive travel, so that between court sessions and the two circuits, he would be forced into almost full-time service. (Rutledge, of course, had found his own solution to the problem.)

Iredell proposed that circuits be rotated, so that each of the three pairs might experience both the comforts of the north and the rigors of the south. Jay demurred. A northern sophisticate to his bones, Jay, who had decided that he did not much like circuit-riding anyway, certainly had no intention of bouncing over ruts and staying in primitive inns in the wilds of Georgia.

Jay told Iredell that rotation would destroy continuity, since different justices might take different positions on an issue from one session to the next and, exercising the prerogative of his office, declared that justices would be assigned permanently to the various circuits. What Jay and Iredell did agree on, along with the three other justices present, was that circuit-riding was a hare-brained idea. Jay went so far as to draft a joint letter to Congress decrying the practice and even intimating that the overlap of circuit courts on the Supreme Court violated the Constitution, but the letter was never posted. The question of circuit-riding was shelved but hardly resolved.

With no cases to decide, after less than a week the justices once again returned home to prepare for the fall circuit. Jay left New York in September and would not return home until late December, this time in a foul humor. Although Boston had been to his liking, he had also been forced to stop at an increasing number of towns, including one in Rhode Island, which had finally ratified the Constitution and joined the Union. Some of the inns were dirty, the food often not to his liking, and his coach forced to travel on less well-repaired roads as the circuit ranged farther afield. Although the spring 1791 journey was improved—Jay took along his wife and eldest son—the chief began to detest circuit-riding. The associate justices' experiences were, if anything, worse, with Iredell complaining that circuit-riding had reduced him to a "traveling post boy."[9]

Antipathy to circuit-riding notwithstanding, with not a single action yet reaching the Supreme Court, circuit courts were the only venues in which the justices could actually adjudicate cases. More importantly, loath to admit it as they were, circuit courts were the only means to bring the full bearing of the new national government to the provinces. "It was, in fact, almost entirely through their contact with the Judges sitting in these Circuit Courts that the people of the country became acquainted with this new institution, the Federal Judiciary."[10] The states, accustomed to doing much as they pleased under the Articles, were reluctant, even blatantly antipathetic, to come to grips with the realities of subordinate authority. Washington, Jay, and other strong nationalists were equally determined that the states be forced to acknowledge the higher sovereignty of the national government. With Congress and the president largely occupied by foreign affairs, finance, and establishing a new capital, the judiciary was the obvious vehicle with which to assert federal authority over local government. As a result, some of the cases that the justices encountered on circuit turned out to be of great significance.

In May 1791, for example, Jay's circuit court, meeting in Hartford, was presented with an appeal to a Connecticut law that did not allow interest to accrue on debts to British or Tory creditors unless the creditors were available to be paid, in effect forgiving interest on American debt for the entire war. This was to be the first test of Washington's resolve to ensure that British creditors were treated fairly, and Jay was up to the challenge. The circuit court struck down the Connecticut law on the grounds that there was no provision for withholding interest in the peace treaty between the United States and Great Britain. Since treaties supersede any law that a state might pass, the law was therefore void.[11] The court, either by design or coincidence, had chosen an apt case with which to assert federal supremacy. The decision, although repugnant to debtors, was cheered by Federalists. The *Hartford Courant* observed, "Numerous spectators beheld the corpse [of the law] . . . hoped that it might never rise again in this world to our shame or in the world to come to our confusion."[12]

Seemingly lost in the debate over the annulment of the law itself was Jay's assertion of national supremacy. None of the contemporary accounts mentioned that, for the first time, the newly created federal judiciary had struck down a local law on the grounds of vested sovereignty. Federalists were fortunate that this test came in Connecticut, rather than Virginia or Maryland—or even New York—where such a ruling by a federal circuit court might easily have been ignored and a constitutional crisis thus precipitated.

The next year, Jay's circuit court, this time sitting in Rhode Island, struck down a state law interfering with the obligation of contract, and in 1793 another Connecticut law was struck down. In those first years of the judiciary, in fact, the circuit courts, which the justices disliked with varying degrees of intensity, were proving to be precisely the sort of vibrant institutions that the Supreme Court itself was not. The problem, in addition to the entropic nature of the circuits and the difficulty in getting there, was that a decision in circuit court lacked the heft to rise to the level of policy or even Constitutional interpretation. While Jay seemed to be making exceptional progress in establishing national authority—there was certainly tacit acceptance, at least in the North, that circuit courts could deal with state statutes on a case-by-case basis—few in any of the states were prepared to yet acknowledge an inherent statutory superiority of the federal judiciary over state law.[13] The limits of circuit-court rulings were not lost on the justices.

In any case, these small, local victories did little to obviate growing depres-
sion within the Court's ranks brought on by the dual melancholies of circuit-
riding and inactivity in the high tribunal. As Chief Justice Rehnquist later
remarked, "During the first decade of the new republic, the Supreme Court
decided a total of sixty cases—not *sixty* cases per year, but about *six* per year,
because there was so little business to do."[14] Indeed, after the August 1791
term, the Supreme Court's fourth, it had yet to hear a single case.

In the absence of legal work, the justices' semi-annual meetings in these
first years were almost entirely devoted to trying to find a way to end circuit-
riding. When the Court moved to Philadelphia, the new national capital, in
1791, the rigors of the southern circuit were to some degree ameliorated.
Jay's travel burden only increased, however, as the Court was no longer in
his home city.

All this became too much for Rutledge. Although he had never attended
a Supreme Court session, he nonetheless decided that a man of his stature
deserved better than the ragtag band he felt the Court had become. In November 1791, he quit.[15] Rutledge's resignation left President Washington in a
quandary. Jefferson's Republicanism was making great inroads in the South,
and South Carolina was the only remaining Federalist bastion in the region.
The president was therefore desperate to appoint a man of prestige from that
state to take Rutledge's place. He wrote a joint letter to Edmund Rutledge,
John's brother and the youngest signer of the Declaration of Independence,
and Charles Cotesworth Pinckney, imploring either of them to take the job,
but both refused, opting to remain in state government.

Washington cast about further, but so marginal was the Court in the nation's affairs that the only man he could find was not a South Carolinian,
but rather fifty-nine-year-old Thomas Johnson of Maryland. And Washington could only cajole the aging Johnson to take the job by assuring him that
"the arrangement had been made or would be so agreed upon that you
might be wholly exempted from performing this tour of duty [circuit-riding]
at that time." In fact, Washington had only persuaded the other justices to
agree not to assign the new man to the southern circuit, not to give Johnson a complete pass. Washington felt safe in the finesse, however, since he
went on to observe to Johnson that he was certain circuit-riding would soon
be eliminated entirely.*

---

* Washington's prognostication was a bit off. Circuit-riding was not wholly eliminated until 1891.

By this time, Jay was seriously reconsidering his decision to take the job. With Congress and the president engaged in tumultuous activities, it was deeply frustrating for a man who had been at the center of the political maelstrom to spend more than half his year bouncing along bad roads, living like "a post boy," while his friends and former colleagues forged a new nation.

In early 1792, the chief justice decided to hedge his bets. While remaining on the Court, he injected himself back into the political mainstream by agreeing to be nominated as a candidate in the upcoming gubernatorial race in New York against George Clinton.[16] Jay did not campaign actively, but nonetheless enthusiastically encouraged his supporters. Clinton, as an enemy of the new Constitution, seemed particularly vulnerable, but Jay, alas, had picked an unfortunate moment to enter electoral politics. For a race in which one of the parties was the highest judicial officer in the nation, the gubernatorial election of 1792 was one of the dirtiest in New York's history, rife with backroom deals, questionable vote-counting, and allegations of fraud flying back and forth. Jay remained largely above the fray—he was on circuit during the actual voting and during the most acrimonious period of vote-counting—but even vague association with such a seamy affair did little to enhance his reputation or that of the Court. Also, that a sitting chief justice would even consider seeking other office was an unfortunate testament to the esteem of the nation's highest tribunal. Most ironically, when he lost to Clinton, he was then forced to remain in a job whose standing he had weakened by the decision to seek state office.

In April 1792, Jay was victim of politicking of another sort. Although no written record survives, Justice Iredell must have made known his complaints about the chief justice's refusal to rotate circuits. On April 18, a law was enacted that circuit assignments "shall be made in such a manner that no judge, unless by his own consent, shall have assigned to him any circuit which he hath already attended, until the same hath been afterwards attended by every other of the said judges."[17] There is also no record of Jay's response, but he could not have been pleased that Congress and the president had seen fit to overrule his authority as head of the Court by enacting into law that which he had refused in discussion. He was, at least, sufficiently fortunate—or sufficiently obstinate—to be assigned Virginia and the middle circuit, rather than the South.

There was more bad news for the judiciary. In March 1792, Congress had passed the Invalid Pension Act, under which circuit courts were charged with evaluating petitions from disabled war veterans to determine whether the petition was proper and, if so, what amount of pension the petitioner should receive. The courts' ruling would then be evaluated by the secretary of war, and then, if rejected, by Congress. Worthy though the new law may have been, the justices seemed to have been reduced to clerks for the secretary of war and Congress. Jay, as well as all five associates, also thought the law violated the Constitution by infringing on the judiciary's independence by subjecting its decisions to congressional and executive oversight. (They were also none too thrilled at the prospect of sitting an extra five days each term to hear the pensioners' claims.) They made their feelings clear in numerous writings, but rather than force a confrontation over the issue, agreed to perform the task.[18]

With the pension issue shunted to the side, the justices met for the August 1792 term, to find that a case had finally come before the Court—but it had arisen out of that very Invalid Pension Act. A pension request by one William Hayburn of Pennsylvania had been denied in circuit court, and Attorney General Edmund Randolph, appearing as a private citizen, insisted that the Supreme Court issue a writ of *mandamus* ordering the circuit court to deliver the pension. Randolph noted that he was appearing "without an application from any particular person, but with a view to procure the execution of an act of congress, particularly interesting to a meritorious and unfortunate class of citizens."[19]

The Court refused to entertain Randolph's motion in what was, in effect, a class action. Randolph shifted gears, and presented the specifics of Hayburn's case. "He entered into the merits of the case, upon the act of congress, and the refusal of the judges to carry it into effect." The Court might not be able to eliminate being postboys, but the justices decided to dig in their heels on being clerks as well. The justices took no action on Hayburn's application, holding it "under advisement, until the next term," but expressed doubts that they would ever be in the position to act, as the judiciary's duties delineated in the Invalid Pension Act were in violation of the Constitution. Jay had written, on circuit in New York, "That by the constitution of the United States, the government thereof is divided into *three* distinct and independent branches, and that it is the duty of each to abstain from, and to oppose, encroachments on either. That neither the legislative nor the executive branches, can constitutionally assign to the judicial any duties, but such as are properly judicial, and to be performed in a judicial manner."[20]

Hayburn presented a memorial to Congress asking for relief, but the House also chose to take the matter under advisement. Hayburn's case was never decided in court—Congress ultimately did change the Invalid Pension law to remove circuit courts from the evaluation process—but the Court had succeeded in establishing its independence from extrajudicial tasks.

As to their principal bête noire, rotating the circuits had not mollified the justices (except perhaps Iredell), and in that same session they finally sent formal letters to Washington and the Congress denouncing a practice than left them "existing in exile from their families." Neither Washington nor Congress could afford the unpleasant prospect of full-scale revolt and possibly even mass resignation among the justices. Still, from both a fiscal and a political perspective, expanding the judiciary to provide a separate circuit court system was not feasible. Johnson at this point realized that, the president's assurances notwithstanding, he would be required to ride circuit after all. He resigned, effective the beginning of the next term, citing his antipathy to the loathsome practice as the reason.[21]

A compromise of sorts was reached the next year, when, on March 2, 1793, Congress passed and Washington signed amendments to the Judiciary Act of 1789. The very first provision of the new law stated: "The attendance of only one of the justices of the supreme court, at the several circuit courts of the United States, to be hereafter held, shall be sufficient, any law requiring two of the said justices notwithstanding."[22] The provision was greeted with relief by the justices, but hardly elation. One circuit per year was more than enough, and justices would remain in the position of hearing cases on the high bench that they had already adjudicated on circuit.

As it turned out, halving the circuit-riding requirement was the second piece of good news the justices received in early 1793. During the February term, which convened as the Judiciary Act of 1793 worked its way through Congress, the Court finally heard a case of significant importance. *Chisholm v. Georgia* was an amalgam of debt repayment and state sovereignty, and therefore allowed the Jay court its first opportunity to cement Federalist doctrine on a national scale. As with most cases in which great law is made, the particulars were straightforward and uncomplicated. During the war, a South Carolina Tory, Captain Robert Farquhar, had sold £64,000 worth of clothing and dry goods on credit to the State of Georgia. Farquhar had since died and his executor, Alexander Chisholm, also from South Carolina, had been rebuffed in his attempts to collect the debt. Georgia had announced haughtily that it had no intention of paying off a British sympathizer, no matter what those Federalists in Philadelphia said. Chisholm filed suit in circuit court in Georgia, asking £100,000—principal plus interest and damages.[23] Georgia declined to appear, refusing to acknowledge the court's right to render judgment. As a sovereign state in its own right, Georgia argued, it could not be sued without its consent, and therefore Chisholm's argument was moot. Justice Iredell, as circuit court judge, agreed with Georgia, citing both constitutional grounds and a failure of the Judiciary Act of 1789 to authorize circuit courts to hear cases where a state was party to a lawsuit.* Chisholm died, but his executors then appealed the ruling to the Supreme Court, placing the issue squarely on constitutional grounds.

In its claim of equal sovereignty, Georgia had thus precipitated not simply the first real test of the national court system, but a test of the limits of constitutional power. Article III, Section 2, clearly stated: "The judicial Power shall extend to all Cases, in Law and Equity, arising under this Constitution, the Laws of the United States, and Treaties made, or which shall be made, under their Authority . . . to Controversies . . . between a State and Citizens of another State." If the Court failed to enforce this provision, the Constitution would be weakened and the entire edifice that Washington and the Federalists were so carefully constructing might well come tumbling down. Underscoring the importance of the issue, Chisholm's attorney, hired by the executors, was again none other than Attorney General Edmund Randolph, appearing, as he had in *Hayburn*, not in his official capacity but as a private citizen.

The case was argued on February 5, 1793. Randolph pointed out that, since Article III made no distinction between whether a state could be a

---

* State sovereignty had been one of the most hotly contested points in debate over the Judiciary Act of 1789, but had, as with most issues, been left unresolved.

plaintiff or defendant, Georgia's argument was spurious. Randolph's remarks
went unchallenged, since no one in the courtroom chose to speak for the
defendant.

Georgia's absence notwithstanding, the case aroused enormous interest,
the first time the Supreme Court had taken center stage since its opening session three years before. Before a packed courtroom on February 18, the Court
convened to render its verdict. Justices followed the English precedent and delivered opinions seriatim—one at a time—in reverse order of seniority. (The
practice of producing an "opinion of the court" would not be introduced until 1801, by Chief Justice Marshall.) First up, therefore, was Justice Iredell,
who favored the defendant, arguing that the Constitution never intended to
grant either Congress or the courts such sweeping powers over the states,
whose continued sovereignty it had taken such pains to ensure. Therefore, he
concluded, Georgia could not be sued in federal court without its consent.[24]

When Iredell was finished, the remaining associates read their opinions,
each of them disagreeing, ruling for the plaintiff. Justices Cushing and Blair
rendered short, concise opinions, relying almost entirely on the wording of
Article III. That left Wilson and Jay, one the chief justice and the other the
man passed over for the job. Wilson began:

> This is a case of uncommon magnitude. One of the parties to it is a
> State—certainly respectable, claiming to be sovereign. The question to
> be determined is whether this State, so respectable, and whose claim soars
> so high, is amenable to the jurisdiction of the Supreme Court of the
> United States? This question, important in itself, will depend on others
> more important still, and, may, perhaps, be ultimately resolved into one
> no less radical than this: "do the people of the United States form a
> Nation?"[25]

Had Wilson chosen to answer that question in terms of the Constitution,
the country might have been the beneficiary of one of the great treatises
on national sovereignty. Instead, as if to demonstrate to the world the great
legal theorist Washington had ignored—or perhaps, after three years, he
was happy just to be able to write something—Wilson produced a long,
rambling, philosophical discourse on political and legal theory. His opinion, ultimately supporting Chisholm, was heavily footnoted, citing Cicero,

Blackstone, and Frederick of Prussia, among others. Rather than a trenchant legal opinion, almost all that Wilson wrote, one scholar notes, "seems largely irrelevant."[26]

Jay, as chief justice, was to read the final opinion. Like Wilson, he had waited a long time for this opportunity, and must have been thrilled, at long last, to be at the center of an issue of great import to the nation. Jay seized his opportunity. Not to be outdone, also like Wilson, he opened with an extended discourse on the theoretical underpinnings of sovereignty and subordinate power; but then, unlike his colleague, calling on his experience as part of the Publius triumvirate, he moved into the practical question of the role of the Constitution itself.

> The people, in their collective and national capacity, established the present Constitution. It is remarkable that, in establishing it, the people exercised their own rights, and their own proper sovereignty, and, conscious of the plenitude of it, they declared with becoming dignity, "We the people of the United States, do ordain and establish this Constitution." Here we see the people acting as sovereigns of the whole country, and, in the language of sovereignty, establishing a Constitution by which it was their will that the State governments should be bound, and to which the State Constitutions should be made to conform. Every State Constitution is a compact made by and between the citizens of a State to govern themselves in a certain manner, and the Constitution of the United States is likewise a compact made by the people of the United States to govern themselves as to general objects in a certain manner. By this great compact however, many prerogatives were transferred to the national government, such as those of making war and peace, contracting alliances, coining money, etc. etc.[27]

From here, Jay embarked on an extended and sometimes rambling discourse on state versus national sovereignty as practiced in Europe and in the United States. There were, however, some hints of the Federalist–Republican divide that would fracture the nation in the coming years.

> Prior to the date of the Constitution, the people had not any national tribunal to which they could resort for justice; the distribution of justice

was then confined to State judicatories, in whose institution and organization the people of the other States had no participation, and over
whom they had not the least control. There was then no general court of
appellate jurisdiction by whom the errors of State courts, affecting either
the nation at large or the citizens of any other State, could be revised
and corrected . . . it was proper for the nation—that is, the people—of
all the United States to provide by a national judiciary, to be instituted
by the whole nation and to be responsible to the whole nation.[28]

Throughout, Jay used "the people" as synonymous with "the central government," a position with which Republicans would have taken great issue.[29]
On the other hand, he also stated that "the United States were," rather
than "the United States was," implying that he continued to view the central government as a compact rather than an overriding entity. In any case,
none of this was necessary—all Jay needed to do was to quote Article III, as
had Randolph in argument and Cushing and Blair in opinion, and assert
that the Constitution meant what it said, since, as did his two colleagues, he
ultimately ruled for Chisholm on those very grounds.

Whatever satisfaction Jay, Wilson, and the others might have felt at asserting federal power was mitigated almost immediately by the hue and cry
that rose up against the decision. Some critics insisted it be ignored by sovereign Georgia; others demanded that the Constitution be amended. On
February 9, four days after the case had begun, anticipating the decision, a
bill prohibiting lawsuits by individuals against states had already been presented and read in the Senate. Within days of the decision, a move began
in Congress to amend the Constitution, and by February 20, a motion was
introduced:

"Resolved, by the Senate and House of Representatives of the United
States of America, in Congress assembled, two thirds of both Houses concurring That the following article be proposed to the legislatures of the
several states, as an amendment to the constitution of the United States;
which, when ratified by three fourths of the said legislatures, shall be
valid as part of the said constitution, viz: The judicial power of the
United States shall not extend to any suits in law or equity, commenced
or prosecuted against one of the United States by citizens of another
state, or by citizens or subjects of any foreign state."[30]

The motion was quickly enacted and sent to the states for ratification. Although the eleventh amendment was not adopted until 1795, the rebuke to Jay and the Court was unmistakable. To make matters worse, opposition came not just from Republicans, but from Federalists.

Jay was to gain a potentially powerful ally, however. To replace Thomas Johnson, Washington nominated the feisty William Paterson. The Senate confirmed the appointment unanimously and, on March 4, 1793, one of the primary authors of the Judiciary Act of 1789 joined the Court.

But Paterson would not begin serving until August. In May, when a chastened Jay, along with Justice Iredell, left to ride circuit (the last term that would require two justices), their first stop was Richmond. They were not to escape the controversy surrounding the war debt issue. British creditors had filed more than one hundred suits since 1790, and some of these were on Jay's docket. One of these, *Ware v. Hylton*, promised to be particularly incendiary. Representing the defendants was an unlikely duo—the arch-Republican Patrick Henry and the on-the-rise Federalist John Marshall.*

---

* Henry, in addition to his political skills, was considered the finest trial lawyer in the nation. His ability to sway a jury was, not surprisingly, phenomenal.

EIGHT

ONCE AND FUTURE CHIEFS: JAY
AND MARSHALL COLLIDE

MARSHALL'S FIRST INTERSECTION with the office of chief justice, albeit on the other side of the bench, coincided with yet another up-turn in his career. After his performance at the Virginia ratifying convention, he had been retained by none other than General Washington to act as the future president's personal attorney. He had also been pressed to run for Congress, but declined. Then, on September 30, 1789, in the aftermath of the passage of the Judiciary Act, Marshall was nominated by Washington and unanimously confirmed as United States Attorney for Virginia. Unfortunately, no one had asked Marshall if he wanted the job. With hefty legal fees finally coming his way, and his reputation better served by remaining in private practice, Marshall wrote to Washington and declined the position.[1]

Marshall concentrated his practice on appeals cases—they paid the highest fees—in which he would plead before his old ally at the ratifying convention, President of the Virginia Supreme Court of Appeals Edmund Pendleton. Many of those appeals were by debtor Virginians who balked at Article IV of the Treaty of Paris of 1783, which specified: "It is agreed that creditors on either side shall meet with no lawful impediment to the recovery of the full value in sterling money of all bona fide debts heretofore contracted." In other words, British creditors had to be paid in value that corresponded to British currency. In Virginia, Article IV had immense import, as almost half of the nearly £5 million owed to British creditors had been accrued by Virginians.

The provision had been insisted on by Crown negotiators largely because of two Virginia laws. The first, passed in 1777, confiscated British property and allowed debtors to discharge their obligations to absentee creditors by paying what they owed into the Virginia treasury. Payment could be in sterling or Virginia paper currency. The intent had been to use British property to help finance the war against Britain. Soon after the law passed, however, Virginia currency plummeted. The effect was to allow loyal Virginians to rid themselves of obligations to the enemy at something under ten cents on the dollar. War financing was thereby imperiled, but clearing the books—no small thing to cash-strapped Virginians—became a serendipitous option. Even these depreciated payments, however, were to be denied British merchants. In 1782, the Virginia legislature also decreed that no debt to a British creditor could be recovered in a Virginia court.

The theory, then, in inserting Article IV was that a provision of the Treaty of Paris would supersede the law of an individual state and compel Virginians to pay up. Under the Articles of Confederation, this reasoning would have been moot, since states retained sovereignty and, in any event, Congress had no enforcement power. Under the new, stronger Constitution, however, with its own Article VI proclaiming treaties to be the supreme law of the land and binding state judges to enforce their provisions, local law notwithstanding, Virginians faced the very real prospect of forking over millions of pounds to absentee creditors.

Premonitions of doom seemed justified when, in the first year after a federal court system had been established to hear the cases, those one hundred suits had been filed by British creditors. More than twice that many were filed in the following year. Debtors needed an advocate who was not only competent in the law but clever in circumventing it. Almost all chose John Marshall.[2]

Marshall, who had hailed the Treaty of Paris, was now in the position of Anti-Federalist advocate. He structured a careful, four-tiered argument in the debtors' defense. First, he asserted that clients who had paid their debts into the treasury in adherence to the 1777 statute had done so in good faith and under the law, so they could not be penalized after the fact. Second, the law passed in 1782 was still in force, so British creditors had no standing to sue. (This was, to be sure, an odd position even in advocacy, for the man who had argued so forcefully for a federal judiciary and national supremacy in the ratifying convention.) Third, Marshall pointed out that since England had failed to live up to other sections of the treaty—they still manned forts in the Northwest and had not compensated Americans for freed slaves—Englishmen had no right to apply the treaty selectively. Fourth,

Marshall made the additional, vague argument that, since the government had changed in 1776, all earlier debts had been annulled. Whatever the eventual outcome, by throwing up this fence of legal thorns, Marshall had at least succeeded in delaying adverse judgments for his clients.

Now, more than three years later, Chief Justice Jay, who had been one of the American negotiators in Paris and knew exactly why Article IV had been inserted, rode into Richmond for circuit court with the opportunity to use the judiciary to cement a cornerstone of Federalist doctrine. With Marshall and Henry in attendance, Jay, who was joined by Justice Iredell and district court judge Cyrus Griffin, left little doubt of the outcome of *Ware* when he announced: "Justice and policy unite in declaring that debts fairly contracted should be honestly paid . . . the man or nation who eludes the payment of debts, ceases to be worthy of further credit, and generally meets with their deserts in the entire loss of it."[3]

Henry, as always, was undeterred by adversity. He railed against the British as being unworthy of being repaid. "Our inhabitants were mercilessly and brutally plundered," he cried. "Our slaves [were] carried away, our crops burnt, a cruel war carried on against our agriculture. . . . We had a right to consider British debts as subject to confiscation, and seize the property of those who originated that war."[4] Henry was so masterful that when he concluded his remarks, Iredell exclaimed, "Gracious God! He is an orator indeed."[5]

As had been the case in the ratifying convention, Henry's appeal to emotion was followed by Marshall's appeal to reason. He presented his four-tiered defense in what was, by all accounts, a masterful performance, all the more so as he was arguing against his own beliefs.[6] Since Virginia had been a sovereign nation when the 1777 law was enacted, he insisted, it had a right to confiscate property from another nation with which it was at war. What was more, it could not then be bound by a treaty concluded after it had become a state.

The court delivered its opinion in June. All three judges agreed that the Declaration of Independence did not void the rights of creditors, thus negating Marshall's fourth point. Jay also ruled that British lack of compliance with other sections of the treaty did not impact Virginia's obligations. The third defense was disposed of. Nor could the Virginia law of 1782, barring recovery by British creditors, survive in a conflict with a provision in a duly ratified Constitution asserting the supremacy of treaties, overturning Marshall's second defense.

But with Jay the sole Federalist on the court, Virginia debtors ended up winning a huge victory on Marhsall's first line of defense. Iredell and Griffin declared that any Virginian who paid money into the Virginia treasury under the 1777 law had legally discharged his obligation. If British creditors wished to recover those monies, they had to seek redress from the government of Virginia, not individual debtors. Since the *Chisholm* decision was in the process of removing that option, the two judges had effectively ruled that Virginia could keep the money.

Although this ruling applied to only a portion of the debt, and three of Marshall's four lines of defense had been overrun, Federalists had nonetheless suffered a stinging defeat. By asserting that private property rights had survived the treaty—as Iredell and Griffin did—the power of the central government to enact a uniform set of standards that would apply equally to every state in the Union had been threatened. Marshall, while enhancing his personal reputation, might very well have helped undermine the very system of government that he so passionately wished to see in place.

NINE

A QUESTION OF PRIORITIES: THE ABSENT CHIEF JUSTICE

WITH THE COMING OF THE FRENCH REVOLUTION, opinion in the United States divided sharply, a trend exacerbated by the execution of Louis XVI in January 1793. Anti-Federalists, growing as a force as they evolved and coalesced into the Republican Party, continued to support revolutionary France. Some even applauded Louis' death as the appropriate response to despotism by a people who had, for too long, been ground under its heel. The more conservative Federalists, on the other hand, found the events in France repugnant and tending to anarchy. Hamilton, for example, "saw the chaos in France as a frightening portent of what could happen in America if the safeguards of order were stripped away by the love of liberty."[1] They wished for the United States to condemn France and ally with England.

The split in point of view had practical as well as philosophical implications. Washington was determined to pursue a policy of neutrality, but England and France, now at war, each sought to ensure that the United States did not aid its adversary. Both attacked and seized American merchant vessels that were suspected of engaging in commerce with the other. The French had gone so far as to fit out American ships as French privateers, and then set up French prize courts on American soil to sell off American vessels captured by heretofore American ships. The practice infuriated Federalists—to say nothing of the owners of the captured vessels—but there did not seem to be any law against it. In fact, when the original owners had brought suit against the French in district courts, they had been rebuffed.

Jay, as a Huguenot, personally loathed Catholic France; but politically, as did the president, he understood the need for his weak new nation to navigate between the warring powers. The August 1793 term of the Supreme Court lasted but two days. A virulent yellow fever epidemic had begun to settle on Philadelphia, and everyone fled who could. Nonetheless, in that time, Jay took an action highly significant to American governance. Washington had asked the justices to render an opinion, officially, on those French auctions. A good deal of correspondence had passed back and forth between the president and the chief justice. Finally, during its two-day term, Jay informed Washington that advising on questions not before the Court was an inappropriate role for the justices. (This precedent of the Supreme Court not acting in an advisory capacity has been followed ever since.)

Jay and his colleagues could not duck neutrality indefinitely, however. Although the February 1794 term featured only four cases, one of them was *Glass v. Sloop Betsey*, in which a merchant ship owned by Americans and Swedes had been seized by a French privateer, condemned as a prize, and brought to Baltimore to be sold by the French consul.[2] The owners sued, but the district court in Maryland ruled against them, claiming the court had no jurisdiction in such a maritime case. Republicans in Maryland hailed the decision. Federalists were once again revulsed. The owners then appealed to the Supreme Court.

Jay delivered a unanimous opinion.* Basing his ruling not so much on jurisdiction as to whether a foreign power had the right to empanel a prize court on American soil, the Court ruled for the owners and against the French. Jay determined that district courts had an inherent right to rule on prize cases within their jurisdictions, and, in any event, the French consuls had no right to conduct prize hearings on American soil.[3]

Although *Chisholm* is generally cited as the most important case to come before Jay as chief justice, *Glass* was of far greater significance. The decision not only upheld the doctrine of neutrality, but also, by inference, proclaimed the sanctity of American borders. No decision ever did more to assert the nation's international rights.[4] Federalists, of course, were overjoyed. By ignoring the letter of the law—by opting for broad construction—Jay had established principles necessary for the United States to establish long-term sovereignty.

---

*Although most decisions were delivered seriatim, there was no prohibition against the Court speaking on occasion through one voice.

Glass was Jay's first genuine triumph on the Court. It was also to be his last. Just after the February 1794 term ended, Washington approached the chief justice with an offer.

Federalist favor notwithstanding, threat of war with England was far greater than with France. American ships were being seized in the West Indies with regularity, and British forts in the Northwest—still manned and ready, despite the treaty—were generally seen as jumping-off points for invasion. Yet, as Washington and most Federalists surmised, British belligerence was less a question of specific antagonism toward its erstwhile colonies than of thwarting France. The solution, therefore, should be diplomatic and not military. Washington decided to send a special envoy to London to negotiate terms of rapprochement. For the task, he chose Chief Justice Jay.

Nothing bespeaks the lack of prestige of the Supreme Court more than the terms of Jay's acceptance. Not only did he agree to go to England, probably for months, but he felt no need to resign his position as chief justice in order to do so. No specific provision of the Constitution prohibited him from serving in both capacities concurrently, though the practicalities of the job would dictate that the highest judicial officer in the land should be available to the people that he served. There is evidence that Jay considered the *propriety* of accepting, but not whether his absence would have an adverse impact on the affairs of state.[5]

In any event, Jay's mission was a success. On November 19, 1794, he signed a treaty with Britain's Lord Grenville, later called "Jay's Treaty," which, while controversial—Jay was widely seen as having given up too much to get too little—effectively eliminated the threat of war with England. France's enmity, however, was irreparably aroused. Eschewing a winter crossing, Jay did not sail for the United States until the following March. Absent a chief justice, the Court did little business, adjudicating but two cases in the February 1795 term.

While Jay was at sea, New York was electing a governor. Once more Jay was a candidate, his name having been placed in nomination—with both his knowledge and consent—by Federalist associates. Jay arrived in New York in late May just in time to learn that this time he had won. Although not the slightest doubt existed that Jay would accept the governorship, he waited a full month, until June 29, 1795, three days after the Senate adjourned, to submit his resignation as chief justice to the president.[6] Washington was therefore able to appoint a chief justice for the August term without gaining Senate approval. No record exists of why Jay delayed, but Republicans had been making gains in Congress, and saving Washington the embarrassment of an acrimonious confirmation hearing would have been very much in character for Jay.

With the chief justice's chair vacant, the remaining justices assumed that the replacement would be drawn from their ranks. Wilson, in particular, must have salivated at the prospect of gaining that which had been denied him five years earlier. Paterson, although new to the Court, was held in high regard and widely believed to be under serious consideration. But, far to the south, another, cleverer, supplicant was also waiting in the wings.

John Rutledge had seethed for five years at being passed over for Jay, and never abandoned the view that high national office was his due. While in 1789 he had employed surrogates to plead for his appointment, this time he communicated with Washington himself.

Anticipating Jay by three weeks, he wrote:

Finding that Mr. Jay is elected Governor of New York and presuming that he will accept the office, I take the liberty of intimating to you *privately* that, if he shall, I have no objection to take the place which he holds, if you think me as fit as any other person and have not made choice of one to succeed him, in either of which cases I could not expect nor would I wish for it. Several of my friends were displeased at my accepting the office of Associate Judge (although the senior) of the Supreme Court of the United States, conceiving (as I thought, very justly) that my pretensions to the office of Chief Justice were at least equal to Mr. Jay's in point of law-knowledge, with the additional weight of much longer experience and much greater practice. . . . When the office of Chief Justice of the United States becomes vacant, I feel that the duty which I owe my children should impel me to accept it, if offered . . . I have never solicited a place, nor do I mean this letter as an application. It is intended merely to apprise you of what I would do if selected.[7]

Astoundingly, Washington, who had been so adroit in 1789 in frustrating the ambitions of Wilson, Livingston, and Rutledge by choosing Jay, now leapt on Rutledge's fawning entreaty. The president wrote back to the South Carolinian on July 1, just three days after he had received Jay's resignation, informing him that he was drawing up a commission.

The delighted (and probably stunned) Rutledge received the letter in mid-July and was off to Philadelphia like a shot, arriving in time for the August term. While Rutledge was en route, however, Washington's precipitous appointment acquired a suspicious odor.

The president had considered Jay's Treaty, for all its flaws, a brilliant diplomatic stroke, a triumph of neutrality. He expected Francophile Republicans to grouse, but Washington was never one to be deterred by yelping detractors. He had, however, expected his fellow Federalists to close ranks behind the treaty.

What Rutledge had not bothered to mention in his June 12 letter was that he opposed the treaty, and opposed it vehemently. In fact, on July 16, mere days before Washington's letter arrived in Charleston, Rutledge, who probably thought he was to be passed over once more, delivered an address in which he excoriated the Jay treaty. Northern newspapers received word of the speech late in the month. They reported that Rutledge had announced that he preferred Washington should die rather than sign the loathsome document.

As Rutledge traveled north for the August term, scathing attacks began to circulate, impugning not just his loyalty but also his sanity. Attorney General William Bradford, who had recently replaced Randolph, called the speech "crazy" and observed that Rutledge was "daily sinking into debility of mind and body." Timothy Pickering hinted at "private information" that indicated Rutledge's commission "ought to be withheld." Oliver Wolcott called him "a driveller and a fool." Edmund Randolph observed that "reports of his . . . puerility and extravagances together with a variety of indecorums and imprudencies multiply."[8]

Rutledge arrived in Philadelphia unaware that word of the speech had preceded him. He was, not surprisingly, taken aback by his reception. Most Federalists refused to speak to him. The exception was Washington who, incredibly, overlooked Rutledge's outburst and continued to press for his confirmation when the Senate next met. Federalist senators, in most cases utterly loyal to the president, demurred on this issue. Rutledge, they asserted, would never be confirmed. But Rutledge's will was as strong as that of Congress. Having waited five years for high national office, he was not about to relinquish it. On August 12, he took the oath of office and assumed his seat as second chief justice of the United States.

John Rutledge

Fortunately for Rutledge—and likely the nation as well—only two cases were decided in the August term, both prize cases and neither of the sort of lasting significance that attended *Glass*. The term mercifully ended and the new chief justice left for circuit duty, no doubt pleased to be done with Philadelphia. He would return neither to the Court nor the city.

When the Senate returned to session, Rutledge's nomination was finally presented for confirmation. Although Washington refused to withdraw his name, it took the Senate a mere six days to refuse to ratify the appointment. On December 15, the office of chief justice was once again officially vacant.[9] Chief justice was not the only vacancy, however: during the interregnum, another seat had opened when John Blair resigned.

Washington, burned by Rutledge, was not about to make a similar error in his next choice. In the interest of unity, he offered the position of chief justice to Patrick Henry, but Henry, who was by then almost sixty, declined. Washington next chose William Cushing, the eldest associate. (Upon

Cushing's confirmation, Washington would fill his seat.) For Blair's seat, at the urging of James McHenry of Maryland, a Washington friend, ally, and new secretary of war, the president nominated the huge, volcanic Samuel Chase.

Well over six feet tall and upwards of three hundred pounds, Chase was outsized in every way. Able, quick-witted, and completely without tact, he had at various times been accused of swindling, financial chicanery, misuse of office, and violation of oath, all with some degree or other of accuracy. Chase had also signed the Declaration of Independence, stuck by Washington in the darkest days of the Revolution, and was so intellectually incisive that some of his opinions stood for more than a century. He had a mane of white hair, and the constant flush to his skin earned the sobriquet "Bacon Face." He was as ferocious a Federalist as existed anywhere in the Union.

On January 26, 1796, Washington reported both nominations to the Senate, and both confirmations were rendered the following day. But Cushing had decided against accepting the position, thinking himself too old. He informed Washington that he intended to remain an associate.

With only one of the two open seats filled, the Court was short one justice for the beginning of the February term, just in time to hear, among others, John Marshall argue the appeal of the circuit court ruling in *Ware v. Hylton.*

TEN

A Taste of the Future: Marshall Visits the Court

B Y FEBRUARY 1796, John Marshall was firmly established among both Virginia's legal and political elite. As an attorney, he had been retained not only by Washington, but also by George Mason, one of the richest men in the state. So successful had his practice become that Marshall himself became engaged in an effort to purchase part of the vast holdings of Lord Fairfax.

Politically, his fortunes were, if anything, greater. With the nation evolving into a distinct two-party system, Marshall had become perhaps the most prominent Virginia Federalist. Washington needed him since Jefferson, Monroe, and the now fully converted Madison had made Virginia into a bastion for the Republican opposition.

In 1795, Washington had solicited Marshall to be his attorney general, but, once again citing the weight of his practice, Marshall declined. When a vacancy later appeared for secretary of state, Marshall was again Washington's first choice, but the president by then knew that Marshall could not be pried out of Virginia.

Marshall had not been north since his war days but, in early 1796, he left Richmond for Philadelphia to argue *Ware*. Only one of his original four defenses remained, that those who had paid into the Virginia treasury under the 1777 statute had legally discharged their debts. But even that defense had become thornier. With Jay's Treaty now in force and under assault by Republicans, an attack on constitutional supremacy had greater ramifications than when the case had been heard in circuit court.

Thus, by necessity, Marshall's argument to the Supreme Court differed from the construction he had offered in Virginia. He intended to steer clear of state sovereignty and dance around Article VI, Section 2 of the Constitution, which states, "This Constitution, and the Laws of the United States which shall be made in Pursuance thereof; and all Treaties made, or which shall be made, under the Authority of the United States, shall be the supreme Law of the Land; and the Judges in every State shall be bound thereby, any Thing in the Constitution or Laws of any State to the Contrary notwithstanding."

Marshall's presentation to the Court contained some interesting assertions. The Constitution might be the supreme law of the land, but only for the "United States." Marshall insisted that "Virginia, at the time of passing her law, was an independent nation." In 1777, the United States, as it was now understood, did not exist. Neither the Declaration of Independence nor the Continental Congress created a single nation. That did not occur until the ratification of the Articles of Confederation in 1781.[1] Yet, just moments later, Marshall noted, "It will be allowed, that nations have equal powers; and that America, in her own tribunals at least, must from the 4th of July 1776, be considered as independent a nation as Great Britain."[2] Thus, it seems, as an independent nation, Virginia had the power of confiscation, but as a part of a larger nation, previous debts had been canceled when the nation was formed.

Having demonstrated Virginia's right of confiscation, Marshall then noted, "So, when the government of Virginia wished to possess itself of the debts previously owing to British subjects, the debtors were invited to make the payment into the treasury; and, having done so, there is no reason, or justice, in contending that the law is not obligatory on all the world, in relation to the benefit, which it promised as an inducement to the payment."[3] That brought Marshall to the main question. "Having thus, then, established, that at the time of entering into the Treaty of 1783, the Defendant owed nothing to the Plaintiff; it is next to be enquired, whether that treaty revived the debt in favour of the Plaintiff, and removed the bar to a recovery, which the law of Virginia had interposed?"[4]

Unwilling to attack the treaty power itself, Marshall employed the sort of light-footed logic that he would later employ in Marbury. "There cannot be a creditor where there is not a debt; and British debts were extinguished by the act of confiscation. The [treaty] articles, therefore, must be construed with reference to those creditors, who had bona fide debts, subsisting, in legal force, at the time of making the Treaty; and the word recovery can have no effect to create a debt, where none previously existed." In other words, the constitutional authority to enter into treaties and expect those treaties to be enforced throughout the nation was moot; the repayment terms of the treaty did not apply to those Virginia debtors who had paid money into the state treasury in worthless currency. Lest anyone remained confused, Marshall added, "Without discussing the power of Congress to take away a vested right by treaty, the fair and rational construction of the instrument itself, is sufficient for the Defendant's cause."[5]

The Court, however, was having none of it. With Justice Iredell absent, the remaining four justices were all staunch Federalists, and undermining fragile relations with Britain was not on their agenda.[6] Chase, the newest justice, delivered the first (and longest) opinion. He actually agreed with Marshall that, at the time of passage of the law, Virginia had been independent, since the Articles of Confederation were not ratified until 1781. In fact, Chase agreed with all of Marshall's points, even so far as that any Virginian who had paid money into the treasury was no longer a debtor.

But none of that mattered. If the United States was to be able to operate as a nation, to end wars (which, according to Chase, could only be done by treaty), then the power vested in Article VI was absolute. "Our Federal Constitution establishes the power of a treaty over the constitution and laws of any of the States; and I have shown that the words of the fourth article were intended, and are sufficient to nullify the law of Virginia, and the payment under it."[7]

The other Federalist justices agreed, although differing on grounds. Cushing was terse, but no one stated the case more effectively. He wrote: "A State may make what rules it pleases; and those rules must necessarily have place within itself. But here is a treaty, the supreme law, which overrules all State laws upon the subject, to all intents and purposes; and that makes the difference."[8]

And so Marshall and the Virginia debtors lost. But, unlike his clients, Marshall had also won. A cornerstone of Federalist policy was now firmly in place, while Marshall himself had enhanced his reputation for fairness and intelligence, bringing both, for the first time, to a national stage.

Marshall reveled in his new status. Describing his visit to Philadelphia "to argue the cause respecting British debts," he observed, "I became acquainted with Mr. Cabot, Mr. Ames & Mr. Dexter & Mr. Sedgwic[k], of Massachusetts, and Mr. Wadsworth of Connecticut and with Mr. King of

New York. I was delighted with these gentlemen. The particular subject which introduced me to their notice was at the time so interesting, and a Virginian who supported with any sort of reputation the measures of the government was such a rara avis, that I was received by them all with a degree of kindness which I had not anticipated."[9]

ELEVEN

YANKEES WIN: ELLSWORTH AT THE HELM

A FTER JUSTICE CUSHING declined his nomination to be chief justice, Washington could easily have nominated Wilson, Iredell, or Paterson, but the nomination of one might well have aroused the enmity of the other two. Rather than risk internecine conflict, Washington once again chose to go outside the Court and, on March 3, 1796, nominated Oliver Ellsworth of Connecticut.

Also a Convention delegate, Ellsworth, the other key author of the Judiciary Act of 1789, was intelligent, learned, pragmatic, and a reliable Federalist. With Paterson and Wilson, he gave the Court a strong scholarly base; if anyone knew what the Constitution meant, or did not mean, it would be these three. Ellsworth agreed to serve, and was confirmed the following day with only one dissenting vote.[1]

As the August 1796 term approached, Washington, who had wanted to leave the presidency in 1792, made the irrevocable decision not to seek a third term. He would leave the nation on precarious footing—ongoing war in Europe threatening to suck it in at any moment, and party divisions becoming deeper and more intractable at home.

Divisions were rife not just between Federalists and Republicans, but also within the Federalist Party. An extreme faction, led by Hamilton—soon to be called "High Federalists"—competed for party supremacy with a more moderate wing, led by Vice President Adams. Hamilton and Adams were already beginning to loathe one another. Washington was closer to the moderates philosophically, although his personal intimacy with Hamilton remained as strong as ever. The president, in fact, showed Hamilton a draft of his farewell address months in advance but, even with foreknowledge, Hamilton was unable to block Adams from standing in Washington's place.

The first term of the Ellsworth Court, August 1796, took place just one month before Washington would formally announce his resignation from public life. The Federalist Party was still theoretically united, and policy prerogatives remained Washington's. The docket held a number of admiralty cases that were of minor significance, but that allowed the Court to expand and clarify America's maritime sovereignty, indispensable if the nation were to maintain Washington's aggressive neutrality.

Before the Court could meet again, the election of 1796 was held, the first time the presidency was contested. Adams, the Federalist nominee, ran with Thomas Pinckney of South Carolina, the only even potentially Federalist slave state. Thomas Jefferson ran with Aaron Burr of New York, a Republican hotbed whose twelve electoral votes would likely swing the election.

Campaigning was fierce and bitter, exacerbating the deep fissures between Anglophile Federalists and Francophile Republicans. According to

Oliver Ellsworth

their opponents, Republicans were thinly disguised anarchists who applauded the terror in France (as indeed some did), while to *their* opponents, Federalists were thinly disguised monarchists who favored an oppressive and aristocratic central government (as indeed some did). Jay's Treaty was either a capitulation to Britain or a masterstroke to prevent war, depending on which newspaper one read or which speaker one listened to.

Adams's problems were compounded by the southern states' disproportion in the House of Representatives, created by counting for apportionment three-fifths of their slaves (who could not vote, of course).

In the end, Adams won every electoral vote in New England, New York, New Jersey, and Delaware—61 in all—while Jefferson won all of Georgia, South Carolina, Tennessee, and Kentucky—only 19. The other states split. Jefferson won twenty of twenty-one votes in Virginia, fourteen of fifteen in Pennsylvania, and eleven of twelve in North Carolina, while Adams won seven of eleven in Maryland. When the tally was complete, Adams had defeated Jefferson by a mere three electoral votes, even though he had won the popular vote 53.4% to 46.6%.

Jefferson had not lost entirely, however. Because of the anomalies of presidential selection in Article II, Section 1 of the Constitution (which had not anticipated the rise of political parties), Jefferson had polled more electoral votes than Pinckney and was therefore elected vice president. So Adams, who as vice president had been utterly loyal to Washington, began his own term as president with a vice president who was his most intense rival.

Within this stew, the Supreme Court met for its February 1797 term, once again with little to do. "At the February and August Terms in 1797, eight cases were decided, none of which were of great importance. The Terms in 1798 were equally barren."[2]

But if the Court was in stasis, Adams was floundering. Desperately trying to hold to Washington's policies, out of both loyalty to his predecessor and a genuine conviction that war could sink America, Adams was assailed mercilessly both by his vice president and his party. He was accused of stubbornness, shortsightedness, stupidity, and mental illness. He was laughed at, sneered at, and disparaged for every flaw, real and imagined. Vilification was open, willful, and vicious. But through it all, Adams—who certainly was stubborn, if nothing else—held true to his beliefs.

In such times, a man is grateful for allies, especially influential and powerful ones, and President Adams discovered that just such a man was living in Virginia. The president was determined to supplement Jay's Treaty with Britain with a similar accommodation with France. He decided to send a three-man commission to Paris to achieve his goal, bring peace to the United States, and stifle his enemies. One of those three men would be that Virginia ally, John Marshall.

TWELVE

As Simple as XYZ: Marshall Ascendant

HISTORIANS HAVE DEBATED whether or not John Marshall was a man ruled by driving ambition, but he certainly at least did not wait passively for opportunity to be thrust upon him. Throughout his long career, his achievements were defined more by acute political instincts and deft manipulation of chance than by intellect, personality, or integrity. No more compelling an example of his political deftness, self-mythologizing, and seizing of opportunity exists than in the XYZ Affair.

Almost from the day he took office, John Adams had been obsessed with avoiding what he was convinced would be a disastrous war with France. While Jay had turned out to be an ideal emissary to England, no single individual seemed to have sufficient skill and reputation to achieve a similar result in Paris. (Jefferson might have filled the bill, but Adams thought it improper to send him, and the vice president would certainly have refused to go.[1]) Adams then settled on a three-man commission consisting of Charles Cotesworth Pinckney, Elbridge Gerry of Massachusetts, and James Madison. The commission was geographically and politically diverse, and all three men had been delegates in Philadelphia. Pinckney, as it happened, was already in Europe. He had been sent by Washington on a special diplomatic mission to France to help resolve the crisis, but, after trying unsuccessfully to be taken seriously by the French government, he had been expelled from the country and forced to travel to Amsterdam.

The commission idea received, at best, a lukewarm reception on all sides. Adams's fellow Federalists were in particular none too pleased with Madison as an emissary to anywhere, but their opposition became moot when the

Virginian refused to consider the idea. Adams was determined to press on, however, and in Madison's place chose John Marshall.

Marshall had rejected numerous overtures from Washington to national office, but this commission he could not turn down. Although Marshall was "engaged with some others in the purchase of a large estate," and thus reluctant to leave, he also "felt some confidence in the good dispositions which I should carry with me into the negotiations, and in the temperate firmness with which I should aid in the investigation which would be made."[2] Others did not find Marshall's explanation convincing, feeling instead that his decision to accept the commission was due to an inability to finance the Fairfax purchase. In Europe, he might assist his brother James in securing the funds.[3] Whatever the reason, Marshall journeyed to Philadelphia, stopping to see Washington at Mount Vernon on the way, and, after meeting with Adams, set sail for the Netherlands in July 1797, to join Pinckney.

He arrived in late August, met the South Carolinian, and sat about waiting for Gerry. When Gerry had still not arrived by mid-September, Pinckney and Marshall debarked for Paris without him. In the first week of October, Gerry finally arrived and the delegation was ready to begin its vital undertaking.

France was as much a revelation to Marshall as it had been to every American on his or her first trip across the Atlantic. Not only were the buildings older and more grand, the fashions more extravagant, the theater and opera more vital, but the manners and mores seemed to be from another planet.

The mission itself soon descended into the kind of Molièresque social farce that the French so enjoyed. In the midst of a Paris in the throes of a revival of cultural excess following the dour brutality of the Terror, three earnest, sober, hopelessly unsophisticated Americans (by French standards) lay ensconced in a hotel, expecting to enter into grave negotiations with the very highest powers in the French government. The Americans were convinced they would quickly be granted access to any or all of the five members of the Directory, the ruling executive in France after Robespierre and the Convention. If, however, they could not meet the Directors immediately, they expected little difficulty in engaging the new foreign minister, Charles-Maurice de Talleyrand-Périgord, Bishop of Autun.

French priorities, however, turned out to be far different. Talleyrand, a master diplomat, rake, seducer (despite a crippled leg), atheist, churchman, philosopher, and most of all survivor, had once quipped, "Regimes may fall and fail, but I do not." Hailing from one of the oldest and most distinguished families in France, Talleyrand had come to prominence during the monarchy, converted during the Revolution, avoided the Terror, and, by 1797, after two years in America where he had become friends with Alexander Hamilton and been a houseguest of Aaron Burr, had been appointed to head foreign affairs for the Directory.*

A more severe contrast in style and outlook could not have existed than that between the bluff, plain-spoken Americans and the evasive, unctuous French, for whom paying for the privilege of access to government officials was standard practice. Bribery to the Americans, perhaps, but a legitimate cost of doing business in France.

Talleyrand received the three ministers immediately, spoke to them in fluent English, provided them "cards of hospitality" (the lack of which had gotten Pinckney banished earlier), and assured them that the French were every bit as desirous of normal relations as were they. He then disappeared for a week, returning to regretfully inform the Americans that none of the five Directors would meet with them. More weeks of exasperating delays, false promises, and interminable waiting followed before Talleyrand ceased his accessibility altogether.

Instead, a series of "colleagues" showed up at the Americans' hotel claiming that, for a fee, the wheels of progress might be slathered with the proper grease. The three were outraged, considering the demand not only excessive—the Treasury could scant afford the $250,000 demanded—but a slur on America's honor. They refused.

The emissaries from Talleyrand—labeled "X," "Y," and "Z" in Pinckney's dispatches—continued to press the Americans, but neither side would budge. Only Gerry was willing to even consider paying the money. Ultimately, Marshall and Pinckney decided to depart France, leaving Gerry behind, powerless, to deal with Talleyrand and his minions.[4]

Marshall was the junior member of the commission and is said to have appointed himself as the recorder of its proceedings. He also composed the dispatches. His motives for becoming the commission chronicler have been a subject of speculation, but Marshall's is the only record of what transpired

---

* A famous anecdote had one of his ancestors accosting tenth-century monarch Hugh Capet and demanding, "Who made you king?"

in Paris. He could thus "impose his definition of what each succeeding phase of the commission's dealing meant."[5] So, when Marshall's account of the scandalous behavior of the French and the refusal by the American delegation to knuckle under reached America in early spring, Pinckney and Marshall were hailed as heroes.

But Marshall had not yet returned to America to hear the accolades. Despite the frustrations, Marshall was in no hurry to leave Paris. Like Jefferson, he had become enchanted with the city and its people. There is even reason to suspect that he engaged in a romantic dalliance with a beautiful widow, the Marquise de Villette, during his stay. In any event, when the talks, such as they were, finally collapsed, and after penning a memorial to Talleyrand eloquently defending American neutrality, Marshall and Pinckney sailed for home.

When Marshall docked in New York on June 17, 1798, he learned that his dispatches had stoked the nation's ire and there were widespread calls—at least among High Federalists—to declare war. Self-righteous patriotism ran riot. The slur on America's honor had even temporarily silenced Republicans, who found it easier to defend the Terror than Talleyrand. Congress approved a number of measures to strengthen the navy and, on July 7, rescinded all treaties with France. Hamilton himself would begin to raise an army with Washington titularly at the head, but which Hamilton himself intended to lead.

But John Adams was nothing if not resolute, more determined than ever not to enter into a war he was convinced could destroy the nation he had helped to build. Allies were scarce, however. Even in his own cabinet, Washington holdovers James McHenry at the War Department, Timothy Pickering at State, and Treasury Secretary Oliver Wolcott made little secret that they would have preferred working for Hamilton. Adams did discover a new collaborator, however—John Marshall, who had traveled from New York to Philadelphia in late June to a hero's welcome.

THIRTEEN

FIRST IN QUASI-WAR: ADAMS ON A TIGHTROPE

A DAMS MIGHT HAVE REFUSED to declare war on France, but that did not mean hostilities were over. From the time of Marshall's return in 1798 until the presidential election in 1800, the United States and France engaged in what has been dubbed "The Quasi-War." The conflict was fought exclusively at sea. French privateers seized American merchant vessels, and the newly strengthened American navy assaulted French vessels in the Atlantic and the Caribbean. Though hostilities were regular and intense, neither side seemed anxious to escalate to land war.

At home, Congress, in high dudgeon, passed four laws in the summer of 1798 destined to be among the most notorious in American history. Now lumped together as the "Alien and Sedition Acts," they consisted of the Naturalization Act, which extended the residence requirement for citizenship to fourteen years (from five); the Alien Friends Act, which allowed the president to deport any resident alien he, on his sole authority, considered dangerous to the peace and safety of the United States; the Alien Enemies Act, which allowed the president to deport resident aliens if their home countries were at war with the United States; and, most controversial, the Sedition Act, which made publishing "false, scandalous, and malicious writing" against an official of the government a criminal offense.

Any chance at rapprochement that might have been possible between Federalists and Republicans vanished with the passage of the Sedition Act on July 14, ironically Bastille Day. The bitterness that the restrictions on free speech engendered was so intense that, in the carryover during the presidential election of 1800, Republicans considered military action to prevent Federalists from retaining the presidency.[1]

Nor was the Sedition Act for show. Federalist prosecutors were in no way shy about indicting and jailing Republican critics, including Benjamin Bache, Benjamin Franklin's grandson, whose newspaper, *The Aurora*, was vituperatively partisan. (Bache died of yellow fever before he could stand trial.)

The judicial branch, however, appeared as though it might remain above the fray and not be called on to rule on the constitutionality of the acts. The First Amendment had yet to be applied to the states, so there were no grounds for judicial challenge there. Jefferson and the Republicans opposed the acts on Tenth Amendment grounds—that Congress had usurped state sovereignty by extending its powers to those that the Constitution had reserved for the states. This opposition eventually took form in the Virginia and Kentucky Resolutions, declarations of states' rights, rather than a challenge in the Federalist-dominated Supreme Court.

As the storm raged on, just after the end of the August 1798 term of the Supreme Court, James Wilson died. Adams solicited Marshall to fill the vacancy, even instructing Secretary of State Pickering to prepare a commission. Playing on Marshall's newfound notoriety, Adams told Pickering that Marshall had "raised the American people in their own esteem."[2] But he also realized that Marshall, who had repeatedly refused Washington's entreaties to assume national office, might decline. So, in addition to asking him to take the job, Adams also inquired as to whether Bushrod Washington would be willing if Marshall was not. Only thirty-four, George Washington's favorite nephew and heir to Mount Vernon, Bushrod Washington was small, fragile, blind in one eye, and very much Virginia gentry. Like Marshall, he was moderate in his Federalism. Marshall did indeed once more decline to leave Richmond. Bushrod Washington was nominated in his place and quickly approved by the Senate.

Marshall's avoidance of national office ended soon after, however. He was summoned to Mount Vernon, where George Washington, now just months from death, "gave Marshall a stern directive to run for office."[3] Washington wanted Marshall in Congress, and Marshall agreed. In Republican Virginia, despite Marshall's now impeccable credentials, only his reputation for moderation allowed him a chance for election. Playing up his centrism and distancing himself from the Alien and Sedition Acts, Marshall was elected and arrived in Philadelphia in early 1799 as Virginia's, and possibly the entire South's, most prominent Federalist. He also quickly be-came John Adams's most valuable congressional ally.

Adams understood that if the Quasi-War could be terminated success-fully, the other issues might, if not disappear, at least become manageable. The president had not given up on negotiating with France. In early 1799, he proposed another special commission, this time nominating William Vans Murray, a diplomat who knew the ins and outs of the Byzantine French government (as well as was possible); Patrick Henry; and Chief Justice Oliver Ellsworth. Ellsworth, who would be senior, was of impeccable reputa-tion and, after all, sending the sitting chief justice had worked with Jay and Britain. Henry declined, and Adams eventually chose William Davie, gover-nor of North Carolina and the man most responsible for that state's ultimate ratification of the Constitution.

By the time the three finally left for France in the spring of 1800, there was reason to believe that this second delegation would have more luck than the first. Napoleon had succeeded the Directory and, with grand ambi-tions in Europe, was thought to favor terminating a conflict that was gain-ing him little and beginning, thanks to increased American naval power, to cost quite a lot. Adams hoped a diplomatic victory would gain him an ad-vantage in the presidential election due later that year.

With Ellsworth's departure, the Supreme Court was once again left with-out a sitting chief justice. Ironically, in the August 1800 term, with the presidential election in full swing, the Ellsworth Court, after years of irrele-vance, finally received a case of significance.

Bas v. Tingy was a prize case, but once again with far-reaching implica-tions. In March 1799, an armed American merchant ship, *Ganges*, had re-captured from the French an American vessel, *Eliza*, then asked for and was granted one half the value of ship and cargo as salvage. Three acts of Con-gress came into play. According to a June 25, 1798, law:

> In all cases of recapture of vessels belonging to citizens of the United States, by any armed merchant vessel, aforesaid, the said vessels, with their cargos, shall be adjudged to be restored, and shall, by decree of such courts as have jurisdiction in the premises, be restored to the former owner or owners, he or they paying for salvage, not less than one eighth, or more than one half of the said vessels and cargos, at the discretion of the court.[4]

That law had been amended three days later:

> Whenever any vessel the property of, or employed by any citizen of the
> United States . . . shall be re-captured by any public armed vessel of the
> United States, the same shall be restored to the former owner or owners,
> upon due proof, he or they paying or allowing, and as for salvage to the re-
> captors, one eighth part of the value of such vessel, goods and effects, free
> of all deductions and expenses.[5]

On March 2, 1799, a statute was enacted regulating the navy, which included the following passage:

> For the ships or goods belonging to the citizens of the United States . . . if
> retaken from the enemy within twenty-four hours, the owners are to allow
> one-eighth part of the whole value for salvage, if over twenty-four hours,
> and under forty-eight, one fifth thereof, if above that and under ninety-
> six hours, one third part thereof, and if above that, one-half.[6]

The *Eliza's* owners sued, claiming that the March 1799 act restricted wartime salvage laws to declared "enemies," and thus could not be enforced
here since, lacking a formal declaration of war with France, the two countries could not be considered combatants. The defendants claimed, given
French depredations, that a "qualified" or partial state of war existed, and
that a formal declaration was not needed to prove the obvious. Both the district court and circuit court had rebuffed Bas, master of the *Eliza*, and upheld the award.

Bas is one of the great war-powers cases. Although only Congress had the
power to declare war, where that power began and ended when there was no
real shooting, no genuine battles had occurred, and one side denied that an
actual state of war existed was in question. To Adams and his fellow Federalists, of course, "war" was something of an amorphous concept and could
exist without a formal declaration or armies facing off on the battlefield.
Action thus taken in defense of the nation or its commerce was the province
of the president, and laws in support of the president might be passed in lieu
of a formal war declaration by Congress. To Jefferson and the Republicans,
that position was mere sophistry. Either a state of war existed or it didn't. If
it did, Congress had to so declare it. In the absence of such a declaration,

Congress could not pass wartime laws, and the president could not exercise war powers.

Adams, of course, had no intention of committing the United States to a full-scale conflagration with France. He had risked his presidency on avoiding war. But nor could he ignore the increasingly intense provocations by French ships. Until a diplomatic solution could be achieved—and Ellsworth was in Paris trying to attain that very goal—the president was forced to skate around the war-declaration requirement by asserting that a state of "partial war" existed. *Bas* would test that notion.

Still, the president could not have been too worried. The Court, even without the chief justice, was reliably staffed with Federalists, though only three were present for the August 1800 term. Cushing was ill and Chase was off in Maryland, electioneering for Adams's reelection. Paterson, Bushrod Washington, and the newly appointed Alfred Moore of North Carolina (James Iredell had died late in 1799) seemed more than capable of upholding Federalist doctrine.

There was no definition of "war" in the Constitution beyond the implication that it had to be declared. The president was commander-in-chief, but could he constitutionally take military action without congressional approval? Little guidance was to be gained even from former Convention delegates. What was certain, Jefferson and the Republicans continued to insist, was that partial war was a specious concept. The Supreme Court was supposed to base its decisions on the rule of law, not political expediency, but few Republicans had any anticipation that it would. Federalists, on the other hand, expected a court comprised almost entirely of, and appointed by, members of their party to perform their political duty and mold the Constitution to fit the circumstances.

Which is precisely what the justices did. Their contortions ranged from laughable to impressive. Newly appointed Justice Moore chose the philosophical:

It is, however, more particularly urged, that the word "enemy" cannot be applied to the French; because the section in which it is used, is confined to such a state of war, as would authorise a re-capture of property belonging to a nation in amity with the United States, and such a state of war, it is said, does not exist between America and France. . . . But, if words are the representatives of ideas, let me ask, by what other word the idea of the relative situation of America and France could be communicated, than by that of hostility, or war? And how can the characters of the parties engaged in hostility or war, be otherwise described than by the denomination of enemies?[7]

Justice Washington did it better. He began by taking as given that the crew of the *Ganges* deserved some award. The question was whether it would be one eighth, as stipulated by the 1798 statute, or one half under the more recent naval organization law. Thus, very deftly, Washington made the question of whether France was indeed an enemy subordinate to a larger issue, that of which law governed salvage on the *Eliza*. Then, even more deftly, Washington, as an aside, disposed of the only issue that actually mattered, unaware of the extent to which debate over this definition would reverberate throughout American history.

It may, I believe, be safely laid down, that every contention by force between two nations, in external matters, under the authority of their respective governments, is not only war, but public war. If it be declared in form, it is called solemn, and is of the perfect kind; because one whole nation is at war with another whole nation; and all the members of the nation declaring war, are authorised to commit hostilities against all the members of the other, in every place, and under every circumstance. In such a war all the members act under a general authority, and all the rights and consequences of war attach to their condition. But hostilities may subsist between two nations more confined in its nature and extent; being limited as to places, persons, and things; and this is more properly termed imperfect war; because not solemn, and because those who are authorised to commit hostilities, act under special authority, and can go no farther than to the extent of their commission. Still, however, it is public war, because it is an external contention by force, between some of the members of the two nations, authorised by the legitimate powers.[8]

From there, of course, only a short leap was necessary to demonstrate that France was, in fact, an enemy, a leap Washington took. Left unanswered is why the Convention delegates granted Congress the sole power to declare war if the president was free to prosecute a war without it. Having established that

France was an enemy, Washington ruled that the *Ganges* captain and crew were entitled to one half the value of the *Eliza*.[9]

Chase, who had hustled back to Philadelphia, went next.[10] He was forced to speak more or less off the cuff—all that politicking had left him no time for judicial chores.[11] Nonetheless, he had no problem also upholding the ruling of the circuit court. Chase more or less regurgitated Washington's argument. "If France was an enemy, then the law obliges us to decree one half of the value of ship and cargo for salvage: but if France was not an enemy, then no more than one-eighth can be allowed," he observed before agreeing that France was an enemy. Partial war had three votes.

Justice Paterson went last and was brief. "The United States and the French republic are in a qualified state of hostility," he claimed. "An imperfect war, or a war, as to certain objects, and to a certain extent, exists between the two nations; and this modified warfare is authorised by the constitutional authority of our country."[12]

So Adams, who had assiduously avoided a disastrous war on the battlefield, now had the partial war he needed in the courts. All he needed was Ellsworth to succeed in Paris and a successful reelection campaign back home.

PART III

MAKING THE COURT SUPREME

FOURTEEN

DEFAULT JUDGMENT: MARSHALL
TO THE BENCH

A DAMS HAD BEEN PRESSING for a judicial reorganization bill since late in 1799, when he asked Marshall to draw up recommendations. Whether Adams was motivated by statesmanship or the foresight to exploit an undervalued asset has been the subject of debate almost since the moment the request was made. There is little question, however, that the court system as sketched out in the Judiciary Act of 1789 had proved woefully inadequate. District courts were alternately bogged down or ill-attended, depending on the availability of judges, and there was a disjointed flow from the district courts on the bottom of the system to the Supreme Court at the top. Two of the three chief justices had seen fit to accept diplomatic assignments while continuing to technically serve on the bench, and Jay had twice accepted nominations for governor. The third had been run out of Philadelphia. These failings were, in one way or another, inevitable results of the unwillingness, first in Convention, and then in Congress, to create a truly dedicated circuit court system.

The circuit courts that had been provided for in the 1789 act, slapdash affairs, manned by a combination of district court judges and Supreme Court justices, had proved unwieldy. District court judges disliked participating in circuit courts because it meant an absence from their own bench, but that dislike paled next to the loathing Supreme Court justices felt for circuit-riding. From a functional standpoint, justices were often forced to hear on appeal to the Supreme Court a case they had already helped decide on circuit (as district court judges often dealt with cases in circuit court that they had decided locally). The main gripe, however, was that the physical demands of a pilgrimage to the farthest reaches of an expanding nation were proving increasingly onerous.

If circuit-riding were to be eliminated, however, a way would then need to be found to re-create the circuit court function, an indispensable link between district courts and the Supreme Court. For Adams and the Federalists, the easiest and most obvious solution to the problem was an expansion of the federal court system to include a layer of circuit courts, which, by coincidence, would also create lots of vacancies along the way.

Republicans wanted no part of court expansion. Philosophically, they opposed any measure that would centralize power and strengthen the national government, as an additional layer of courts would. An inefficient federal court system was preferable, since it seemed inevitable that state courts would ultimately be forced to step into the breach. From a fiscal point of view, a new layer of courts would shift desperately needed resources from the myriad of financial crises faced by the young nation to an additional layer of federal bureaucracy. Politically, with Federalists maintaining a firm majority in the Senate where judicial nominations needed to be confirmed, any expansion of the courts would result in a spate of lifetime appointments for their opponents.

For most of the short history of the nation, Republican intransigence would not have come to much; but, as 1800 dawned, with Adams under siege not just with the electorate but within his own party, delay offered a chance at victory. If Republicans could deter judicial expansion until March 4, 1801, a new and possibly Republican president and Congress would be sworn in, and Federalists might well have lost their power to add new federal judges.

For precisely that reason, Republican interest in delay was matched by a new urgency for Federalists to ram some sort of measure through. When supremacy in the legislature and executive had been unchallenged, expanding the judiciary had been a low priority for Federalists, as they had had little to gain from adding power to an independent third branch of the government. The shift in the political winds was anything but subtle, however, and by early 1800 Federalists began to sense that in another year the third branch might be all they had left. A broader and more powerful judiciary suddenly became appealing, and, on March 11, 1800, "A bill to provide for the better establishment and regulation of the Courts of the United States" was introduced in the House. It was a hefty and detailed document, forty-one pages long, covering everything from reorganization to districting, to rules for witnesses, to method of adjournment in the case of "infectious sickness."[1]

Washington City in 1801

The bill stipulated that the Supreme Court would move to the planned new capital, to be in the District of Columbia, then popularly called "Washington City," and sit for two sessions per year, one commencing June 1 and the other on December 1, a change from the February–August schedule under which the Court was then operating in Philadelphia. While the alteration probably indicated no more than a desire to free the Court from meeting at the height of the oppressive summers on the Potomac, it was to have great significance in the drama to be played out in 1802.

Another provision stipulated a reduction in the number of justices from six to five. As a sitting justice could not be removed unless impeached, the reduction could only become effective with the next vacancy by death or resignation, after which the open seat would not be filled. While constituting the court with an odd rather than an even number of justices was an obvious improvement, the Federalists' decision to reduce to five rather than raise to seven the size of the panel indicated an apprehension as early as March that they might not be the ones doing the appointing.

To ensure that the new, leaner, odd-man Supreme Court had the means necessary to discharge its function, the bill granted it the power to issue "all writs not specifically provided for by statute, which may be necessary for the exercise of its jurisdiction, and agreeable to the principles and usages of law." Expressly included in this power was the authority to issue writs of *mandamus*. Once again, conspicuously absent in any of the forty-one pages was a definition or delineation of the Court's role in constitutional interpretation or power of nullification.

The most contentious provisions, of course, were those to reorganize the judiciary and eliminate circuit-riding by Supreme Court justices. The bill divided the nation into twenty-nine districts created within nine circuits. An additional judge, called a circuit judge, would be appointed for twenty-six of the districts, and paid the agreeable sum of $2,000 per year. Excluded were only sparsely populated and sometimes inaccessible Vermont, northern Kentucky, and western Tennessee, where currently sitting district judges would perform the circuit-judge function but receive a pay raise to bring them up to the $2,000 salary. Marshals and United States attorneys "learned in the law" were also to be appointed for all the districts.

Circuit courts, consisting of circuit court judges of each district, would meet twice yearly in each of the districts within the circuit, thus eliminating any overlap among the three layers of courts. While some circuit-riding by the circuit judges would be required, the distances would generally not be excessive nor the travel especially onerous. The new circuit courts were to be hybrids—required to empanel juries in "issues of fact" but entitled to rule from the bench in cases of equity or maritime law. (An entire section of the bill dealt with Courts of Admiralty, which were to be extensions of district courts.) Jurisdiction of the national courts would be expanded, since cases, especially suits in which the plaintiff was a resident of the district and the defendant was an "alien" or resident of another district, were ordered removed from state to federal court if the defendant or plaintiff so petitioned.

Reading the bill out of political context—which Federalists urged Americans to do—obscured its partisanship. Reducing the number of Supreme Court justices could easily be justified by the difficulty of finding qualified men willing to accept the position. Nor were the Federalists unmindful of the demands of the common man (most of whom were Republican). Circuit courts, since they were permanent fixtures of a district, would actually bring the appeals process closer to the people. To prevent citizens from being dragged across districts to play against a stacked deck, there was a provision in the bill specifying that "no person shall be arrested in one of said districts for trial in another; and that no civil action or suit shall be brought before any of the said courts, by any original process, against an inhabitant of the United States, in any other district than that whereof he is an inhabitant, or which he shall be found at the time of serving the writ." The bill also guaranteed trial by jury.

To Republicans, however, any potential benefit to the common citizen was overwhelmed by the incendiary prospect of scores of new Federalist judges, and so the bill was fiercely debated in Congress during the final week of March. On March 25 and again on March 28, Republicans tried to defer debate until December 1—after the voting for president was done—but failed each time, the first time by six votes and the second by eight. After the March 28 vote, the bill was returned to committee and redrafted.

On March 31, 1800, an amended bill, now called "An act to provide for the more convenient organization of the Courts of the United States," was presented to the full House.[2] The Republican minority had been unable to derail the reorganization, but had nonetheless made inroads. The number of districts had been reduced from twenty-nine to nineteen, all of which would have a circuit judge, and the number of circuit courts from nine to six. President Adams would thus have fewer judgeships to fill with loyal Federalists.

In the interim, Adams's popularity had plummeted still further and his chances of reelection had become slimmer. Securing a Federalist judiciary had become a top priority. One Federalist congressman wrote, "the close of the present executive's authority was at hand, and, from his experience [Adams] was more capable to choose suitable persons to fill the offices than another."[3] On April 1, the bill was given two of three readings necessary before it could be voted on, and then consigned to a committee of the whole House.*

Finally, after two weeks of additional debate, on April 14, a motion was made to postpone consideration of the bill until December 1. To the shock of most Federalists, the motion passed, 48–46. The vote to postpone was made possible by four New England Federalists who abandoned their party and changed sides: Jonathan Freeman of New Hampshire; William Shepard of Connecticut; and Dwight Foster and John Davenport of Massachusetts.

---

* The committee of the whole House, in which the Speaker yielded the chair to another representative, was a device that allowed the members more latitude in debate.

They did not make their reasons for siding with the Republican minority clear, although Foster did write later that he thought parts of the bill (which he did not specify) were ill-considered and needed amendment. It was not beyond possibility that some Federalists were so furious with Adams that they were willing to deny him the appointments out of spite.

With reorganization of the judiciary on hold, attention turned to the coming national elections. There was no specific national election day in 1800; each state decided when and in what manner its presidential electors were chosen. Electoral votes would be reported (but not made public) in the various state capitals on December 3 and then transmitted to Congress, where they would be revealed with great ceremony before a joint session on the following February 11. In eleven of the sixteen states (Vermont, Kentucky, and Tennessee having joined the Union), electors were appointed by the state legislatures, while Kentucky, North Carolina, Maryland, Virginia, and Rhode Island chose electors by popular vote. Thirteen states had a general ballot, winner-take-all rule, while Pennsylvania, North Carolina, and Maryland chose electors by district, allowing for a split in their delegations' electoral votes.

Rules in each state were subject to change at the whim of its legislature, and whether or not changes were made was based on which rules would favor the party currently in power. In 1796, for example, Virginia electors had been chosen by district, but the Republican-dominated Virginia legislature had changed to general ballot in 1799 to ensure that Jefferson would receive all twenty-one electoral votes in 1800. Massachusetts had similarly switched from a district system to general ballot to ensure that all its electoral votes went to Adams. New York had chosen electors by general ballot in 1796, but in early 1800 Federalists beat back a Republican effort to change to a district rule, a gamble since the state had exhibited increasingly Republican tendencies, but a necessary one since it was widely assumed that Adams needed all twelve of its electoral votes to be reelected.

This jockeying could not have been more vital, since, Adams's woes notwithstanding, the election promised once more to be razor-close. In 1796, as Republicans never tired of pointing out, Adams had won by the tiny margin of three electoral votes.* This time, Adams was certain to carry

---

* There was nothing that rankled Adams more than the epithet "President by three votes."

New England and Jefferson was equally certain to carry most of the South, including Virginia's now-unified bloc of twenty-one electoral votes. Pennsylvania had turned sharply Republican in the four years since the last election, as had Maryland, and both states' votes promised to split roughly 50–50. New York, as during ratification, would be a major test of the political winds, and that test would come early: voting for the New York legislature—the body that would choose electors—was scheduled for three days in the last week in April, the result of which might very well decide the next president.

The vote in New York City would determine who would carry the state, and each party threw its best men into the breach. For the Federalists, Alexander Hamilton led the charge, riding about the city, speaking on street corners and in meetings. Aaron Burr, who saw a path to the vice presidency if he could deliver New York for the Republicans, was prepared to meet Hamilton's challenge. "That April, New Yorkers out for a stroll could have stumbled upon either Alexander Hamilton or Aaron Burr addressing crowds on street corners, sometimes alternating on the same platform."[4]

But whereas Hamilton had banked on his own abilities and spoke in support of a lackluster Federalist slate of nominees, Burr had been more clever and persuaded some well-known—albeit long-in-the-tooth—Republicans, such as George Clinton and Horatio Gates, to stand for election. Burr himself was everywhere. He spoke; he cajoled; he charmed; he organized. He threw open his home to campaign workers, providing food and mattresses for the two months leading up to the vote. Burr employed some remarkably farsighted techniques, maintaining detailed notes on any influential citizen who might be able to deliver votes. Everyone in the organization knew what to say to whom and, more importantly, what not to say. It would not be an overstatement to assert that, in the spring of 1800, Aaron Burr invented the modern political campaign.[5]

By May 1, it was clear that Burr had bested Hamilton and almost single-handedly engineered a Republican victory in the elections for the New York legislature. "We have beat you by superior *management*," Burr said afterward.[6] Federalists were stunned, none more so than Hamilton. He tried to salvage partial victory by proposing to Governor Jay that the now lame-duck Federalist state assembly vote to change New York's method of selecting electors from general ballot to district rule, the precise measure that the

Federalists had killed just months before. Jay considered the scheme under-handed and refused to support it.[7]

The only strategy left for the Federalists was to try to steal a Southern or middle state, as the Republicans had stolen one in the North. In Maryland, one of the three states with popular vote where electors were chosen by district, a move was initiated to shift the choice to the state legislature, which would mean general ballot. Maryland's legislature, which had recently adjourned, had traditionally been Federalist and thus could have delivered its ten electoral votes to Adams. But with Republicanism on the rise, Federalists needed to maintain control of the legislature in the new elections in order to change the voting rules, as uncertain a prospect as it had been in New York. Although Federalists spent a good deal of money, made an enormous public effort, and said some particularly nasty things about Jefferson, Republicans won a majority in the legislature and so Maryland retained its by-district system. Prominent among Federalist campaigners was a Baltimore merchant and financier named William Marbury.

In another attempt to steal a Southern state after the loss in New York, Hamilton urged the nomination of Charles Cotesworth Pinckney of South Carolina as Adams's vice president. Unfortunately for Adams, to many High Federalists—including Hamilton—Pinckney was seen as not just a number two, but possibly as a better presidential candidate than the incumbent. A plot was hatched by Hamiltonians, abetted if not actually fomented by Hamilton himself, to have Federalist electors dump Adams and vote in the South Carolinian, and the plotters made virtually no effort to keep the details secret from the president.

Adams, for all his faults, was being treated detestably. He had stuck to a moderate course to keep the country out of war and disbanded Hamilton's army to keep the nation solvent. Adams was repaid for moderation and statesmanship with invective and personal attack. Members of his own party speculated publicly as to whether or not the president had lost his reason. Hamilton, behaving like a petulant child, scurried about, planting rumors and hatching plots, furious that he was being denied the preeminent position in government that he thought should be his by right.[8] Even worse, Adams was by this time being actively undermined by members of his own cabinet, the group he had held over from the Washington administration as a gesture of loyalty and to ensure continuity.

The three main culprits were unabashed Hamiltonians: Wolcott, Pickering, and McHenry. Adams fumed at the divided loyalties—if they were indeed divided—but chose to tolerate the situation rather than rip the party apart. On May 3, 1800, however, the party held a nominating caucus in which it more or less adopted a plan that called for "equal support" for Adams and Pinckney, an open slap to a sitting president, and Adams had had enough.

Within a week, he demanded the resignations of McHenry and Pickering. The timid, poetry-writing McHenry's dismissal was particularly disagreeable. Adams subjected him to a screaming harangue about disloyalty, one of the displays of temper that would later be cited as proof that the president had come unhinged.[9] During the tirade, Adams assailed Hamilton as "a man devoid of every moral principle," and "a Bastard." Adams even declared that Jefferson, his other archenemy, was "an infinitely better man" and "a wiser one."[10] McHenry dutifully resigned on May 5.

John Adams

On May 7, 1800, Adams sent a message to the Senate naming his replacement: "I nominate the Honorable John Marshall, Esq. of Virginia, to be Secretary of the Department of War, in the place of the Honorable James McHenry, Esq. who has requested that he may be permitted to resign, and that his resignation be accepted to take place on the first day of June next."[11] Unfortunately, Adams had neglected to consult Marshall before submitting his name, and Marshall was forced to tell Adams that he had no wish to be secretary of war.

At this point, Adams's need of Marshall's skills and ability to negotiate the Federalist minefield was far too acute to let him simply remain in Congress. A few days after he assailed McHenry, Adams had also demanded the resignation of Pickering, but Pickering, contentious and prickly, had haughtily refused. Marshall found Pickering's job at State, however, more appealing than McHenry's at the War Department, so on May 12 Adams fired Pickering and sent another message to the Senate: "I nominate the Honorable John Marshall, Esq., of Virginia, to be Secretary of State, in place of the Honorable Timothy Pickering, Esq. removed."[12] The Senate approved the nomination the following day; the day after that, they recessed in Philadelphia for the last time "until the third Monday in November next, to meet in the city of Washington, in the Territory of Columbia."[13]

Marshall quickly became Adams's most trusted adviser, perhaps by then the president's *only* trusted adviser. The wounds that had been opened by the defeat in New York and the forced departure of the two cabinet officers had brought what had heretofore been largely a simmer, at least in public, to a full boil. In June, Hamilton wrote to McHenry of his disgust for the president. "The man is more mad than I had ever thought him and I shall soon be led to say as wicked as he is mad."[14] By then, McHenry had published a letter of his own detailing Adams's tirade, including the reference to Hamilton's illegitimacy, the most profound insult possible to a man who had fought his entire life to overcome the circumstances of his birth.

The battle between the Madman and the Bastard raged all summer, as the coming battle between the Madman and the Great Lama of the Mountain, as Marshall sometimes referred to Jefferson, simmered. In the midst of all this good feeling, the nation began to choose the electors who would decide the next election.

Both Adams and Jefferson tried to play the statesman. Adams left Philadelphia shortly after the cabinet purge, heading south, through Pennsylvania and then Maryland, to inspect the new federal city, before turning back north through New Jersey on his way home to Quincy, Massachusetts. The reception he received would certainly have encouraged him. In small towns, large and enthusiastic crowds turned out to hear the president speak.[15] He arrived in the new capital just as summer was dropping a thick blanket of heat, humidity, and malaria over the region. He spent ten days there, briefly overseeing the transfer of government documents from Philadelphia, and then left for home.[16] The trip north was not as encouraging: the president was ignored in New Jersey and was forced to avoid stopping in New York entirely.

Jefferson, eagerly anticipating New York's twelve electoral votes, conducted his affairs from Monticello. He received visitors, wrote letters, commissioned pamphlets, and dispensed optimism from his hilltop home. Well aware of the implosion of his opponents, Jefferson was content to draft a series of position papers laying out Republican principles while competing Federalists ripped at each other's throats.

While his party fought for survival, Secretary of State Marshall was charged with the unenviable task of remaining for the entire summer in the miasma of the new federal city. In addition to his official duties, which were not excessive, Marshall was also to oversee the ongoing construction of both the new capitol and the president's residence. After his ten-day visit to the Potomac in June, Adams would remain in Massachusetts until November. Congress was not in session and virtually every other member of the government had gone home, so, in the summer of 1800, John Marshall for all intents and purposes *was* the government of the United States.

By October, fifteen of the sixteen states had chosen electors. Although, in theory, the results were under lock and key, secrets as potent as voting results were difficult to keep, and unofficial state-by-state tallies began to leak out. Federalists absorbed the sketchy news with growing concern. Republicans exulted. Adams's last hope seemed to rest with South Carolina, the only state yet to choose electors, since state legislative elections had not been held there. If Federalists could manage to win control of the South Carolina legislature, they would be certain to vote for Pinckney, who, as a matter of honor, would have also instructed them to vote for Adams. The gain of South Carolina would then balance out the loss of New York, and Adams would be elected to a second term.

South Carolina had been a state divided since the Constitutional Convention, its low-country, coastal gentry overwhelmingly Federalist, while back-country pioneers were just as fiercely Republican. At the Convention, the planters had squeezed out the pioneers and dominated the Philadelphia proceedings, but the ensuing decade had seen many changes. Although the early election returns for the legislature favored the Federalists, as votes drifted in from the countryside, the Republicans easily overtook them. The South Carolina legislature would not be Federalist.

It seemed clear that Adams had probably lost.

Probably, but not for certain.

The vagaries of the electoral-vote process left open any number of scenarios, some of which would deny Jefferson the presidency in favor of the incumbent, some in which Pinckney would prevail, and one or two that would actually see Jefferson defeated by his own vice presidential candidate, Burr. Obscuring the picture still further was the question of whether or not electors would actually vote for those whom they had been selected to support. Electors had behaved with maverick independence in 1796, and many expected a similar performance here. With months to go before the votes were actually delivered, scheming by both parties ratcheted up still further.

The second session of the Sixth Congress opened on Monday, November 17, 1800, in the District of Columbia, the first time the business of government would be conducted in the new national capital on the Potomac. The city was anything but imperial. Described by one observer as "almost a wilderness," much of Washington City's land remained undeveloped and swampy, and the 1½-mile stretch between the President's House and the Capitol contained "thick groves and forest trees, wide and verdant plains, with only here or there a house along the interesting ways, that could not yet be properly called streets." The Capitol itself was largely unfinished, but the surrounding area was a center of activity, "seven or eight boarding houses, one tailor, one shoemaker, one printer, a washing woman, a grocery shop, a pamphlets and stationery shop, a small dry-goods shop, and an oyster house," being in the immediate vicinity.[17]

On Saturday, November 22, President Adams rode a carriage to the Capitol and addressed a joint session of Congress in the Senate chamber. He began by congratulating himself and the country. "May this territory be the residence of virtue and happiness!" he trumpeted. "In this city may

The Capitol building as depicted by William Russell Birch in 1800

that piety and virtue, that wisdom and magnanimity, that constancy and self-government which adorned the great character whose name it bears, be forever held in veneration! Here, and throughout our country, may simple manners, pure morals, and true religion, flourish forever!"[18]

Aware that the nation might have to flourish under a Republican president after March 4, Adams then called once more for reform of the judiciary. "It is, in every point of view, of such primary importance to carry the laws into prompt and faithful execution, and to render that part of the administration of justice which the constitution and laws devolve on the federal courts, as convenient to the people as may consist with their present circumstances, that I cannot omit once more to recommend to your serious consideration the judiciary system of the United States. No subject is more interesting than this to the public happiness, and to none can those improvements which may have been suggested by experience be more beneficially applied."[19] Despite his entreaties, by December 3, the day the electoral votes were to be cast in secret in the state capitals, the courts bill had not been reintroduced in the House.

With so much riding on whether or not electors would adhere to their parties' orders, both Federalists and Republicans were determined to do everything possible to ferret out the outcome. Within days, results began to trickle out, and they suggested a stunning outcome. Two weeks later, Jefferson wrote to Madison:

> The election in S. Carolina has in some measure decided the great contest. Tho' as yet we do not know the actual votes of Tennessee, Kentucky, & Vermont, yet we believe the votes to be on the whole, J. 73, B. 73, A. 65, P. 64. Rhode isld withdrew one from P. There is a possibility that Tennessee may withdraw one from B., and Burr writes that there may be one vote in Vermont for J. But I hold the latter impossible, and the former not probable; and that there will be an absolute parity between the two republican candidates. This has produced great dismay and gloom on the republican gentlemen here, and equal exultation on the federalists, who openly declare they will prevent an election, and will name a President of the Senate, *pro tem.* by what they say would only be a *stretch* of the constitution.[20]

Only days after Jefferson posted his letter, a full, state-by-state tally was published in a number of American newspapers, and the numbers matched Jefferson's. Not only had the South Carolina electors failed to vote for Pinckney, but only one of the 276 electoral votes had been cast against strict party discipline, the Federalist elector in Rhode Island who had cast a vote for John Jay instead of Pinckney.

The nation now knew—John Adams had lost.

But, as Jefferson had noted in his letter, just because Adams had lost did not necessarily mean that he had won. The Republicans had blundered. The Tennessee elector had evidently not withheld his vote for Burr. Each of the seventy-three Republican electors had dutifully cast votes for Jefferson and Burr. Sixty-four of the sixty-five Federalist electors cast their votes for Adams and Pinckney, while one voted for Adams and Jay. If even one Republican elector had avoided voting for Burr—and it had been widely speculated that the Georgia electors had intended do just that—the result would have reflected the clear intention of the voters to put Jefferson in the presidency. As things stood, however, the tie between Jefferson and Burr meant that the election would be decided between them in the House of Representatives instead of by the electors.*

The Federalist defeat had extended farther than just the presidency. The party had lost both houses of Congress as well, and by wide margins. On March 4, 1801, Republicans would control the House 69–36 and the Senate 18–14, and Jefferson's Republicans would be the beneficiaries of the first genuine transfer of power in the nation's brief history.[21] As the results became public and accepted, at least as far as the parties were concerned, Federalists' resentment at the magnitude of their defeat was exacerbated by the knowledge that Jefferson's victory in the presidential race had been enabled by the three fifths of the slaves that had been counted for apportionment in the Southern states. If slave electors had been eliminated, Adams would have been reelected 63–61.[22]

Yet despite the debacle, Federalists, as Jefferson had also noted, would remain in power for three more months. On February 11, when the House would choose the president and vice president, the old Federalist Sixth Congress, not the new Republican Seventh Congress, would be in power. Federalists therefore had the power to produce all sorts of mischief, including blocking an election altogether and appointing a president *pro tem* to run the country from Congress. Leading Federalists denied that they intended what amounted to a coup, but Republicans suspected that some trickery was in the works, particularly because of the odd distribution of seats in the House.

The Sixth Congress was an incongruity. Although Federalists held a 64–42 majority in seats, because of the extreme concentration of Federalist seats in New England and the all-Federalist delegation from South Carolina, Republicans actually controlled more state delegations, eight to seven, with Vermont's two-man delegation consisting of one from each party. To complicate matters further, although Federalists controlled five of Maryland's eight seats, one of the five quickly announced his intention to vote for Jefferson, thus creating a potential 4–4 deadlock. With sixteen states in the Union, nine delegations would be required to elect the president. Jefferson was one state short, but Federalists did not control enough state delegations to force a deal.

---

* Had the situation been reversed, Adams, by virtue of the single vote for Jay, would have been president and Pinckney vice president.

During the course of the following weeks, rumors flew, plots were hatched, conspiracies initiated. One idea was for Congress to claim voting irregularities in the South and invalidate enough of Jefferson's electors to keep Adams in office. Another had members procedurally damming up the process in such a way as to perpetuate rule by the current Congress past March 4. A rumor circulated among Republicans that certain arch-Federalists were plotting to have Jefferson assassinated and another that recent fires in the new buildings housing the Treasury Department and War Department had been intentionally set by Federalists eager to destroy documents that incriminated the Adams administration in unspecified malfeasance.

In the end, however, few Federalists were willing to risk the nation's future or even civil war by trying to overturn the election and retain power.[23] The only real issue was which poison the Federalists would ultimately swallow—Jefferson or Burr—and on this, the party was deeply divided. Burr was widely considered unscrupulous and untrustworthy, but without real ideology and with a greater mercantile sensitivity than the agrarian Jefferson. And he was a Northerner. Jefferson, on the other hand, was seen as essentially honest, but an ideologue and tool of French radicals, a man who would destroy the nation's business and turn the country over to the rabble.

Most High Federalists preferred Burr, with whom it was widely assumed a deal could be struck. Some thought Burr could even be converted to Federalism out of gratitude, if the party satisfied his immense ambition to gain the presidency. Alexander Hamilton favored Jefferson, whom he detested, over Burr, whom he both detested and mistrusted. Adams also favored Jefferson, with whom, despite their current estrangement, he had a history of mutual struggle and triumph not easily forgotten. Also, to Adams's credit, he knew that Jefferson had been the choice of the voters and felt it would be far better for the nation if that choice was acknowledged.

In early January, Burr justified Hamilton's mistrust. After assuring Jefferson that he would accept the vice presidency and refuse any entreaty to the higher office, Burr began circulating feelers, letting it be known that he would gladly be president if offered the job. When there were no repercussions, Burr took the logical next step and told acquaintances that he intended to actively seek the position. That was all High Federalists like Oliver Wolcott needed to hear, and they decided to back Burr.

Yet even if they could persuade the divided states to go their way, Federalists knew they still could do no better than a tie. Assured of remaining in power only until March 3, Adams and his party, now somewhat reconciled by adversity, were determined not to waste what could be their last weeks in office. A torrent of legislation was introduced in the House and Senate. While a number of favored bills regarding lighthouses, post roads, and other pet projects were eventually voted into law, by far the most attention was paid to the judiciary.

The judiciary was the only branch of government not susceptible to shifts in the electoral wind, now blowing a gale to Jefferson, and the only way to retain a semblance of nationalism in what was sure to be a wave of Republican decentralization was to create a stronger federal court system.

On December 11, virtually at the moment this reality was sinking in with Adams and his fellow Federalists, William Davie arrived in New York from France, bearing two documents from Chief Justice Ellsworth. Davie made immediately for Washington City, where both documents were delivered to the president.[24]

The first was the long-sought-after agreement with France. Called the Convention of 1800, it had been signed with great pomp at Joseph Bonaparte's estate at Môrtefontaine on October 3. Although he would later be roundly criticized for giving away too much to get too little—precisely how Jay's Treaty was characterized—Ellsworth had, in fact, brought about an end to the Quasi-War with both American honor and the American navy intact. The agreement required Senate ratification, but the mere fact of its existence was an enormous boost to Adams's flagging spirits.

The second document brought less-welcome news. In a letter dated September 30, Oliver Ellsworth informed Adams that he was resigning as chief justice of the Supreme Court for reasons of health. Ellsworth would not even return to the United States to make himself available for persuasion, choosing instead to winter in England.

Ellsworth's resignation had more profound significance than simply creating a vacancy on the Court. The previous April, it will be remembered, four obscure New England Federalists had voted to defer debate on the court reorganization bill. Had they not done so, if the bill had completed debate in April, then been passed by a Federalist Congress and signed into law, President Adams would not be allowed to fill the Ellsworth vacancy—he would have been required to appoint one of the sitting justices as chief so that the Court would consist of only five members. And if that happened, as no one else resigned during Adams's term, John Marshall could not have been nominated to the Supreme Court. Since the only way Marshall would get near the Court in a Jefferson presidency was as an attorney, those four Federalists had cast their votes not for a trivial motion on procedure, but rather, as it turned out, to enable the Marshall court. With the bill only pending at the time Ellsworth's resignation reached the capital, Adams was free to appoint a Federalist chief justice. After the bill passed, two more resignations would be required before Jefferson was allowed to nominate his first Supreme Court justice. Freeman, Shepard, Foster, and Davenport had thus been unwittingly responsible for one of the seminal appointments in American history.

Adams was well aware that Ellsworth had set him in a procedural trap. If a new chief justice was not approved by the Senate before Adams signed the judiciary bill—which he would have to do sufficiently before March 4 to get all those new judges, clerks, United States attorneys, and marshals appointed and confirmed—the seat would be lost when the Court was reduced to five justices.

The president was therefore under enormous pressure to act quickly. On December 18, just days after Davie arrived in Washington City, the Senate received the following communication from the president: "Gentlemen of the Senate: I nominate John Jay, Esq. Governor of the State of New York, to be Chief Justice of the United States, in the place of Oliver Ellsworth, who has resigned that office. JOHN ADAMS." The president dashed off a letter to Jay, then in Albany, informing him that he had been re-nominated as chief justice. "Nothing will cheer the hopes of the best men so much as your acceptance of this appointment," Adams added.[25]

Jay was an excellent choice. He was considered a moderate, yet was respected by all wings of the party, and he had served as chief justice before. Even Jefferson was relieved. "Jay was yesterday nominated Chief Justice," he wrote to Madison. "We were afraid of something worse."[26] Unfortunately, as he had done with Marshall's secretary-of-war nomination, Adams had not bothered to consult with Jay first and was unaware that the New Yorker, who had recently stepped down as governor, had informed friends of his intention to retire from public life.

The next day, December 19, the Senate confirmed Jay while, in the House, "the bill to provide for the more convenient organization of the

courts" was finally reintroduced. It was again given its first and second reading before being referred to the committee of the whole house for debate.
Jefferson wrote to Madison one week later and first gave his younger colleague a rundown of the situation. "All the [electoral] votes are now come
in except Vermont and Kentucky, and there is no doubt that the result is a
perfect parity between the two republican characters." He was less flip about
the courts bill. "[The Federalists] have got their judiciary bill forward to
commitment. I dread this above all the measures meditated, because appointments in the nature of freehold render it difficult to undo what is
done."[27]

Jay received his signed and sealed commission in the last days of December, along with a letter from Secretary of State Marshall urging him to accept the position. Jay, by this time only fifty-five years old, might have
deferred his retirement and heeded this one last call to public service except
for the rigors of the position. He had made it known during his first term in
the Court that he loathed riding circuit and, with the court bill yet to be
passed, that was still officially part of the job. He wrote back to Adams in
early January that his health was too tenuous to expose himself to "the fa-
tigues incident to the office."[28] Unaware that Adams planned to ram through
the reorganization bill, he was also unwilling to return to a Court still under
the aegis of the Judiciary Act of 1789, which he had fruitlessly hoped would
be revised. "Under a system so defective," he had written, "[the judiciary]
would not obtain the energy, weight, and dignity which are essential to its
affording due support to the national government, nor acquire the public
confidence and respect which, as the last resort for the justice of the nation,
it should possess."[29] Jay returned the commission to Marshall, on the grounds
of poor health.*

Almost two weeks elapsed before Adams received Jay's letter. Although
most who knew him had assumed that Jay would decline the appointment,
Adams was devastated. He summoned his secretary of state, who arrived to
find the president standing disconsolately with Jay's letter in his hand. According to Marshall, Adams "said thoughtfully, 'Who shall I nominate
now?' I replied that I could not tell, as I supposed that his objection to Judge
[Paterson] remained.[30] He said in a decided tone, 'I shall not nominate him.'

---

* The excuse turned out to be unconvincing—Jay lived for another twenty-nine years.

After a moment's hesitation he said 'I believe I must nominate you.'"[31] Marshall's nomination was sent to the Senate the following day, January 20, and, despite some foot-dragging by High Federalists who wanted Adams to withdraw the nomination in favor of Paterson, the nomination was approved one week later. John Marshall thus became the fourth chief justice of the Supreme Court of the United States.

Marshall, who had intended to return to his law practice and land speculation when Adams's term ended, was not altogether thrilled with the appointment. Until he himself joined its ranks, strong indications are that Marshall shared Hamilton's *Federalist 78* assessment of the judicial branch as "beyond comparison, the weakest of the three departments of power." Placed in charge of the government's transition from Philadelphia to the District of Columbia by Adams, Secretary of State Marshall thought so little of the Supreme Court that he either did not notice or did not care that planners of the new capital had made no provision for its accommodations. No chamber had been set aside for the Court to meet, nor were any plans in place for a law library, office space, housing for the six justices, or even staff. Marshall received two letters from the district commissioners, one in December 1800 and the other in January 1801, asking him to recommend remedies, but he apparently did not reply to either until he realized it was his own working space that he had been ignoring.

On January 20, 1801, Marshall's nomination came before the Senate and the courts bill passed the House. With the February term of the Court due to begin in just over a week, "The Speaker laid before the House a letter from the Commissioners of the city of Washington, requesting that an arrangement may be made for the lodging of the Supreme Court of the United States, in the Capitol."[32] Three days later, the House "Resolved that leave be given to the Commissioners of the city of Washington to use one of the rooms on the first floor of the Capitol for holding the present session of the Supreme Court of the United States."[33] The Senate acceded to the resolution the following day.

Marshall may well have regretted his inattention to the Court when he saw the room that had been assigned to it, a noisy, unfinished Committee Room 2 on the Senate side of the first floor, next to the main staircase, "meanly furnished and very inconvenient."[34] The justices were to sit at desks on a raised platform instead of behind a bench, and the Court had still not been assigned a secretary or staff. The Supreme Court of the United States lacked even an official reporter, since the man who had held the job in Philadelphia, Alexander Dallas, had refused to abandon his sophisticated city to pioneer in the new capital.

Far more significant than second-rate accommodations was that the Court itself had sunk to such low repute. The one time the Court had asserted itself on a constitutional question—the *Chisholm* case—Congress had responded by passing the Eleventh Amendment to nullify the ruling. While in theory most legislators and members of the executive acknowledged that the Supreme Court should have some role in constitutional interpretation, after a decade, the nature of that role had not yet begun to be determined. Judicial review as it was to be established in *Marbury* was not remotely an accepted notion, and "both Congress and the executive could lay greater claim to constitutional finality than the Court."[35]

No one was more aware of the inconsequence of the Court than the justices themselves. For the February 1801 term, Marshall's first, two justices, Paterson and Moore, stayed home, averse to wasting their time in swamp-ridden Washington City. Circuit-riding had been often abandoned as well, and circuit courts, which relied on the willingness of the justices to undertake a semi-annual tour, had withered.

In accepting the position of chief justice, Marshall was taking on not only the judicial task of establishing relevance for the nation's highest court, but the political task of creating a judiciary that could serve as the only counterbalance available to a government controlled by Republicans. Until his elevation to the highest judicial office in the nation, Marshall's experience with the law had been solely as an advocate. Whether in the courtroom, at the ratifying convention, or on the floor of the state or national legislature, Marshall had never before been in a job one of whose requirements was, at least in theory, the suppression of his own personal politics for a higher good. Until this point, Marshall had had the luxury of maintaining that his political beliefs would inevitably lead to a higher good. Although affability often disguised it, Marshall was an intensely political man, skilled in achieving consensus but even more skilled at winning.

His first term in office began in humbling fashion, however. In that grim committee room in the Capitol, with only three of his five colleagues and almost no spectators present, the greatest chief justice the United States has

ever known was sworn in at 11 A.M. on February 4, 1801. Eschewing the scar-
let robes or grand accoutrements favored by other judges, Marshall dressed
simply, in a plain black robe. He did not specify whether this was fitting for
the surroundings, a function of the general lack of interest in appearances
for which he was well known, or a symbolic message that the Supreme
Court would no longer hold itself above the people, but soon all the associate justices were wearing plain black robes, as they do today.* Six days later,
without passing on a single case of note, the Court adjourned the February
term, and Marshall once again became full-time secretary of state.

---

* In January 1995, Chief Justice William Rehnquist shocked Court watchers when he appeared in
a gown with four gold horizontal stripes on each sleeve.

FIFTEEN

TWO BILLS: ADAMS'S LAST STAND

T O THE SURPRISE OF MANY, the courts bill had not sailed through the Federalist Congress. After the first two readings on December 19, the bill was not even discussed until January 5. Possibly this was a result of the vacancy in the chief justice's chair, or simply a reflection of the general chaos that seemed to surround a government poised for its first political transition; but, whatever the case, once the measure did come to the floor, determined Republicans persisted in prolonging argument throughout January by introducing extraneous topics of debate. In one case, the better part of a day was spent deciding whether Virginia should be one circuit or two and, if two, whether the line of division should be by latitude or longitude.[1] Two days later, Republicans initiated an extended discourse as to whether state courts could be made to adhere to federal law, an important issue, but one that been covered before. Even the House reporter noted that one congressman "went over the same ground as that taken by him in a former debate."[2] There were motions to reduce the judges' $2,000 salary to $1,800, and many others to parse this section of the bill or that.

In session after session, Federalists and Republicans alike droned on about minutiae and little of substance was accomplished. With Jay, the putative chief justice, yet to make an appearance, however, Federalists had no choice but to accept the endless palaver. The *House Journal* for January 5, 1801, gave a sense of the pace. "The House, according to the order of the day, again resolved itself into a Committee of the Whole House on the bill to provide for the more convenient organization of the Courts of the United States; and, after some time spent therein, Mr. Speaker resumed the

chair, and Mr. Rutledge* reported that the committee had, according to order, again had the said bill under consideration, and made a further progress
therein."[3] The exact same entry appeared for January 7 and for January 8, 9,
and 12, except that for the latter three days it was Mr. Morris[4] reporting
progress instead of Mr. Rutledge. Not until January 16 did the House get
around to dealing with amendments.

Finally, on January 20, as Adams's nomination of John Marshall for chief
justice was read in the Senate, the House of Representatives quickly
brought the courts bill to a vote and it passed, 51–43. In the early days of
Congress, votes of specific members were only recorded if one fifth of those
present called for yeas and nays, which happened here. Whether Federalists
or Republicans asked for the roll call was not specified, but the results
showed a strict party-line vote, with not a single Republican agreeing to the
reorganization.

The Jay debacle had cost Federalists precious weeks, and speed was now
of the essence. The following day, the bill was reported to the Senate, received the second reading a day after that, and then sent to a committee that
consisted of five Federalists, four of the five from New England. The committee reported out the bill without amendment on January 29, two days after John Marshall had been confirmed as chief justice.

Republicans were not finished, however. Once again they bombarded the
bill with a series of amendments. They proposed lowering the salaries of the
circuit judges and, when that failed, raising the salary of circuit judges in
Republican Tennessee and Kentucky. They suggested changing the mandated day for the meeting of one of the circuit courts by one month. Had
any of these amendments passed, the bill would have returned to the House.
Finally, on Saturday, February 7, the Senate passed the bill as received, by a
16–11 vote. It was affirmed on the following Tuesday, February 10, and then
brought to the House, where it was signed by the Speaker.[5]

The following day, Wednesday, February 11, was supposed to be one of
high ceremony, when Americans found out for the first time who would be
their next president. According to the plan, the electoral votes from the
various states, suitably endorsed and certified, were to be read in the Senate
chamber by the president of the Senate (who happened to be Thomas Jefferson) and then tallied with great flourish and drama before a joint session

---

* John Rutledge Jr. of South Carolina, son of the former chief justice.

of Congress. When the tally was complete, a proclamation announcing the result would be issued to a breathless and eager nation. Since the result of the election was by this time known to virtually every person in America, many thought that this grand scenario would have lost its allure. But since the tie between Jefferson and Burr had injected a number of heretofore unforeseen variables into the mix, anticlimax had been replaced with excitement of a different sort than what was anticipated by the framers.

On the morning of February 11, the capital's few thousand residents awoke to a driving snowstorm. House members slogged through the mess and dutifully trooped into the Senate chamber, listened to the reading of an outcome that had been more or less public for weeks, affirmed that both Jefferson and Burr had received a majority of the electoral votes, and then dutifully trooped out to return to their own chamber to commence the by-state voting to break the tie.[6]

Federalists kept their vow to vote for Burr, and the result of the first ballot was eight states for Jefferson, six for Burr, and two divided. The result of the second ballot was the same. And the third. After eight ballots, neither side had blinked. By the ninth ballot, even the House reporter had wearied of recording the same outcome and he noted simply, "The States then proceeded to a ninth, tenth, eleventh, twelfth, thirteenth, fourteenth, and fifteenth ballots; and, upon examination of the ballots respectively, the result was declared to be the same."[7]

The delegates took a break for dinner and then returned to the freezing, half-finished Capitol to cast the sixteenth ballot at 9 P.M. After that provided no change, the members voted to take only one vote per hour, thereby allowing time for someone to try to broker a deal. At 11 P.M. a motion to adjourn until the following day was defeated, and at midnight the nineteenth ballot was still eight for Jefferson, six for Burr, and two divided. The votes kept coming through the night, monotonous in their repetition, while America waited to learn the identity of the next president. After the twenty-seventh ballot, which had begun at 8 A.M., the members gave themselves a break until noon. The rest did not help—the twenty-eighth ballot was the same. The House then adjourned until the next day.

Before the voting began, the House had agreed that they would not be interrupted by other business until a president had been chosen. According to the reporter, "During the time the States were employed in balloting, sundry messages from the President of the United States, from the Senate, and

communications from Departments, were received, and reports from committees made; but it being contrary to the rules established on [February 9]
for the House to take them into consideration at that time, they were taken
up and acted upon after the balloting had been completed, and the final result declared."[8] One of the sundry messages was to inform the House that
"An act to provide for the more convenient organization of the Courts of
the United States" had been placed before the president for his signature.[9]

On Friday, February 13, only one ballot was taken, the twenty-ninth,
with the same inconclusive result. Meanwhile, at the President's House,
John Adams signed "An act to provide for the more convenient organization of the courts of the United States," which soon became popularly
known as the Judiciary Act of 1801.[10]

Four ballots were taken on February 14 and, after taking Sunday off, one
on February 16. The nation was facing the very real possibility that, in two
weeks, it would be without a chief executive. On February 17, the first vote
of the day, the thirty-fifth ballot, showed no change. At 1 P.M., the thirty-
sixth ballot was taken. The reporter noted:

> The time agreed upon by the last mentioned vote being expired, the States
> proceeded in manner aforesaid to the thirty-sixth ballot; and, upon exam-
> ination thereof, the result being reported by the tellers to the Speaker, the
> Speaker declared to the House that the votes of ten States had been given
> for Thomas Jefferson, of Virginia; the votes of four States for Aaron Burr,
> of New York; and that the votes of two States had been given in blank; and
> that, consequently, Thomas Jefferson, of Virginia, had been, agreeably to
> the Constitution, elected President of the United States, for the term four
> years, commencing on the fourth day of March next.[11]

The stalemate had been broken not by an arrangement made in the House
chamber, but as a result of the turmoil on the outside.[12] While the congressmen repetitively cast their ballots during that week in February, the United
States had teetered on the brink of dissolution, military coup, or even civil
war. Republicans had been unimpressed that Federalists magnanimously had
not tried to actually seize the government, but remained so incensed by what
they saw as a bald-faced ploy to frustrate the will of the voters that in two
states, Virginia and Pennsylvania, militia had been either alerted or actually
mustered with the intent of marching on the capital if Jefferson's election

was not validated by the House. Virginians threatened to secede or call another constitutional convention. For every actual event, there were ten rumors, one of which was that a mob of Pennsylvanians had seized the federal
arsenal in Philadelphia. Other rumors had key Federalists receiving death
threats that would be carried out if Jefferson was denied the presidency.

In the capital itself, deals and counter-deals were proposed seemingly
by the hour. Federalists were convinced that they could barter their votes
for concessions from one or both of the candidates. Different members of
the party petitioned or were said to petition—fact was becoming increasingly indistinct from fiction—both Burr and Jefferson, trying to wrangle
indulgences.[13]

During the Sunday break, James Bayard, Federalist of Delaware, began to
waver. Bayard was in a unique position in the House—a delegation of one,
the sole representative of the state that, at the time, had the smallest population in the Union. Bayard despised Jefferson and could never bring himself to vote Republican. But, if he turned in a blank ballot, according to the
rules, it would be as if Delaware did not exist. The number of states would
be reduced to fifteen and Jefferson's eight would be a majority.

Bayard apparently engaged an intermediary to determine what Jefferson
was willing to guarantee in return for a blank ballot. It is unclear whether the
intermediary ever brought the offer to Jefferson or, if he did, whether Jefferson
responded. (Bayard later claimed that Jefferson agreed to terms—Jefferson denied it—but the man who put the hated Virginian in the presidency surely
had an agenda of his own.) In any event, Bayard revealed his decision to abstain to a party caucus on Sunday, where it was not received well.[14]

Evidently, the reason that Bayard did not withhold his ballot first thing
Monday morning or for the first ballot on Tuesday was that other Federalists
were waiting for a response to a counter-offer from Burr. By midday Tuesday,
it had either not arrived or was unsatisfactory, so, on the thirty-sixth ballot,
Bayard cast his blank vote. Aware of Bayard's intentions, Maryland's five
Federalists also did not bother to vote, nor did Vermont's, throwing those
states to Jefferson. South Carolina's all-Federalist delegation refused to cast
ballots as well, thereby creating an abstention and the final tally of ten
states for Jefferson, four for Burr and two abstentions. At shortly after 1 P.M.
on February 17, 1801, Thomas Jefferson was finally elected as the third president of the United States, a mere fifteen days before he was scheduled to
take office.

The next day, John Adams sent his first list of judicial nominees to the Senate.

The courts bill Adams signed on February 13 had changed somewhat from the one that had been formulated the previous spring. It established a series of six circuit courts that would sit permanently within twenty-two federal court districts. These districts largely corresponded to state boundaries, but created a separate district for the territory of Maine (then part of Massachusetts) and the Ohio territories, and created a northern and southern district for New York, and eastern and western districts for Pennsylvania, Virginia, and Tennessee. Unlike the previous bill, which created a circuit judgeship for each district, five of the six circuit courts would be overseen by three permanent federal circuit court judges, and the sixth, Tennessee and Kentucky, by one new judge who would sit with the district court judges already in place. Judges would still ride from district to district within the circuit. Passage of this act would therefore enable the appointment of sixteen new federal judges, all of them with lifetime terms and all likely to be Federalists. As before, the act also provided for United States attorneys, federal marshals, and court clerks in each of the newly defined districts to supplement those already in place. All in all, this "convenient organization" promised to provide a convenient number of jobs for outgoing Federalists.

The provision to reduce the number of Supreme Court justices from six to five remained, meaning that, with Marshall now confirmed as chief justice, when the aged Cushing either died or resigned from the bench—one of which was expected imminently—Jefferson could not appoint a Republican replacement.* As had its predecessors, this bill also provided the Court the authority to issue "writs not specifically provided by statute, which may be necessary for the exercise of its jurisdiction, and agreeable to the principles and usages of law," including writs of *mandamus*.

The twelve judicial nominees that Adams sent to the Senate on February 18 were far from a bankrupt lot. The list included Jared Ingersoll and Richard Bassett for the second circuit, both of whom had been delegates to the Constitutional Convention; Charles Lee, the sitting attorney general,

---

* Cushing was another Federalist with unusual resilience. He lived another nine years, all of them spent on the Court.

for the fourth circuit; and even his own unfaithful treasury secretary, High Federalist Oliver Wolcott, for the first circuit.* Nonetheless, all were Federalists, and all stuck in the craw of a Republican Party forced to watch helplessly—for the moment—while Adams packed the courts. On Monday, February 23, Adams sent nominations for judges of the fifth and sixth circuits, as well as for a number of marshals and United States attorneys. All the nominations were quickly approved by the Senate.

The courts bill was not the only piece of legislation with implications for the judiciary that had been making its way through Congress while the struggle to elect a president was playing out. Another reorganization measure, "A Bill concerning the District of Columbia," something of a companion piece to the courts bill, had been initiated in the Senate, but was attracting far less public attention. It created two counties, Washington for that part of the District that lay in Maryland, and Alexandria for that part in Virginia. It established a federal circuit court for the district that would "consist of one chief judge and two assistant judges, resident within the district," giving President Adams three more Federalists to appoint. The chief judge would be paid the same $2,000 salary as circuit court judges, and the assistants would receive $1,600. The bill established terms for the court, and assigned it jurisdiction over "all crimes and offenses committed within said district, and of all cases of law and equity between parties, both or either of which shall be resident or be found within said district, and also of all actions or suits of a civil nature at common law or in equity in which the United States shall be plaintiffs or complainants." As in the courts bill, this legislation provided for all necessary support personnel as well—clerks, a marshal to run the jails, and a United States attorney to handle prosecutions. Although perhaps understood, the bill did not, as had the courts bill, specifically authorize the new circuit court to issue writs of *mandamus*.

Section 11 of the bill stipulated "That there be appointed for each of the said counties, such number of discreet persons to be justices of the peace, as the President of the United States shall from time to time think expedient, to continue in office for five years." Justices of the peace, a local or county

---

* Ingersoll and Lee declined the appointments.

office, did not come up in the courts bill, which dealt with only the federal judiciary, but was required in any definition of District of Columbia government. Although limited by term and lack of salary—compensation came through court fees—it was nonetheless vital to municipal order, "the most powerful public office in the lives of the common people."[15] Justices of the peace manned county courts, and therefore oversaw arrest, arraignment, and a number of other key day-to-day civil and criminal court functions. Excepting the pre-existing towns of Georgetown and Alexandria, the District of Columbia justices of the peace were also to serve as the capital's governing body.

The District of Columbia bill passed the Senate on February 5 and was sent to the House. Republicans once again attempted to stall passage by adding amendments, this time successfully. With the days of Federalist government ticking away, the amended bill was returned to the Senate on February 24, after passing the House by 57–36, all of the nays coming from Republicans. The Senate passed the amended bill on Friday, February 27, and sent it on to the president. Adams wasted no time, signing the bill, now "An act concerning the District of Columbia," the same day.[16]

February 27, 1801, was also the day James Madison's father died. Madison, who was to become the secretary of state, replacing Marshall, wrote to Jefferson that the "melancholy occurrence" would force him to remain in Virginia indefinitely to help settle the estate. Even then, however, politics was never far from Madison's thoughts. Precursing the constitutional crisis to come, he added in the same letter, "The conduct of Mr. A. is not such as was to have been wished or perhaps, expected. Instead of smoothing the path for his successor, he plays into the hands of those who are endeavoring to strew it with as many difficulties as possible; and with this view does not manifest a very squeamish regard to the Constn. Will not his appts. to offices, not vacant actually at the time, even if afterwards vacated by acceptances of the translations, be null?"[17]

Saturday, February 28, and the following Monday, March 2, his penultimate day in office, President Adams persisted in the conduct of which Madison had been so critical and sent a stack of nominations to the Senate to fill the new vacancies in the District of Columbia. These smacked even more of patronage than the nominations under the Judiciary Act. For associate judges of the new District of Columbia circuit court, Adams tapped James Marshall, the younger brother of the chief justice and his partner in land speculations, and William Cranch, his wife's nephew, who had recently gone broke in a land speculation of his own.* Filling out the appointments, Adams nominated two men to be judges of Orphans Court (one for Alexandria County and one for Washington County), another two as registrars of wills, and a third pair as notaries public. Then President Adams nominated an incredible forty-two men to be justices of the peace, twenty-three for Washington County and nineteen for Alexandria.[18] One of the Washington nominees was one "William Marberry."[19] Another was John Laird, and a third was the sitting secretary of the navy, Benjamin Stoddert.[20] While party affiliation played the most important role in who was nominated, not all the nominees were ardent Federalists. There were even some Republicans among the nominees.[21]

Judicial appointees accounted for only 93 of the 216 nominations that Adams sent to the Senate in the final month of his presidency. There were also nominations for military and diplomatic posts. In as pure a demonstration as possible that Adams was pleased that Jefferson had prevailed over Burr, he nominated James Bayard, congressman from Delaware, as ambassador to France, but Bayard declined.

On March 3, the last day of the Sixth Congress, the Senate approved the appointments of almost one hundred of Adams's last-minute nominations— among them, but not specifically mentioned in the *Senate Executive Journal*, William Marbury. The commissions were then sent by messenger to the President's House, where John Adams was spending his final hours in office.

---

*Adams blundered in his choice for circuit court chief justice, however. Thomas Johnson declined the appointment—to John Marshall's horror—by which time Jefferson was already in office and could fill the post with a Republican—which he promptly did.

SIXTEEN

SUNSET AT MIDNIGHT

WHAT OCCURRED AT THE PRESIDENT'S HOUSE once the approved commissions were delivered from the Senate was a source of conjecture, rumor, hyperbole, and, in the months following, more than a little vitriol. Few of the details can be discerned with certainty, but, even from the fragmentary evidence that is available, a reasonable picture can be drawn.

On the night of March 3, Adams signed and Marshall countersigned the commissions that the Senate had rammed through earlier in the day, as well as some earlier commissions that had not yet been processed. Marshall also affixed the Great Seal to each. Included was the commission for James Marshall for circuit court in the District of Columbia. (John Marshall had earlier helped process commissions for three current or future brothers-in-law.[1]) Most evidence indicates that all of the commissions were processed, but subsequent testimony, not altogether reliable, indicated that some were not. While it is also widely assumed that John Marshall was with Adams at the President's House—James Marshall may have been present for part of the time as well—similar testimony maintained that Adams was alone and Marshall never left his office at the Department of State.[2]

Wherever the signing and countersigning actually took place, Republicans later branded the whole crew, including those who had been confirmed the previous week, "Midnight Judges." A story quickly circulated in Republican circles that Adams and Marshall sat in the President's House, signing and affixing seals until the very moment, midnight, that Adams's term officially ended. Jefferson's granddaughter even told of Levi Lincoln, the incoming attorney general, surprising the pair a few moments after that and, pointing to Jefferson's watch, which for some reason he was carrying, demanding that they desist, as Adams was no longer president.[3] This story acquired the authority of the printed word when some credulous Jefferson biographers latched on to it. As for Jefferson himself, he felt that his predecessor had stayed within the law, and he also seems to have held on to his watch. In a letter about a month later, referring to the western district of Virginia, Jefferson wrote, "Mr. Adams, who continued filling all the offices till 9 o'clock of the night, at 12 of which he was to go out of office himself, took care to appoint for this district also."[4]

There is also some question as to Adams's and Marshall's states of mind. Some have portrayed the outgoing president spending his last hours in the President's House relieved at the lifting of what had become a grating burden, thrilled and expectant at the prospect of returning to Massachusetts to become "Plain John of Stony Field." Marshall, although harried by the flurry of activity—he would, at Jefferson's request, be conducting the swearing-in the following day—is said to have proceeded with his duties as he always did: responsibly, with good humor, and, most of all, in a lawful manner.

Yet, after taking such enormous pains to load the judiciary with Federalists in the waning days of a defeated and discredited administration, Adams and Marshall could hardly have proceeded without some degree of grim satisfaction, knowing that they were thrusting one last thumb into Jefferson's eye. This was, after all, to be Marshall's judiciary; beginning at noon the next day, he would be the most powerful Federalist in the nation. The chief justice, too, would clearly have understood that forty-two justices of the peace for a city as small as the District—even if there was a Republican or two sprinkled in—was a patronage giveaway. The presence of not only Marshall's brother and Abigail Adams's nephew among the appointees, but numerous other friends and relatives, and spouses of yet *other* friends and relatives, only underscored the patronage being offered.

Whenever the process came to an end—and there is no way to know for sure if it was before or after midnight—at 4 A.M. on the morning of March 4, 1801, John Adams, now a private citizen, boarded a coach to begin his journey home, thus becoming one of only two outgoing presidents who refused to attend the inauguration of his successor. His son, John Quincy Adams, would be the other.[5]

It was left to John Marshall, Chief Justice of the Supreme Court of the United States and, at Jefferson's request, for another twenty-four hours still secretary of state, to deliver the commissions. Once again, the process by which this was accomplished—and, in some cases, not accomplished—is unclear. Many of the commissions did, in fact, find their way to their appropriate destinations and it seems impossible that Marshall could have achieved this feat alone. Even if he had forgone sleep, he could never have scurried about, in the few hours he had before he was due at the Capitol to swear in Jefferson, to deliver dozens of commissions. Nor is there any record of a line of eager appointees showing up at the President's House or the Department of State in the early morning hours of March 4 to grab up their signed and sealed commissions before slinking off again into the night. Thus, while Marshall must have had help in his labors—and the legality of delegating this task is questionable—whom he employed as couriers is also unrecorded, although now–Associate Justice of the District of Columbia Circuit Court James Marshall was definitely among them.

By mid-morning of March 4, most of the key commissions had in one way or another been dispatched, but many of those for marshals and justices of the peace remained in Marshall's possession. He had been expecting the chief clerk at the Department of State, Jacob Wagner, to help with the deliveries, but Wagner had been pressed into service by Jefferson as a temporary private secretary and was unavailable. James Marshall signed for twelve of the commissions and left to deliver them. When he was unable to complete his rounds, he later returned "several" to his brother's office. As the hour grew late, John Marshall left the Department of State, a stack of remaining commissions still undelivered.

Afterward, Marshall was under some pressure to explain why, after the huge fuss involved in getting the commissions approved by the Senate, then signed and sealed, they were left to their fates at the State Department. He noted in a letter to James a few weeks later that he did not bother with the marshals' commissions because he believed that under the law Jefferson could sack whomever he pleased anyway—as the new president subsequently did—leaving open, of course, the question of why he and Adams had bothered with them in the first place. As to the justices of the peace, Marshall explained to his brother that he believed that, once signed and sealed, the commissions became lawful and irrevocable, and he therefore "entertained no suspicion" that Jefferson could or would fail to uphold their validity. It was only "the extreme hurry of the time and the absence of Mr. Wagner" that caused the commissions of William Marbury and the others to be left behind.[6]

That would be scant consolation to the frustrated appointees. While justice of the peace might seem a relatively minor post in the scheme of things, it had ceremonial and symbolic value quite important to a striver like William Marbury.

Marbury was born in 1762, son of a failed tobacco farmer, great-grandson of a successful plantation owner who, by distributing his property through inheritance, had subdivided his heirs into subsistence. By the time Marbury's father died, there was nothing left to inherit at all.[7] The Marburys were poor and patriotic; three of Marbury's older brothers fought in the Revolution. William Marbury, after a hardscrabble youth, eschewed military service and instead got himself a job in the Maryland state capital, Annapolis, clerking for a minor state official. He eventually held a series of low-level secretarial positions in Maryland government, acquiring a reputation for intelligence and hard work, until, in 1789, after Alexander Hamilton persuaded Congress to assume all state war debts, Marbury finally had an opportunity to make some money of his own.

Marbury's associates, all Federalists with a penchant for speculating, not surprisingly owned a sizable quantity of Maryland debt instruments. When the value of the paper increased with the government guarantee, they therefore profited handsomely. Marbury, a de facto junior partner, was allowed to buy some small quantity of the notes at their depreciated value and then benefit from the appreciation, a transaction that today would be called "insider trading" but which in the early days of the Republic was standard speculative practice.[8] Marbury's friends eventually chartered a bank in which Marbury was allowed to invest. The bank became enormously successful, and Marbury profited along with the rest. He would eventually be named a director.

Marbury was not content to simply slipstream behind his associates, however. He was highly ambitious and possessed a natural acumen for finance to turn ambition into reality. In the early 1790s, he was named a "Deputy Agent for the State of Maryland," then, in 1796, got the top post and with it, a chance to make some real money. As agent, Marbury "engaged in complex financial dealings, collecting back taxes, selling estates, exchanging debt certificates for federal stock, and brokering on his own."[9] While never quite breaking into either Maryland's political or financial elite, Marbury

William Marbury

amassed substantial wealth and became a well-known figure in the state. He sat for a portrait by Rembrandt Peale and even began lending funds to friends and associates.

The Federalist rift during the Adams presidency was as deep in Maryland as anywhere else, and Marbury found himself in the thick of the fray. The battle was as much financial as ideological with one contingent, under the leadership of Samuel Chase, vying with Adams loyalists to carve up the spoils of assumption and speculation. Marbury's circle aligned with Adams. Deft as he was as a financial practitioner, Marbury's expertise was invaluable and he became a key player in the Adams camp. He moved to Georgetown to be closer to the new capital and, when his close friend Benjamin Stoddert was appointed secretary of the navy, Marbury's political fortunes seemed on the rise as well.

After Adams purged his cabinet in May 1800, Marbury's associates gained even more sway with the president. One of them, an intimate named Uriah Forrest, asked Marbury to spearhead the effort to gain Maryland's ten electoral votes for Adams. Had he been successful and Maryland's ten votes all gone to Adams instead of splitting 5–5, Adams would have been re-elected and Marbury would have been in line for a major government post, the culmination of a remarkable American success story.

Despite unstinting efforts, however, Marbury could not deliver Maryland, but his tireless and loyal support did not go unrewarded by the outgoing president. He was not sufficiently senior for a circuit court nomination, so, to show his appreciation, Adams named William Marbury as one of the forty-two new justices of the peace for the District of Columbia.

SEVENTEEN

THE NEW DAY

THOMAS JEFFERSON WAS INAUGURATED as the third president of the United States at noon on March 4, 1801, before a special joint session of Congress and a packed gallery in the Senate chamber. He had been conciliatory in asking the Federalist Marshall to swear him in—as had been Marshall in agreeing to administer the oath—and the new president appeared at first to be even more conciliatory in his inaugural address, in which he called on those of all parties to join him.[1] "Let us then, fellow citizens, unite with one heart and one mind, let us restore to social intercourse that harmony and affection without which, liberty, and even life itself, are but dreary things. And let us reflect, that, having banished from our land that religious intolerance under which mankind so long bled and suffered, we have yet gained little, if we countenance a political intolerance, as despotic, as wicked, and capable of as bitter and bloody persecutions." He added, "We are all republicans; we are all federalists."[2]

As Jefferson continued on, however, conciliation gave way to thinly veiled threat. "I know indeed that some honest men fear that a republican government cannot be strong; that this government is not strong enough." The "honest men" to whom Jefferson referred were, of course, Federalists. "But would the honest patriot, in the full tide of successful experiment, abandon a government which has so far kept us free and firm, on the theoretic and visionary fear that this government, the world's best hope, may, by possibility, want energy to preserve itself? I trust not. I believe this, on the contrary, the strongest government on earth . . . Let us then, with courage and confidence, pursue our own federal and republican principles; our attachment to union and representative government."[3] It was lost on no one

that, by "representative government," Jefferson was referring not to the elit-
ist centralization of the Federalists, but to the populist majority rule that he
favored. Rather than a call for moderation on all sides, then, the speech offered an olive branch only to those Federalists willing to set aside their own
views and accept the principles of the victors, an extremely clever ploy to
create an even deeper rift in the divided party and isolate and marginalize
Hamilton and the High Federalists.

Thursday, March 5, was officially the first day of the Seventh Congress,
but the only day that it would sit until the new session began in December.[4]
Jefferson nominated Madison for secretary of state (Levi Lincoln would
man the post until Madison's return), Samuel Dearborn to be secretary of
war, and Lincoln to be attorney general. Dearborn and Lincoln were both
from Massachusetts, meaning, with Madison's absence, Jefferson's entire
initial cabinet was from Adams's home state.* Robert Livingston was nominated ambassador to France, the post James Bayard had declined. The senators waived debate on the nominations and approved all four immediately,
and then Congress adjourned for its eight-month recess. With the Senate
confirmation of Madison, John Marshall left the executive branch forever.

Jefferson was inundated with requests for appointments from hungry Republicans, but the savvy Virginian knew all too well that a mass purge of
federal (and Federalist) officials would not only throw the government into
chaos, but also undermine his plan to co-opt as many moderate Federalists
as possible. Nettling some of his supporters, he thus removed few Adams appointees of long standing. Even Rufus King, Adams's ambassador to Britain,
kept his job. Appointments made in the closing days of Adams's presidency,
however, would be treated quite differently.

In a letter of March 23, 1801, responding to a Republican office-seeker,
Jefferson laid out his criteria. "All appointments to *civil* offices *during pleasure*, made after the event of the election was certainly known to Mr. A, are
considered as nullities," he wrote. "I do not view the persons appointed as
even candidates for the office, but make others without noticing or notify-
ing them. Mr. A's best friends have agreed this is right."[5] Jefferson never
specified which of Adams's friends had agreed that all appointments made
after the election results were known were void—nor did he specify whether

---

*Albert Gallatin of Pennsylvania was appointed interim secretary of the treasury soon afterward,
an appointment made permanent when the Congress reconvened later in the year.

he meant the results announced February 11 or December 3—but this threat was clearly directed at the judiciary and might possibly have included Marshall himself. After Jefferson then promised to remove anyone guilty of official misconduct, an unsubtle threat of impeachment, he added: "Good men, to whom there is no objection but a difference of political principle, practised on only as far as the right of a private citizen will justify, are not proper subjects of removal, except in the case of attorneys & marshals. The courts being so decidedly federal & irremovable, it is believed that republican attorneys & marshals, being the doors of entrance into the courts, are indispensably necessary as a shield to the republican part of our fellow citizens, which, I believe, is the main body of the people."[6] Jefferson kept to his promise, replacing virtually all Adams's marshals and United States attorneys, and announced his intention to eliminate the Midnight Judges by a repeal of the Judiciary Act of 1801, "which we trust will be at the next Congress."[7]

To the justices of the peace, Jefferson showed both the carrot and the stick. The stick came first. Shortly after his inauguration, upon a visit to the State Department, the new president discovered the signed, sealed, but undelivered commissions sitting on a table. He instructed that none of the commissions be delivered and then proceeded to void the lot.[8] Years later, Jefferson justified this decision by likening the commissions to deeds, and "if there is any principle of law not yet contradicted, it is that delivery is one of the essentials to the validity of a deed."[9] Nonetheless, two weeks later, although he cut the number of justices of the peace in the District to a still-hefty thirty, fifteen for each county, Jefferson behaved with remarkable forbearance and reappointed twenty-five of Adams's forty-two nominees. The seventeen who failed to receive commissions were either highly partisan Federalists or men against whom Jefferson bore a personal grudge. Marbury, who qualified on both counts—the Maryland electoral vote gambit had been particularly galling to the Republican faithful—was one of the seventeen who was not appointed.

Marbury's specific reaction is not recorded, but likely he was far more incensed when he learned that twenty-five of his fellow nominees had been allowed to succeed to the position than he was when he learned that Jefferson had simply refused to reappoint all forty-two. To a man who craved public respect like Marbury, the reappointments would have made his firing much more personal—a lawful and well-earned position usurped. To make it all the more frustrating, since the twenty-five were reappointed under the District of Columbia Act, they would get to complete their five-year terms even if the Judiciary Act of 1801 was repealed.

Marbury refused to simply sit still and accept the slight, and so, almost immediately, he visited the Department of State to try to secure his commission. Lincoln, however, would not see him. He then sought out Daniel Brent and Jacob Wagner, the clerks at the State Department and both Federalists, but not only could they not help Marbury obtain his commission, they claimed that they could not even tell him where the physical document was. While it was presumed to have been in the stack that Jefferson had discovered when he took office, nobody had seen the paper since. As Marbury was contemplating how to further proceed, Madison finally arrived in Washington City and was sworn in on May 2, relieving Lincoln.

With the disappearance of the physical commission, any chance Marbury had of buttressing his claim with documentary evidence had vanished. Undaunted, Marbury attempted to press his suit, and eventually succeeded in securing an audience with the new secretary of state, only to be told that nothing could be done if the commission could not be found and, besides, the president considered the matter closed.

With Congress gone until winter and only a few members of the new Republican administration still in town, William Marbury had ample months ahead of him to stew about his bad fortune and contemplate his next step.

EIGHTEEN

"Beyond Comparison the Weakest of the Three": Marshall Takes the Court

WHEN THE JUSTICES of the nation's highest tribunal returned to Washington City for the August 1801 term—the June–December schedule would not begin until the Seventh Congress convened—the capital was all but deserted. Congress would not convene for another four months, and both the president and secretary of state had abandoned the malaria-ridden city for the bucolic rolling hills of western Virginia. In this serendipitous isolation, still ensconced in Committee Room 2, John Marshall set himself the task of molding the Supreme Court.

The Supreme Court that Marshall inherited was thirteen years of pomp over substance. The Court had not become an arm of policy-making but rather a vestigial appendage in the power structure. His first move was to persuade all six justices to live under the same roof. This might have been difficult in sophisticated Philadelphia, rich in choices of first-class lodging, but could almost be achieved by default in Washington City. Marshall chose Conrad and McMunn's, the same boardinghouse at which Jefferson had stayed before his inauguration and considered easily the best hostelry in town. It also boasted some of the finest food in the area and was well stocked with good wine, both vital considerations for the convivial chief justice. By forcing the justices to live, work, eat, and drink with each other, Marshall forged a tight, insular unit in which teamwork became mandatory and egos were forced under control. For the remainder of Marshall's thirty-four-year tenure, whenever court was in session, all the justices would live in the same abode.

It was fortunate that Marshall possessed the social skills to pull off such a coup, because the five associate justices he inherited represented extremes in size, temperament, age, and—though all were titularly Federalists—political philosophy. The most senior associate was the gentle, erudite Yankee, William Cushing, now almost seventy and in frail health. While Cushing's intellect seemed undiminished, he moved slowly, both physically and in contemplation. He was still considered the Court's foremost authority on comparative constitutional law. The youngest associate, at thirty-eight, was the genteel Bushrod Washington. Not at all genteel was William Paterson. No one had been more zealous in enforcing the Sedition Act. Adams had come to detest him. Alfred Moore was forty-five, Marshall's age, and was also a moderate Federalist. Tiny—he weighed less than one hundred pounds—he was able, quick-witted, and affable. Then there was Samuel Chase, who had enforced the Sedition Act with gusto, harangued defendants from the bench, and openly campaigned for Adams against Jefferson.[1]

While galvanizing these five men into an effective working body would be no small feat in itself, Marshall's bigger challenge was to forge a power base for the Court. His first step was to discontinue the practice of delivering opinions *seriatim*, each justice speaking separately and independently, and replace it with an "opinion of the court," each opinion delivered by a single justice, usually the chief, which represented a synthesis of the views of whichever justices participated in the case. In addition to creating a single voice for the Court, this practice required that the justices confer in advance on the opinions being written.

The first case on the August 1801 docket was *Talbot v. Seeman*. *Talbot* had been scheduled for the February term, but Marshall had decided to carry it over to August. The official reason was the absence of Moore and Paterson, but it is more likely that Marshall did not want to begin his tenure on the Court by hearing a politically charged case amidst the maelstrom of a contested election, with frantic Republicans and Federalists prowling the halls of Congress, muttering and plotting within earshot of Committee Room 2. It was an astute decision, since the Court could never have had more freedom to maneuver than was present in the empty capital that August.

Talbot, like *Bas*, was a prize case, involving the seizure of a vessel on the high seas. In 1799, at the height of the Quasi-War, the *Amelia*, a merchant ship owned by Hans Seeman of Hamburg, had set sail from Calcutta bound for its home port, filled to the gunwales with pricey Indian exotica. To deter pirates, the ship carried eight small guns. Once in the Atlantic, however, the *Amelia* had been seized by a French man-o'-war. Seeman's crew was replaced and the *Amelia* was placed under a French flag and redirected to the West Indies. There, both ship and cargo, valued at a whopping $190,000, were to be declared prizes by a French admiralty court—a process known as condemnation—and then sold, the proceeds going to the captors.

Before it could reach its new destination, however, the *Amelia* was sighted by yet another warship, this time Old Ironsides, the USS *Constitution*, Silas Talbot commanding. The *Amelia* was no more successful in avoiding the *Constitution* than it had been with the French warship, and was seized once more. Captain Talbot sailed the *Amelia*, now under an American flag, to New York, where he claimed from Seeman, by international law of salvage, half the value of ship and cargo for himself and his crew for rescuing them from the French. (The laws cited in *Bas* did not apply, since the *Amelia* was not originally American-owned.)

Seeman sued in federal district court, claiming that salvage was not owed since Hamburg was neutral in the ongoing British–French conflict and the *Amelia* thus would not have been considered a fair prize in French

"Old Ironsides," the USS *Constitution*

court and should have been returned to him for nothing. Talbot countered that the French actions spoke for themselves and, since the *Amelia* was flying the flag of a combatant of the United States as defined by Congress and the president, he and his men were entitled both to seize the ship and to claim their $95,000.* While the money involved was substantial, the principal point of contention was political. Federalists, who insisted Congress's and President Adams's actions against France during the Quasi-War were legitimate, favored Talbot, while Francophile Republicans, who had always believed that both Congress and the president had exceeded their authority, backed Seeman.

At the heart of the case, as it would be in *Bas*, was whether or not, at the time of the seizure, a state of war existed between the United States and France and, if so, how it had come to be. Adams had, of course, never asked for a formal declaration, nor had Congress provided one. Instead of a declaration, the Federalist Congress had enacted a good deal of bellicose legislation, which Adams had interpreted to suit his policies. Adams had issued a number of directives as commander-in-chief based on his reading of Congress's intent, but what role the president could actually play in this process under the Constitution was equally vague.

The district court had agreed with Talbot and awarded salvage, but Seeman appealed to the circuit court in New York, over which Bushrod Washington presided. The potential volatility of the case—as well as its true political nature—was reflected by the advocates for the parties. Previewing their duel in the April 1800 New York legislative elections and another duel in 1804 of a more permanent nature were Alexander Hamilton for Captain Talbot and Aaron Burr for Hans Seeman.

The verdict was highly anticipated, but Justice Washington was not the sort to introduce a spark into a container of gunpowder. Rather than rule on the Quasi-War or attempt to define the power and limitations of the executive and legislative branches to make war, Washington chose a narrower, less risky path. Tiptoeing past the political questions entirely, he overturned the district court's ruling and found for Seeman, but only on the grounds that an American warship did not have the right to seize a neutral vessel, which the *Amelia* was under international law. As it was not a lawful prize

---

* *Talbot* was heard in district court before *Bas* had been decided.

and would have been returned at no cost by the French court, Seeman was at no risk. On the dubious proposition that a French court would have ruled against French sailors, Washington declared that Talbot was therefore not entitled to salvage.

By the time *Talbot* reached the Marshall court in 1801, *Bas* had already been decided, and the notion of "imperfect" war was a part of the law of the land. In his opinion in *Bas*, Justice Washington had hastened to emphasize that his circuit court ruling in *Talbot* did not contradict this principle, but had been decided on narrower grounds. Washington wrote, "The opinion which I delivered at New York, in *Talbot v. Seeman* was, that although an *American* vessel could not justify the re-taking of a neutral vessel from the *French*, because neither the sort of war that subsisted, nor the special commission under which the American acted, authorized the proceeding; yet, that the 7th section of the act of 1799, applied to recaptures from *France as an enemy*, in all cases authorized by congress."[2]

Representing Talbot before the Supreme Court were two prominent Federalists, Jared Ingersoll of Philadelphia, who had declined Adams's nomination to the new second circuit court, and none other than February's tie-breaker, Congressman James A. Bayard of Delaware. For Seeman were equally distinguished Republicans John Thomson Mason of Maryland, nephew of George Mason IV, the most significant member of the 1787 convention who refused to sign the Constitution, and Alexander Dallas, another well-known Philadelphia advocate who had reported for the Court before its move to the Potomac. (Looking around at the Court's incommodious chambers, Dallas must have congratulated himself on his foresight.)

The hearings lasted four days. Reiterating the arguments in circuit court, Talbot's side claimed that the captain's actions were justified, since he had seized an armed combatant vessel and saved it from condemnation. Mason and Dallas returned to the original assertion that the French admiralty court would have returned Seeman's property and therefore Talbot had done him no service for which compensation was required. As they had in circuit court, both plaintiff and defendant inevitably gravitated to the political question of whether or not the *Amelia* could possibly have been a neutral vessel under a French flag. Washington had ruled that it could, but that was before *Bas*.

Once the concept of imperfect war was introduced, Adams's directives to the navy could also come under scrutiny. While *Bas* had confirmed Congress's power to create limited war, the decision had not dealt specifically with a president's power to engage the nation in war, limited or full, unless he was specifically following the dictates of Congress. As a result, arguments in *Talbot* focused on whether or not President Adams's interpretation of Congress's declarations had exacerbated or obviated the limited state of war that Congress had seemed to create between the United States and France. Marshall was thus to be faced with the question of whether or not his old boss had exceeded his constitutional authority as commander-in-chief.

Mason and Dallas asserted that Washington had more or less backed into the correct decision in circuit court. Since the *Amelia* was neutral, Talbot's seizure exceeded the conditions Congress had imposed by which Americans could engage the French in battle, and was thus illegal and the resulting prize could not be held for salvage. What's more, President Adams's statements were irrelevant or worse, since the president was not granted the power to declare war by the Constitution. Bayard and Ingersoll maintained that the *Amelia* was an armed vessel, flying a French flag, which, as the president had made clear, fell squarely within the boundaries that Congress had imposed. They tried to read Adams's comments about the relevant legislation into the record but were refused.

In his very first case as chief justice, Marshall faced the same conundrum that he would in *Marbury*. He could play safe and rule narrowly on the *Amelia*'s neutrality, thus avoiding war powers and the Quasi-War entirely, or, using *Bas* as a starting point, take the opportunity to extend the Court's constitutional authority by sharpening the definition of war powers. Safety was certainly supported by some compelling arguments. Since the Quasi-War was over and the nation was now run by Jefferson and his Republicans, there seemed little need to rekindle the fires and rule on war powers. Unfortunately, if the Court found for Seeman, it would invalidate Adams's actions and thus, with its maiden decision, abdicate its role as guardian of Federalist values.

If the Court found for Talbot, however, it would be forced to affirm Adams's interpretations of war powers, which would outrage Republicans and, with the threat of impeachment looming in December when the Seventh Congress convened, outrage might well soon translate into action.* Adding to

---

* Constitutionally, of course, Supreme Court justices could only be impeached for misconduct, but neither Federalists nor Republicans were under any illusions that the letter of the law would be adhered to. No one would have been surprised to see Marshall impeached, and many in Washington expected it.

the difficulty was that a finding for Talbot would reverse Justice Washington's ruling and therefore work against the musketeer spirit that Marshall was trying fervently to develop among his justices.

Marshall and his colleagues needed almost a week to find a solution, while the lawyers sweltered in empty Washington City. Since "what little social life there was in the scraggly village revolved around" the off-limits Conrad and McMunn's, they were forced to sit idly in inferior living quarters having no one to speak with except each other. The decision, delivered by Marshall, the first "Opinion of the Court," was a masterpiece of legal reasoning, political necessity, conciliation, and misdirection, all the elements that would, in two years, distinguish *Marbury*. That Marshall could be so successful in crafting pragmatism to sound like legalism, eelishness to appear as clarity, is testament to his political skill.

The chief justice began by reaffirming *Bas*. "It is not denied . . . that congress may authorize general hostilities, in which case the general laws of war apply to our situation; or partial hostilities, in which case the laws of war, so far as they actually apply to our situation, must be noticed." But then Marshall extended *Bas* and asserted: "The whole powers of war being, by the constitution of the United States, vested in congress, the Acts of that body can alone be resorted to as our guides in this enquiry."[3]

Having thrown a sop to Republicans by declaring that Adams's interpretation of Congress's actions had no bearing on the case—which also carried the implication that the president had exceeded his constitutional authority—Marshall then examined Congress's actions and came to the dubious conclusion that Talbot's seizure was justified under existing law. There was no specific legislation that supported that conclusion, nor had there been a declaration of war. Most importantly, Marshall did not specify by what authority he could interpret Congress's action when the president could not. Still, the chief justice concluded, "the real intent of Congress" was for American naval vessels to protect American commerce and, since the *Amelia* "was an armed vessel commanded and manned by Frenchmen," that Talbot had had "probable cause" to bring her to a United States port.

Had he stopped there, the decision would have enraged Republicans, the implied slap at Adams notwithstanding. But Marshall was too smart for that. He danced on the question of whether or not Talbot was entitled to salvage, which in turn depended on whether or not Seeman would have gotten his ship and cargo back from a French court. It troubled Marshall not one whit to use as a linchpin of an important constitutional decision his determination of the probable actions of a foreign court. This round went to Talbot as well. Marshall decided, contradicting Washington, that under French law the *Amelia* would have surely been condemned, as it was carrying goods loaded in a part of the British Empire, to wit India. Talbot had therefore performed "an essential service, and the Court is therefore of the opinion that the re-captor is entitled to salvage."[4]

Until this point, the opinion had been, at least by Marshall's standards, more or less straightforward. But no one understood better than John Marshall that the essence of mediation is to leave neither of the parties totally happy, but both with something to lose. So, adding the twist that would characterize all his great decisions, Marshall then hefted his scalpel and went to work on the award.

While she *appeared* to be a combatant vessel, he observed, the *Amelia* was actually *neutral,* and a neutral vessel "according to the law of nations . . . is generally restored without salvage." Having defined the ship as two things at once, Marshall went on to assert that, under the circumstances, one half— about $95,000—was far too great a sum. Talbot, after all, had only saved a part-neutral vessel. One sixth—$31,500—seemed fairer, Marshall decided, pulling a number out of the air. Moreover, for reasons that were not expounded, he determined that Seeman, even though he had lost, should be able to deduct his costs from the total. In the end, Hans Seeman paid Captain Talbot $26,405.77. (Talbot was forced to pay his own costs as well.)

If Jefferson had been in town or Congress had been in session, Marshall would likely have been impeached on the spot. But, as it was, in the vacuum of Washington City in August, he had been allowed to achieve everything he wanted, and the decision would be allowed to mellow for four months before the new Congress or the new president could act against it. The Court had acted as one, exercised constitutional authority, and everyone was both happy and unhappy at the result. The enduring legacy of *Talbot,* like that of *Marbury,* is found not in the essentials, but rather in the incidentals, in this case in Marshall's assertion that only Congress is invested by the Constitution with the power to make war.[5] Marshall's propensity to, in effect, legislate from the bench did not pass totally unnoticed. In 1823, Thomas Jefferson wrote: "The practice of Judge Marshall of travelling out of his case to prescribe what the law would be in a moot case not before the court, is very irregular and censurable."[6]

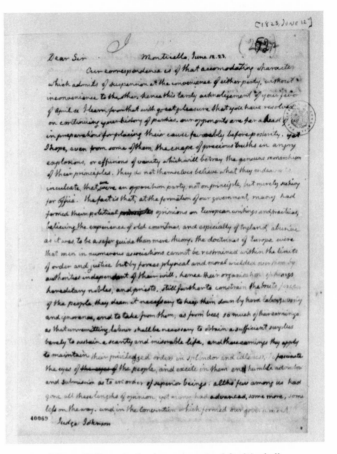

Thomas Jefferson's 1823 letter censuring John Marshall

No such sentiments were expressed at the time, however—no one was in town to do so—and thus, operating in the shadows, Marshall had laid precedent not only for Congress's power to make war, but for the chief justice's power to say what the law is, even if no one had asked him. All in all, a brilliant coup. That Republicans chose ultimately to accept the *Talbot* decision simply provides even more proof that when John Marshall drew a line in the sand, he knew exactly how many grains should be on either side.

With *Talbot* concluded and a political victory in his pocket, after disposing of some minor matters, Marshall adjourned the Court until December, a term that promised to lack the peace and tranquility of the one just concluded.

NINETEEN

REPEAL: THE SEVENTH CONGRESS

O N DECEMBER 7, 1801, when the Seventh Congress reconvened, this time fully and aggressively Republican, President Jefferson ironically found himself faced with the same problem of reining in the extreme members of his party that had bedeviled his predecessor. Radical Republicans were bristling for revenge and were only grudgingly willing to aid their leader in achieving consensus with their routed enemies. Jefferson had already stretched their patience the previous March when he had reappointed the twenty-five justices of the peace and left a number of key Federalists in their posts. It particularly galled radical Republicans to see Rufus King still in London.

In an attempt to avoid kindling partisan bickering—or at least to forestall it—Jefferson broke with tradition and chose to submit written remarks to Congress rather than deliver them in person. As he explained in a letter shortly afterward, "By sending a message, instead of making a speech at the opening of the session, I have prevented the bloody conflict to which the making an answer would have committed them." As a result, he noted optimistically, "Our winter campaign has opened with more good humor than I expected."[1]

Jefferson's speech was read to Congress on December 8, and emphasized state power, smaller federal government, and lower taxes. Although he referred only briefly to the courts bill, he left no doubt as to his intentions. "The judiciary system of the United States, and especially that portion of it recently erected, will, of course, present itself to the contemplation of Congress." To help Congress in this task, the new president added, "and that they may be able to judge of the proportion which the institution bears to the business it has to perform, I have caused to be procured from the several states, and now lay before Congress, an exact statement of all the causes decided since the first establishment of the courts, and of those which were depending when additional courts and judges were brought in to their aid."[2]

Most congressional Republicans had no qualms about forgoing niceties and proclaiming publicly that they wanted to repeal the Judiciary Act of 1801 simply to boot Adams's judges out of office, but Jefferson was after the moral high ground. Conciliation would fall flat if he could not find some justification for repeal beyond mere spite. Nonetheless, submitting statistics to establish that the extra layer of courts created by the act was unnecessary—to, in effect, prove that the judiciary of an expanding nation should contract—was an uncertain undertaking. Even if court volume did not warrant a dedicated circuit court system and all those new judges at that moment, even the most partisan Republican would admit that the existing judiciary would inevitably become inadequate in the coming years. Their solution to the problem—simply to dump Federalist judges through repeal, then add Republicans to the courts as the need arose—was not, however, what Jefferson was looking for.

Jefferson's call for statistics, then, was a way to deter the sort of vindictive internecine bickering that had sunk Adams and, at the same time, persuade Federalists to accept the inevitable. After all, what fair man could argue with the facts? Jefferson, riding a wave, had every reason to be optimistic that the strategem would be successful. Unlike his predecessor, who had inherited a party spoiled by unbroken success and then seen it demonize him when its hegemony was threatened, Jefferson was the leader of a newly empowered party whose members almost universally credited him with their ascension. Using reason and the power of his office, he had thus far been masterful in co-opting Federalists while blunting the point of the Republican spear. As for the judiciary itself, the last Federalist bastion, Marshall had demonstrated in *Talbot* that he joined the president in the conviction that confrontation served no one. An orderly repeal, based on sound statistical evidence, would leave Marshall and his five Federalists no choice but to acquiesce.

On December 8, 1801, the same day that Jefferson's message was read to Congress, the Supreme Court began a new term. Marshall adjourned the proceedings in the morning to allow the justices to hear the president's address read in the Senate chamber—it was, after all, only a short walk—then, in the afternoon, heard arguments in another volatile Federalist-against-Republican prize case, United States v. Schooner Peggy. Unlike Talbot, however, which concerned the actions of the departed Adams, in this case the Court was to rule on an alleged abuse of authority by Thomas Jefferson himself.

Like the Amelia, the Peggy was an armed merchantman, French-owned, that had been seized and condemned in circuit court as a prize during the Quasi-War. Before the ship could be sold, however, Oliver Ellsworth signed the Convention of 1800 at Môrtefontaine. The treaty stipulated that captured vessels that had not been "definitively condemned" should be returned to their owners. After he took office, Jefferson had therefore directed that the proceeds of the sale go to the French owners, not the Peggy's captors, who then appealed Jefferson's directive to the same circuit court in Connecticut that had awarded them the prize in the first place. Justice Cushing, presiding in circuit court, agreed that Jefferson had no right to stick his nose into the affair and, as a result, the court clerk in Federalist Connecticut refused to hand the money over to the French owners. Jefferson's new Republican United States attorney for Connecticut appealed Cushing's ruling to the Supreme Court.

Like Talbot, which had been on the February docket but was held over until August, United States v. Schooner Peggy had been scheduled for the August term but Marshall had held it over until December. It was one thing to rule on an Adams administration case in a deserted capital, but quite another to risk being seen as end-running Jefferson. Once again, delay had proved wise. By the time Schooner Peggy was heard, Marshall had taken the measure of the new president and could feel reasonably confident that his cousin would be tolerant of the Court as long as it did not directly challenge his power.

Arguments were the same as they been in circuit court, the defendants maintaining that the original decision, rendered before the treaty was in existence, was quite obviously a "definitive condemnation." Jefferson therefore had had no authority to instruct the court to do anything, since the ruling had been within the law at the time it was made. As to the Supreme Court, since it acted only in an appellate capacity, it could only overturn Cushing's decision if the circuit court had committed a judicial error—which it had not—not because the president had decided to inject himself into the process.

If Adams had been reelected, Marshall, with his enduring commitment to separation of powers, almost certainly would have agreed. Here, however, in his opinion of the court, he dodged the question of Jefferson's meddling with characteristic legerdemain. "It is in general true," he first conceded, "that the province of an appellate court is only to inquire whether a judgment when rendered was erroneous or not." However, he continued, ignoring the constitutional ban on *ex post facto* laws, "if subsequent to the judgment and before the decision of the appellate court, a law intervenes and positively changes the rule which governs, the law must be obeyed or its obligation denied. In such a case the court must decide according to existing laws, and, if it be necessary to set aside a judgment, rightful when rendered, but which cannot be affirmed but in violation of law, the judgment must be set aside."[3] Having twisted the Constitution to avoid antagonizing Jefferson, Marshall added an additional sop to the executive: he delayed making the decision public, not delivering his opinion until after Jefferson had signed the ratified and amended Treaty of Môrtefontaine on December 21.[4] The proceeds of the sale of the *Peggy* were thus awarded to the French owners over the American captors.

Marshall had retreated to avoid a confrontation he could not win. The hint of collusion on the *Schooner Peggy* decision, however, was unmistakable, "a potential olive branch from the judiciary" and "a vindication of [Jefferson's] desire to repair relations with France."[5] As long as Marshall backpedaled, Jefferson had no cause to risk his grand strategy of cooperation. As it was, Marshall was left to make the law jump through political hoops to create the impression that the two avowed enemies had succeeded in maintaining their rapprochement with remarkable ease.

But that illusion was about to be strained considerably. On December 16, Charles Lee appeared before the Court to demand a writ of *mandamus* for his client, William Marbury.

Marbury had fruitlessly pursued his appointment for seven months. Finally, along with three other denied appointees, Marbury engaged Lee, attorney general under Washington and Adams, to initiate a suit on his behalf. Lee was also an old friend of Marshall's who appeared regularly before the Supreme Court. With the physical commission nowhere to be found, Lee's first act was to establish evidence of the appointment, so he petitioned the Senate to turn over its records of the nomination and ratification. The Senate ignored him. From there, Lee went to Marshall.

In light of the subsequent decision, Lee has unfairly come under criticism for choosing the Supreme Court rather than the recently empaneled District of Columbia circuit court to seek the writ. Lee had excellent reasons for bypassing the circuit court. From a legal standpoint, power to issue writs of *mandamus* had not been specifically enumerated among this circuit court's powers, which had been established under a separate bill from the other circuit courts. From a political standpoint, William Kilty, a Republican, was now chief judge of the District of Columbia circuit court, and Lee's request could easily have been refused. The Supreme Court, on the other hand, headed by Federalist Marshall, was, on two counts, a more promising alternative. In the first place, the Court seemed to be specifically empowered under the Judiciary Act of 1789 to issue a *mandamus*, and, in the second, Lee had every reason to believe that the chief justice, whom he knew well, would be pleased to have a chance to atone for his error in not getting Marbury his commission back in March.

Charles Lee

The chief justice was, in fact, none too pleased to see Lee show up in his court, threatening the carefully constructed truce that he had achieved with Jefferson, particularly for a cause as unimportant as four essentially worthless justice-of-the-peace commissions. Still, he was unable to simply shoo Lee away without appearing to have caved in to the Republicans. To make the question even more delicate, Marshall had to contend with Justice Chase, who, in typical fashion, wanted to grant Lee's request and issue the *mandamus* immediately.

Levi Lincoln must have been told of Lee's intentions in advance, because he was in the tiny committee room when Lee showed up. Marshall asked Lincoln if either he or Madison had anything to say, but Lincoln declined to take a position on the motion. Marshall talked the matter over with his associates, and then once more opted for strategic delay. Mentioning nothing about constitutionality, the appellate process, Section 13 of the Judiciary Act, any other court, or whether Lee had come to the right place to seek the writ, Marshall issued an order requiring Secretary of State Madison to show cause why a writ of *mandamus* should not be issued. Madison was not required to respond immediately, but was given until the fourth day of the next term, which would be some time the following June when Congress was no longer in session and Washington would again be deserted. At that time, as he had done in *Talbot* and *Schooner Peggy*, Marshall could figure out a way to dispose of the matter, steering a path between Jefferson and the needs of his own party without arousing rancor on either side.

Jefferson's hold over the firebrands in his party, however, was more tenuous than either the president or Marshall had thought. For the first month of the legislative session, Congress dealt largely with administrative matters. When it finally got down to business on Wednesday, January 6, 1802, two weeks after the December term of the Supreme Court ended and Marshall had returned to Richmond, the very first item on the Senate agenda was a motion by John Breckinridge of Kentucky: "Resolved, That the act of Congress passed on the 13th day of February, 1801, entitled 'An act to provide for the more convenient organization of the courts of the United States,' ought to be repealed."[6]

Jefferson had great affection for Breckinridge personally—the young man had been something of a protégé and would be the first cabinet member from a Western state when appointed attorney general in 1804—but the president almost certainly did not welcome an open attack on the Federalist judiciary this quickly any more than Marshall welcomed Charles Lee's *mandamus* petition. After all the wooing of moderate Federalists, he would have preferred dealing with other legislation—lowering taxes was his first priority—before risking antagonizing enemies that he had been courting. Jefferson had, of course, anticipated fireworks over the courts bill. In a letter only two weeks before, he had said of the congressional session, "Hitherto there have been no disagreeable altercations. The suppression of useless offices, and lopping off the parasitical plant engrafted at the last session on the judiciary body, will probably produce some."[7]

Breckinridge did not specify why he brought his motion to the floor so quickly but many Republicans had been furious about Marshall's show-cause order to Madison. Lacking the nuance of the president, they could not see the move as a strategic retreat, an attempt by the chief justice to stall and

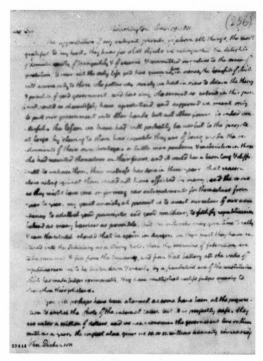

Thomas Jefferson's letter complaining that the Federalists had "retired into the judiciary as a stronghold"

then dispense with the issue quietly. To Republicans in Congress, hauling Madison in front of the reviled Marshall seemed the first salvo in the long-expected orchestrated assault on the executive by the Federalist courts. Demonstrating how tenuous was his détente with Marshall, even Jefferson had expressed that very point of view in a letter on December 19, sentiments that he had also certainly communicated to loyal supporters like Breckinridge. "[The Federalists] have retired into the judiciary as a stronghold. There the remains of federalism are to be preserved . . . and from that battery all the works of republicanism are to be beaten down then erased by a fraudulent use of the constitution."[8] Lee's appearance was therefore not seen as a spontaneous action by four frustrated office seekers, but part of a cabal with the justices to usurp power from Jefferson and the Republican Congress.

Once introduced, the repeal motion occupied the Senate for a month. The debate quickly coalesced around two issues—whether the new judges were needed at all and, more importantly, whether or not the Constitution would allow for the repeal of an act that permitted sitting judges of "good behaviour" to be deprived of their positions. Republicans had anticipated the constitutional issue, and Breckinridge raised it almost immediately in his opening remarks. He posed the question, "Because the Constitution declares that a judge shall hold his office during good behaviour, can it be tortured to mean that he shall hold his office after it is abolished? Can it mean the shadow, to wit the judge, can remain, when the substance, to wit the office, is removed?"[9] Breckinridge added that since Article III stated that Congress may from time to time establish inferior courts, it could also from time to time disestablish them. The senator from Kentucky went on to spend two more hours demonstrating that the Constitution only protected the man when there was an office for him to occupy, using rhetoric that one Federalist senator described as "ingenious."[10]

Gouverneur Morris of New York, one of the best minds in the nation and one of its most acerbic wits, saw it differently. He replied: "You shall not take the man from the office, but you may take the office from the man; you may not drown him, but you may sink his boat under him; you shall not put him to death, but you may take away his life . . . is it not absurd?"[11]

Morris had written the text for the finished Constitution. At least in theory, therefore, no one in the nation could state with greater certainty what the document actually meant. Morris pointed out to his fellow senators that Breckinridge's reading of Article III was incomplete. The article actually stated that "judicial power *shall* be vested in one Supreme Court and such inferior courts as Congress *may* from time to time ordain and establish." The choice of words, he asserted, was not arbitrary. "The Legislature," Morris went on, "therefore had, without doubt, the right of determining . . . what inferior courts should be established; but when established, the words are imperative, a part of the judicial power shall vest in them."[12]

At issue, of course, was not semantics or interpretation—or even law—but power. When another senator described this debate as "one of the most important questions that ever came before a legislature,"[13] the reason was clear—at stake was not only the definition of Article III of the Constitution, but whether or not Congress was empowered to form that definition. Who was to be the final authority on constitutional interpretation?

Republicans insisted that Congress had every right to construe Article III, Section I such as to eliminate judgeships, just as Congress explicitly had the power to create them. The Federalist minority was equally insistent that Article III was not open to congressional interpretation, but must be adhered to only as written. With strict construction and broad construction argued on the Senate floor, everyone present realized that the question would ultimately end up in the very court system that they were seeking to either enable or limit, depending on point of view.*

The question of redundancy was equally tricky, but more immediate and practical. Breckinridge opened the debate by saying, "No increase of courts or judges could be necessary or justifiable, unless the existing courts or judges were incompetent of the prompt and proper discharge of the duties assigned to them. To multiply expensive systems and create hosts of expensive officers, without having experienced an actual necessity for them, must be a wanton waste of the public treasure."[14] To buttress his argument, Breckinridge relied on Jefferson's submission of court records in December. "The document before us shows that, at the passage of this act, the existing courts, not only from their number, but from the suits before them, were fully competent to a speedy decision of those suits."[15] Breckinridge even noticed from Jefferson's documents that the number of suits was actually decreasing and

---

* The Federalists, broad constructionists when they were in power and could interpret the Constitution to their benefit, had now become strict constructionists to deny Republicans the same opportunity. This was not the first occasion, or remotely the last, when philosophy shifted to match political necessity.

promised to decrease still further when state courts took over many of the cases that had misguidedly been assigned to federal court. Under the circumstances, he was quick to point out, it would be the height of irresponsibility to add judges and court personnel that would cost the nation, by his accounting, $137,000.

But Jefferson had blundered. After studying the document, Uriah Tracy of Connecticut discovered that Jefferson's numbers had grossly underreported the actual number of past and present cases in federal court. Jefferson had omitted the records for Maryland entirely. "This omission is unaccountable," Tracy helpfully pointed out a few days later, "since the means of knowledge were near at hand." Jefferson had also neglected to include pending cases in Tennessee, North Carolina, and his own state of Virginia. Records for New York and Massachusetts had been reported incorrectly as well. "I am not disposed to attribute intentional error to any man, much less to the Executive," Tracy was quick to add, "but in point of use the statement amounts to nothing."[16]

Once Tracy had called Jefferson on the errors, all of which involved underreporting, the door was shut on redundancy and Congress could focus solely on the constitutional issue. "But there is another objection to the repeal of the judiciary law," he added, "which in my mind is conclusive: I mean the letter and spirit of the Constitution."[17] He read Article III to his colleagues and then asked, "Are there any words in the English language more explicit? Is there any condition annexed to the judge's tenure of office other than good behaviour?"[18]

Tracy's salvo took Republicans by surprise—in the glow of victory, they had not expected such intense Federalist opposition. Even worse, Republicans seemed to realize only then that, while they held a clear majority in the Senate, it was a small one—four senators—and, with attendance always an issue and defections a possibility, repeal was far from a sure thing. Looking around the chamber at that moment, Republicans could count only thirty of the thirty-two elected representatives, and both of the absentees were from their party.

Their predicament was made more tenuous by the fragility of their arguments. With Jefferson's statistical abstract discredited and loath to admit simple power politics as their motive, Republicans were forced into some rather far-fetched justifications for their position. (One Republican congressman eventually suggested that without the power to abolish judgeships, every outgoing president would create a new layer of judges until the federal government had been overrun with jurists.[19]) The biggest problem for Republicans, however, was not shabby statistics, an unforgiving Constitution, or tortured logic—it was the president of the Senate, Vice President Aaron Burr.

Burr had not simply faded into the night after Jefferson was finally declared the victor. Having been brought so close to ultimate power by Federalist wooing, Burr had apparently decided that they might actually be serious in their courtship. Rumors had begun to circulate that he had met with members of the rival party to build a power base from which to unseat Jefferson in the next election. Whether true or not, when Burr took his position in the Senate on Thursday, January 15, it was certainly not as a loyal second-in-command to his president.*

After only one day of presiding over the Senate, Burr slipped off for dinner with Gouverneur Morris and mentioned to the New Yorker that he was prepared to support the Federalist struggle against repeal if he could do so without seeming to break with his party.[20] Burr did not mention what form this support might take, although both he and Morris were obviously aware that the vice president was empowered to break tie votes.

A tie was certainly not impossible. By the time Burr took the chair, the debates had ratcheted up in intensity even more, since Federalists realized that they actually might win. During days of argument, Federalists and Republicans eschewed virtually all other business and devoted each session to long and often repetitive speeches either in favor of or against repeal. Each side spoke in defense of the Constitution and in the interests of the nation—terms such as "honor," "duty," and "responsibility" were evoked regularly and political motives confined to opponents.

Finally, on January 19, John Colhoun, a newly elected Republican from South Carolina, proposed that a committee be established to formulate amendments to the courts act that would "render the present motion for repeal unnecessary."[21] Although Colhoun was ruled out of order by Vice President Burr, Federalist senator Jonathan Dayton of New Jersey reintroduced a motion to "revise and amend" rather than "repeal" the Judiciary Act of February 13. Although the motion failed 15–13—Colhoun siding with the

---

* Although Jefferson could have little complaint on that score, having been something less than a loyal vice president himself.

Federalists—the close vote heartened the opposition.[22] One more defection would have created a tie. Nonetheless, three Republican senators were assigned to prepare a repeal bill. The bill was duly presented and received its second reading on January 26, after which Dayton moved that the bill be sent to a select committee to formulate rules for the circuit courts in case the February 13 law was repealed. This motion also failed by two votes, 16–14, with Colhoun switching back to the Republican side. Another motion was made to proceed to a third reading of the bill. This vote ended in a tie, 15–15, Colhoun jumping to the Federalist side once more.[23]

Burr's vote was then required. If he sided with the Federalists, the repeal measure might be killed entirely, thus earning him the gratitude of the opposition but also everlasting enmity among Republicans. Burr was not prepared for that degree of bridge-burning, so he broke the tie in favor of the Republicans.

The next morning, Dayton opened the proceedings in a strangely upbeat manner. Although he "had been defeated in two attempts to arrest the progress, or turn the course of the business, he was not, however, so far discouraged as to be making one other." The source of his encouragement, he noted, was because he had learned "that [his second motion] had not been perfectly heard and understood by one of the gentlemen who had voted against it."[24]

Dayton added that "it could not come to good if measures admitted by some to be bold and violent, and believed by many others to be unconstitutional, should be carried by a bare majority, and he trusted, therefore, that this proposition would now succeed." He once again moved that a select committee be appointed "to consider and report the alterations which may be proper in the Judiciary system of the United States."[25]

The wind-blown Colhoun, clearly the man to whom Dayton referred, followed the New Jersey senator by announcing that he would once again vote with Federalists in favor of commitment, producing another 15–15 tie, returning the fate of the repeal bill to Burr. Unlike his previous tie-breaking vote, which might have killed the bill outright, committing the bill to a select committee in a Senate in which Republicans held a majority was likely a mere postponement of the inevitable. Maintaining his balance, this time Burr voted in favor of the Federalists, after which he proclaimed that "he felt disposed to accommodate" the minority party so that the bill "might be rendered more acceptable to the Senate." Republicans need not fear his actions, Burr hastened to add, since he had no intention to encourage "any attempt, if any such be made, that might, in an indirect way, go to defeat the bill."[26] A committee of five was then selected to study the bill. It consisted of two Federalists—Morris and Dayton—and three Republicans. One of the Republicans, however, was Colhoun, leaving the product of the committee's deliberations very much in doubt.

Federalists left the session in high spirits, a minority party that had succeeded in frustrating the majority in perhaps its most prized initiative. But the Republicans were not without artillery of their own. Not once during the debates had the full complement of senators shown up. While Federalists had secured the periodic support of one Republican senator and the vice president, fifteen votes seemed to be the maximum number that they could muster. With full attendance, however, seventeen votes could be counted as firmly Republican, rendering both Colhoun and Burr moot.

Five days later, on February 2, 1802, Republicans succeeded in securing the attendance of one of the absentees, Stephen Bradley of Vermont, and Breckinridge introduced a motion that the committee of January 27 be discharged. Federalists, who had been so close, desperately tried to amend the bill and extend debate, but the fight was over. After furious invective on both sides and with Bradley providing the insurmountable sixteenth vote, the motion passed, 16–14.[27]

Despite an outcome that was no longer in doubt, the two sides debated well into the night. Vermont's Bradley, perhaps in a desire to make up for his earlier inattention, spoke for hours, reiterating arguments made before he arrived. The most telling exchange, however, did not begin until five o'clock in the candlelit chamber, when Breckinridge once more rose to speak. Referring to the power of the Supreme Court to annul acts of Congress, the specter of which had been raised earlier, Breckinridge thought the idea ludicrous. "I did not expect, sir, to find the doctrine of the power of the courts to annul the laws of Congress unconstitutional, so seriously insisted on." Breckinridge continued: "It is said that the different departments of Government are to be checks of each other, and that the Courts are to check the Legislature. If this be true, I would ask where they got that power, and who checks the courts when they violate the Constitution? Would they not, by this doctrine, have the absolute direction of the Government? To whom are they responsible? But I deny the power which is so pretended. If it is derived from the Constitution, I ask the gentlemen to point out the cause

that grants it . . . Is it not extraordinary, that if this high power was intended, it should nowhere appear? Is it not truly astonishing that the Constitution, in its abundant care to define the powers of each department,
should have omitted so important a power as that of the courts to nullify
all acts of Congress, which in their opinion were contrary to the Constitution?"[28] Breckinridge added, "To make the Constitution a practical system,
this pretended power of the courts to annul the laws of Congress cannot
possibly exist."[29]

It fell to Gouverneur Morris to respond. "[Breckinridge] asks," Morris began, "where the judges got their pretended power of deciding the constitutionality of laws? If it be in the Constitution (says he) let it be pointed out.
I answer, they derived that power from authority higher than this Constitution. They derive it from the constitution of man, from the nature of
things, from the necessary progress of human affairs."[30]

Morris spoke for well over an hour, but never provided any other justification for judicial review than vague references to what was implied in the
Constitution rather than what was stated, the very essence of broad construction and diametric opposite of textualism. Even more telling, a man
who had been present at the constitutional debates could not refer to a single delegate or exchange in those debates in which judicial review had been
propounded as an understood power of the court system.[31]

Finally, at about 8 P.M. on the evening of February 3, 1802, the Senate,
by a vote of 16–15, voted to repeal the Judiciary Act of 1801.

The bill went on to the House, where it was debated for another four
weeks. Federalist opposition was led by the ubiquitous James A. Bayard,
but the Republican majority in the lower chamber was sizable and the issue was never in doubt. The House passed the bill on March 3, 59–32, and
when Jefferson signed it five days later, the Judiciary Act of 1801 was officially repealed. With his signature, Jefferson had put sixteen United
States circuit court judges and a host of other recent appointees out of
work.[32]

Beyond the practical impact, by agreeing to the repeal, Jefferson had also
announced that, in his view, the Congress and the executive were legally empowered to interpret the Constitution, to "say what the law is."[33] While the
repeal did not eliminate the judiciary from constitutional interpretation—
neither Jefferson nor his party would have thought that proper—Republicans
had postulated that nothing in the Constitution gave the judiciary an

exclusive right of interpretation. If, after the imminent court challenge to the repeal by Federalists—and Hamilton had demanded that just such a challenge be launched "as soon as possible"—the Supreme Court attempted to invalidate the repeal, a constitutional crisis was inevitable.[34]

In order to prevent chaos, the repeal was not to take effect until July 1. On that date, all cases before circuit courts or district courts as defined in the Judiciary Act of 1801 were to be returned to whatever court in which they would have resided had the courts bill not passed. All writs pending before the new courts would be returned to the old courts as well. With all the upheaval, however, the show-cause order to Madison in the matter of *Marbury et al.* seemed at first to be unaffected, since the two-week June term of the Supreme Court would be completed before the repeal took effect.[*]

Republicans, however, had no intention of simply rolling back the clock. To complete the job of shaping the judiciary—and to thwart any constitutional challenge to the repeal act—the Republican Congress immediately set to work on their own "Bill for the More Convenient Organization of the Courts." Whether they chose the exact same name for their bill as the one for the legislation they had just repealed is not known; but after the third reading on April 8, the name was changed to "A Bill to Amend the Judicial System of the United States."[35] With the new name, the bill passed the same day, 16–10, Senator Colhoun absent and not voting.[36]

The bill was an amalgam of power play and reform, with Marshall's Supreme Court faring badly on both counts. Supreme Court justices would again ride circuit—that had been ensured by the repeal—with circuit courts sitting twice yearly. Court sessions were reduced from two two-week sessions to one four-week session, to be held each February, a month that had conveniently just passed. Both the June and August 1802 terms would thus be eliminated, creating a hiatus of fourteen months between the previous Court session and the first meeting in the future. Elimination of the two terms also meant that Madison would not be required to answer the show-cause order—or choose to ignore it—for another ten months.

---

[*] If the Court returned to the old rules after July 1, there would technically have been an August term as well.

But for the judiciary as a whole, some substantial improvements had been made as well. Republicans retained the Federalists' six-circuit plan—up from three—and a justice assigned to a circuit had to reside within it. (Marshall was assigned the Virginia–North Carolina circuit, within which his home in Richmond was roughly in the center.) Kentucky, Tennessee, and Maine were not included in the circuit court plan, thus eliminating trips to the wilderness.[37] The three-judge District of Columbia circuit court, unaffected by the repeal, was left intact but downgraded to a district court. In their zeal to limit judicial power, Republicans had made no provision in the bill to extend the circuit court system westward as the nation expanded. Circuit-riding to the Mississippi was not an issue that Republicans were anxious to raise, an omission that the Louisiana Purchase would soon bring into stark relief.

The bill moved to the House in the second week of April. Led by Bayard, Federalists stalled, proposed amendments, debated minutiae, but mostly railed against the injustice perpetrated by a Republican majority that cared nothing for a nation's liberty, but were simply interested in grasping power. The arguments were, not coincidentally, exactly those made by Republicans in the previous Congress during the debates on the Judiciary Act so recently repealed.

Nonetheless, Federalists made some telling points. On April 23, after the third reading of the bill, Bayard inveighed against the measure with a mixture of logic, sarcasm, and indignation.[38] He attacked everything from the true aim of the bill to its new name. "This act is not designed to amend the Judicial system," he exclaimed. "That is but pretense. If amendment had been in view, gentlemen would have contrived a better plan than the present bill proposes, which I panegyrize, by calling a miserable piece of patchwork. No sir; the design of this bill is to prevent the usual session of the Supreme Court in next June. It is to prevent that court from expressing their opinion upon the validity of the act lately passed, which abolished the offices of the judges of the circuit courts, until the act has gone into full execution. . . . May it not lead to the abolition of a court, the existence of which is required by Constitution?"[39]

As Federalists had had no answer—nor needed one—to justify the midnight appointments, Republicans had no answer—nor needed one—for Bayard's accusations. That Congress had just put the Supreme Court on hold for fourteen months to save the justices the rigors of travel when it had also just reinstituted the more extreme rigors of circuit-riding was quite beside the point. In the end, Republicans did just what Federalists had done—they simply passed their bill and sent it on to the president. Jefferson signed the measure on April 29, and the "Bill to Amend the Judicial System" became law, known popularly as the Judiciary Act of 1802.

Marshall, who had been in Richmond during the congressional debates, was immediately pressed to both give his opinion as to the constitutionality of the Congress's actions and to reveal whether or not he would accede to the new law. He did not equivocate on the circuit-riding provision, condemning the rule that would once again put the justices in the position of hearing cases on the Supreme Court that they had already decided on circuit.[40] Nor did he make a secret of his distaste for the reduction in prestige that accompanied the traveling judicial show. On the constitutional issue, however, he was far less easy to pin down. While privately Marshall expressed doubts as to the constitutionality of repeal, he mentioned to Bayard during a trip to Alexandria in April that he thought the question probably fell within Congress's purview. Marshall told Bayard—whose father-in-law, Richard Bassett, was one of the midnight judges—that anyone appointed under the 1801 act was now without power and should step aside from any case before them not yet resolved.[41] In defending repeal, it should be noted, Marshall was also asserting the right of Congress to interpret the Constitution—to say what the law is— a right that could not, it seemed, be superseded by the Supreme Court.[42] When Bayard related Marshall's comments to Gouverneur Morris, Morris was disgusted, but thought Marshall's equivocating to be quite in character.[43]

Marshall would not, however, be required to take a more defined position any time in the near future, as there was to be no Court term for another nine months. In rendering moot, at least for the moment, the question of the constitutionality of repeal, Republicans had bought time for Marshall as well as for themselves. The first practical test of the new laws would come in early autumn, not in the courtroom but on the roads, as that was when the justices were due to ride circuit. If they refused, they were, in effect, passing on the constitutionality of the repeal act by fiat, without hearing a case. Marshall polled his associates by letter, asking whether or not they wished to show up.[44]

Predictably, Chase was the most outspoken among the associates in his denunciations of the repeal law—denunciations that he had issued publicly—and he wrote back that on no account should any justice agree to ride circuit. Whether or not Chase wished to precipitate a challenge to the Constitution, he saw such a crisis as inevitable. "I believe a day of severe trial is fast approaching," he wrote, "and we, I fear, must be principal actors, and may be sufferers, therein."[45] The other four associates were prepared to swallow their objections and follow the new law if Marshall agreed to do so.

Chase wanted to fight, but Marshall wanted to win.[46] If he eschewed retreat and refused to ride circuit—chose this moment for his counterattack—Republicans would almost certainly move to impeach the entire Court. Marshall's own position, along with that of the fulminating Chase, was the most precarious. Jefferson's mantle of conciliation had eroded substantially with the passage of the two judiciary acts, and he had of late made little secret of his desire to eventually get Marshall off the Court in favor of his friend and colleague, Spencer Roane.[47] If, on the other hand, Marshall and his fellow justices continued to give ground and agreed to ride circuit, while it might signal temporary acquiescence to Republican authority—again—the Court might preserve the right to rule on constitutionality later. Marshall instructed the associates to resume circuit-riding.

In Marshall's subsequent apotheosis, the calm with which he greeted both the repeal and reorganization acts, his comments later that the bill was an improvement on the previous system, the willingness with which he accepted the return to circuit-riding, are said to prove that he was fair-minded and simply interested in "keeping the Court free of partisan politics."[48] But what choice did he have? Jefferson was spoiling for a chance to rid the courts of as many Federalist judges as he could, and Marshall, whether for personal or ideological reasons, wanted more than anything to keep his job. As the chief justice had demonstrated in *Talbot* and *Schooner Peggy*, and was to prove even more profoundly in events to come, he was a master of going limp. That he would say nothing about a situation in which he could do nothing was the very essence of the man.

Many Federalists, particularly in the Hamiltonian wing of the party, were furious with Marshall for what they saw as a cowardly capitulation. They wanted protest, confrontation, and exposure. If Marshall was not their ally, they reasoned, he must be their adversary. If Marshall would not confront Jefferson on his own, he would be compelled to do so. High Federalists launched a campaign to provoke a constitutional crisis that would inevitably place the chief justice and the Supreme Court in the path of the Republican locomotive and render Justice Chase's warning prophetic.

TWENTY

SUICIDE SQUEEZE: HAMILTON V. MARSHALL

IF MARSHALL HAS TENDED to be lauded for his acquiescence to the new Republican majority, just the opposite has been true of Hamilton and the extreme wing of the tattered Federalist Party. The Hamiltonians, it has been said, frustrated and bitter at being turned out of power, simply flailed about blindly, not so much to gain a tangible victory as simply for spite.[1] That view, however, grossly underestimates the political acumen of men such as Gouverneur Morris, James Bayard, and even Alexander Hamilton himself.[2]

Certainly, Federalists were playing a desperately weak hand, made all the weaker since everyone's cards had already been turned up. Their only choice in such a circumstance was to find some way to have the game called off, and the best way to achieve that was to prove that the winners had cheated. No Federalist could be unaware that, as reluctant to do so as it now appeared, only the judiciary held any possibility of initiating such an action.

But the Marshall Court had proved itself to be less than even a reluctant ally. Despite anything the president might have said, Hamiltonians did not see their party as having strategically fallen back behind the barricade of the judiciary. That had been the plan, certainly, but Federalists had been frustrated by what they deemed a cowardly, equivocating Marshall, who was clearly more interested in retaining his job than upholding the principles under which he had gotten that job in the first place. Compelling the chief justice to take the honorable course, therefore, was going to take a combination of extremely clever politics and a sustained public outcry.

High Federalists decided on a plan that consisted of three interlocking strategies, designed to ultimately isolate the renegade Court and force it to publicly confront the very constitutional issues that Marshall had to this point been so deft in evading. Since the Supreme Court would not sit until February 1803, the battle was begun in circuit court in the fall of 1802.

On September 18, 1802, when Bushrod Washington convened the second circuit court in Hartford, Connecticut, Roger Griswold, a local Federalist congressman who had achieved substantial notoriety for trying to bash a fellow legislator's head in with a hickory stick on the floor of the House of Representatives, issued a challenge to the court's authority to rule on the cases on the docket, since the presence of Supreme Court justices in circuit court violated the Constitution.[3] If Washington ruled for Griswold, he would thus declare the repeal of the Judiciary Act of 1801 unconstitutional.

This same action was initiated in four of the six circuits, Federalists demanding that the Supreme Court justices sitting in those courts declare their own participation void. Regardless of the degree to which the justices loathed circuit-riding, the petitioners could not have expected to prevail in any of these actions—in agreeing to once again ride circuit, the justices had already announced their position.

In Connecticut, Justice Washington dismissed Griswold's motion out of hand. Federalists had the same result in Boston, although they did succeed in persuading Justice Cushing to adjourn for a day. The third test was launched in New Jersey, where Justice Paterson ruled as had his two brethren.

The fourth test case, while sure to receive the same summary treatment in circuit court as the other three, engaged the chief justice himself. Whether or not the parties were aware of it at the time—and there is some indication that they were—this petition placed Marshall in the very political vise the Federalists had sought, and resulted in one of the most crucial Supreme Court decisions—or, more precisely, non-decisions—in the nation's history.

The matter itself was innocuous. In late 1800, John Laird of Maryland had filed suit in circuit court against Virginians Hugh Stuart and Charles Carter for breach of contract in a land dispute.[4] At that point, Supreme Court justices still rode circuit, as specified in the Judiciary Act of 1789. Before the case could be heard, however, the Judiciary Act of 1801 was passed, establishing the new fourth circuit court, consisting of three of Adams's midnight judges. That court had found for Laird and awarded damages in the form of property to be sold, with the proceeds going to Laird. The judges also required Stuart and Carter to post a bond guaranteeing delivery of the property.

In July 1802, before the property could actually be sold and the judgment discharged, the repeal act had been passed and the fourth circuit court as established under the Judiciary Act abolished, so oversight of the case was transferred to the new fifth circuit court, Chief Justice Marshall presiding. That was when Charles Lee—the same Charles Lee who was representing *Marbury et al.*—stepped in, representing Stuart. Lee instructed his client to default on delivery of the property, sending Laird back to circuit court to recover the bond.

In December 1802, one year after he had thrown *Marbury* into Marshall's lap, Lee appeared in front of the chief justice in Richmond. By this time, the midterm congressional elections had been completed. Where the Seventh Congress had been solidly Republican, the Eighth Congress was overwhelmingly so. Jefferson's party enjoyed a 63-vote majority in the House and controlled well over two thirds of the Senate. If confrontation was foolhardy before, it might well be suicidal now.

With even less to lose, Lee stood before the chief justice and claimed that the new, Marshall-led circuit court had no right to hear the case, since only the judges who had originally instituted the judgment could order the release of the bond. These judges, Lee asserted, retained their authority since their removal had violated the Constitution, and, since it also violated the Constitution to require Supreme Court justices to ride circuit, Marshall therefore had no power to rule in their place.

This last point was particularly sore, since Marshall had made no secret that he also thought the circuit-riding provision was unconstitutional, a position of which Lee was doubtlessly aware when he raised the question in court. Still, after months of maneuvering to avoid a direct confrontation with Jefferson, Lee certainly also knew that Marshall had no intention of precipitating a battle from circuit court, a disinclination by now buttressed by the three associates who had also declined to rule against repeal. So, surprising no one, least of all Lee, Marshall avoided the constitutional question, dismissed Lee's assertion, found for Laird, and

ordered the bond vacated.* Lee then announced his intention to appeal
the ruling before the Supreme Court at the next term, February 1803, the
same term in which the Marbury mandamus hearing was scheduled.

Before the Supreme Court term could begin, however, Federalists unveiled
the second prong of their attack. On Thursday, January 27, 1803, eleven of
the deposed circuit court judges—including Bassett, whose protest had received wide circulation in the Federalist press—petitioned the House of
Representatives for a return to duty and back pay. They argued that, as a result of the repeal of the Judiciary Act of 1801, the "rights secured to them
by the Constitution as members of the Judicial department have been im-
paired," and that, "influenced by a sense of public duty," they needed to ask
Congress to review their actions.[5] To justify the petition, the eleven judges
resurrected the same arguments that had been rejected—or, more accurately, ignored—the previous spring.

Griswold, who had returned to Washington after his failure with Bushrod
Washington in Hartford, immediately moved that the petition be sent to a
select committee, and the Republican Andrew Gregg of Pennsylvania just as
quickly proposed sending it to the Republican-dominated Court of Claims
instead. Neither prevailed. Most Republicans wanted the petition summarily
disposed of and voted to debate it on the floor that very day. The House put
aside its other business and once more weighed in on the judiciary.

During the course of the debate, each side evoked the Constitution and
asserted its applicability to its position. Griswold properly pointed out that
in repealing the 1801 law, Republicans "had decided that the Legislature
had the constitutional right to deprive then judges of all judicial power," in
other words, to decide what Article III meant.[6] Republicans at first tried to
dance around the constitutional question, but when John Smilie, a Republican from Pennsylvania, ingenuously asked "whether in a case such as this
the Supreme Court could be denominated as an impartial tribunal," his fellow Republicans were forced to take a specific position on constitutionality.
This they did once again by asserting the Blackstonian argument that the
legislature was the proper venue to decide constitutionality. Wilson Cary

---

* Whether Lee's client, Stuart, realized that his financial interests were to be sacrificed for the cause
is unknown.

Nicholas of Virginia stated: "The people constituted the great tribunal before whom the constitutionality of all laws of Congress should be brought."[7] The debate raged on the entire day, characterized by the same partisan sniping and invective of the previous spring, and the outcome was no more in doubt in this session than in the former. Nicholas's fellow Republican congressmen agreed that they had the right to interpret Article III, and the petition of the eleven judges was soundly rejected.

The following day, Friday, January 28, before the Senate had a chance to debate the petition, the Federalists initiated their third phase. John Howard of Maryland introduced a petition from William Marbury and two of his co-claimants "praying that the Secretary of the Senate may be directed to deliver them a certified copy of their nominations to be justices of the peace for the counties of Washington and Alexandria."[8] In theory, the petition was simply an attempt to gain documentary evidence of the appointments to be used in judicial proceedings, which Marbury and the other two noted "your Secretary has declined giving without leave of the Senate." In fact, of course, the issue was far more inflammatory, another thinly veiled attempt by Charles Lee to induce the Senate to assert prerogative over the executive. Moreover, the records that the petitioners sought were contained in the *Senate Executive Journal*, whose contents were confidential except to the senators themselves.

The Senate let the motion lie over the weekend and took it up Monday morning. Howard opened the debate by asserting that "the request was so reasonable, that he concluded it should pass without objection," to which James Jackson of Georgia replied that "an attempt was made at the last session to effect the same thing . . . then by counsel . . . now from the men themselves." Whatever the source, Jackson continued, it was "an attack on the Executive department . . . and as such [he] would oppose it . . . in whatever shape it might present itself."[9] The debate over Marbury's petition played out according to what was now a familiar script and after a full day of pro forma partisan rhetoric, Marbury's petition was denied by 15–13 in a strict party vote.[10] Three days later, on February 3, the Senate took up the judges' petition and again spent a day in venomous debate before rejecting it by the same 15–13 vote.[11]

Noteworthy, however, in the debates on the Marbury petition was the focus, which was almost exclusively, as Senator Jackson had noted, on the implied rather than strictly defined right of the executive branch to conduct business free from interference from either Congress or the courts. That the entire question should have been moot—after all, Marbury and his fellows hardly needed to prove to the Supreme Court that the commissions had been granted when the man who had signed them was by then the sitting chief justice—did not prevent the senators from staking out the political rather than the legal boundaries of the case.

Because of what had transpired on the floor of Congress, therefore, although Lee and his fellow Federalists had abjectly failed to receive any relief there or in circuit court, they had succeeded in sharpening the focus of the debate and leaving no doubt in the nation at large that the two key cases on the docket for the first Supreme Court term in more than a year—*Marbury v. Madison* and *Stuart v. Laird*—were every bit as much a political test of the Court's role as a legal one.

A political confrontation was precisely what Marshall had been trying to avoid. Nor did he have much time in the wake of Congress's actions to prepare for the showdown. Court was scheduled to convene only three days after the Senate turned down the judges. If Charles Lee's intent was to squeeze his old friend Marshall, he could not have done a much better job.

Remarkable and not a little ironic is that some of the most crucial events in the nation's history have so little source documentation attached to them. The Philadelphia Convention of 1787, in which the Constitution was drafted, was held in secret and, if not for James Madison and, in the first weeks, Robert Yates, Americans would have virtually no idea what transpired behind those closed doors. Records of the proceedings of *Marbury v. Madison* are almost as scant. The official record, the notes of midnight judge William Cranch, seems to be little more than a verbatim rendering of reports in the *National Intelligencer*, a Republican newspaper published in Washington City. A more complete account, particularly of proceedings of the trial itself, appeared in another Republican newspaper, Philadelphia's *Aurora*, on February 15, 1803. Despite the partisanship of each of these periodicals, their records of the trial and Marshall's subsequent decision have been accepted by historians as being accurate.[12]

Lack of primary records, however, in no way implied lack of interest. When the Court convened the following Monday, February 7, the tiny committee room in the Capitol was packed, although conspicuous by his absence was the defendant. James Madison, secretary of state, ignored the proceedings entirely, refusing to acknowledge that the toothless Court was

AURORA

IVROG BY PROBEN.

PHILADELPHIA:

TUESDAY, FEBRUARY 15, 1803.

FROM WASHINGTON,

FEB, 9 1803.

" The supreme court had this day before them the subject of the *mandamus*, in the case of the commissions which were alledged to be signed by John Adams for Marbury and others as justices of the peace for this district. The witnesses examined were *Jacob Wagner*, chief clerk, and *Daniel Brent*, another clerk in the secretary of states office, and Levi Lincoln the present attorney general. The apparent object of the examination was to ascertain the actual existence of such commissions, and the course through which they proceeded and what had become of them. Mr. Wagner's evidence went to shew that a number of commissions for justices of the peace had been filled up in the usual form in the office of state. He had *heard* that the commissions of Messrs *Marbury & Hooe* had been filled and signed by the president (*Adams*) but had understood that the commission of Mr. Ramsay had by some accident not been signed. Being asked from whom he had heard such information, he declined answering and the court acquiesced. He had no particular knowlege of any particular commission, nor had he referred to the books in which commissions are registered for more than a year past.—Mr. Brent's evidence amounted to this in substance. That the various commissions made out for justices of the peace *in the*

Front page of the *Philadelphia Aurora* recounting the trial of *Marbury v. Madison* even worth a perfunctory appearance. In fact, the "trial" was actually an inquest, since "Madison" was not represented at all. The secretary of state had not bothered to retain a personal attorney, and although Attorney General Lincoln was in attendance, he was quite pointedly there as a private citizen and not an advocate.[13] Also absent were two of the justices: Cushing was ill, and Paterson missed the first day of testimony.[14]

Marshall, whose shambling, rumpled mien of private life was replaced with imperial solemnity on the bench, did not lack for a sense of the dramatic. Although *Marbury* and *Stuart* were the reason that local lawyers, newspapermen, and members of the public had squeezed in, Marshall insisted on following protocol and proceeding in the order that cases had been placed on the docket. *Marbury* was to be heard before *Stuart*, but even so, spectators had to sit through a drone of unimportant motions and legal housecleaning since the *mandamus* case did not come up until two days later.*

On Wednesday, February 9, 1803, the drama that had been building for almost two years finally reached center stage. With it, one of the most surreal episodes in American legal history began. For Lee, the first requirement was to establish that his clients had actually been appointed to their posts and that their commissions had dutifully been signed and sealed. The task should have been quite simple: call as a witness a man present at the signing, who had himself applied the seal of office. Even better, that man—who had made no secret of his role in the affair, nor his negligence in creating the problem in the first place—was already in the courtroom.

Lee at that point could have requested that Chief Justice Marshall recuse himself from hearing the case and, once Marshall had acknowledged the blatant conflict of interest and done so, he could then be called as a witness to recount the facts. This, however, Lee was loath to do. The very point of the exercise was to squeeze Marshall into either ruling against Jefferson and demonstrating the Federalists would not just roll over and play dead, or ruling for Jefferson and demonstrating his own moral cowardice. That Marshall would ultimately rule both for and against Jefferson had not crossed anyone's mind, nor had the even more remote possibility that he would do so by evoking a great constitutional principle.

---

* The Supreme Court handled nineteen cases from February 7 to March 3, 1803, its mandated four-week term, but only *Marbury* and *Stuart* involved constitutional questions.

So Lee continued the charade and puttered along as if the man behind the bench was not related to the man who had been party to the affair. Not only did Lee refuse to ask Marshall to step down, he did not seem to ever have made reference at all to the actual process of preparing the commissions for delivery.[15] Instead, he referred to ratification in the Senate—an event for which he had no proof since the Republicans were now trying to thwart the law by refusing to turn over the appropriate records—and then to existence of the signed and sealed commissions at the Department of State—an event for which he had no proof since the two clerks present at the time had, at the insistence of the Republican attorney general, refused to discuss the matter.* It was as if Adams's secretary of state had not existed.

Lee's wraithlike view of the office did not extend to *Jefferson's* secretary of state, however. Lee made a point of emphasizing that *Jefferson's* secretary of state had refused to respond to an inquiry as to whether the commissions had, in fact, been signed and sealed. Lee did not bother to mention that, unlike Marshall, Madison had not even been in Washington when these events transpired and was not to return for another two months, when, in all likelihood, the commissions themselves had already been destroyed.

In his opening remarks, Lee laid out the question before the Court. "It was important to know on what ground a justice of the peace in the District of Columbia holds his office and what procedures are necessary to constitute an appointment to an office not held at the will of the President."

Lee then called as witnesses the chief clerk at the State Department, Jacob Wagner, and his assistant, Daniel Brent. Both were Federalists but neither politically active, and they had been held over by the new administration. Each had refused to provide an affidavit, and they now declined to answer Lee's questions on the grounds that they could not discuss the goings-on of an executive department.

Lee countered, speaking for the remainder of the day, spending hours expounding on the dual nature of the office of secretary of state "as a public ministerial officer of the United States and as agent of the president." In the latter capacity, no cabinet officer could be required to divulge private intercourse with another member of the executive branch, while in the former capacity he would owe allegiance to the people. This argument cut not only

---

* "Reasonable information has been denied at the office of the department of state," was how Lee phrased it.

to the question of whether or not Madison should be required to produce records to demonstrate whether or not Marbury had ever been appointed, but also to the question of his right to withhold any ratified commission, even at the president's specific instruction. Although this narrow definition of executive privilege was Lee's, with no one providing a countervailing view, Federalists might reasonably assume that it would be accepted by the Court.

"The President is no party to this case," Lee asserted. "The secretary is called upon to perform a duty over which the President has no control, and in regard to which he has no dispensing power, and for the neglect of which he is in no manner responsible." Thus, Lee continued, "the Secretary of State, therefore, being in the same situation, as to these duties, as every other ministerial officer of the United States, and equally liable to be compelled to perform them, is also bound by the same rules of evidence. These duties are not of a confidential nature, but are of a public kind, and his clerks can have no executive privileges."

To those in the courtroom, whether or not Marshall would side with his old friend and fellow Federalist and compel the two clerks to testify seemed to be a barometer for the rest of the case. Marshall considered the matter after Lee had taken his seat and then announced that Wagner and Brent must indeed testify, but that they might object to any particular question that they thought violated their responsibility to their office. In that case, the chief justice himself would decide whether or not the question was pertinent. With that, court was adjourned for the day.

Unlike Madison, two clerks were not about to openly flaunt the Supreme Court, and they took the witness stand the next morning.* Wagner's recollections were hazy. He testified that he had heard about the commissions but could not recall whether or not he had seen them. He did recall that Marbury and Dennis Ramsay had succeeded in meeting with Madison, but that the secretary had referred them to him. Wagner had told the two claimants he had heard that some of the commissions had been signed and some had not, and some had been recorded but some had not, and that he could not remember which ones had received which treatment.

---

* The witness stand itself had been hastily thrown together since the Supreme Court chamber, such as it was, had not been set up for trials, but simply for appeals where both sides argued from their respective tables.

Brent was slightly more forthcoming, but the information he provided seemed divergent from what was previously known of the affair and he sometimes contradicted himself. He testified "that he did not remember certainly the names of any of the persons in the commissions of justices of the peace signed by Mr. Adams," but then added, "he believed and was almost certain, that Mr. Marbury's and Col. Hooe's commissions were made out, and that Mr. Ramsay's was not; that he made out the list of names by which the clerk who filled up the commissions was guided."

Brent also testified that "After the commissions for justices of the peace were made out, he carried them to Mr. Adams for his signature. After being signed, he carried them back to the secretary's office, where the seal of the United States was affixed to them." This statement would indicate that Marshall and Adams were not together on the night of March 3, 1801, although Marshall had previously given the impression that he had been at the President's House for at least part of that evening. Whatever was the accurate version of that night's events, the chief justice at no point corrected Brent. Brent then added: "He believed none of those commissions of justices were ever sent out, or delivered to the persons for whom they were intended," a statement obviously inaccurate since James Marshall, the chief justice's brother, had spent much of the early part of March 4 frantically seeking out appointees to whom he could deliver the commissions.

Of greater significance, however, was that neither of the clerks knew what had become of the commissions after Jefferson was sworn in.

Lee next called Attorney General Lincoln, who had been the acting secretary of state as the Adams presidency expired. Lincoln, from the gallery, also expressed a disinclination to testify. He could, he said, not reveal any of his dealings with President Jefferson while acting secretary of state, but, as sitting attorney general, if the chief justice deemed his testimony required, agreed to evaluate any questions Lee wished to put to him if Lee would submit them in writing.

Marshall agreed to the ground rules and instructed Lee that he could submit four questions in writing to Lincoln, and "if Mr. Lincoln wished time to consider what answers he should make, they would give him time, but [the justices] had no doubt he ought to answer." Lincoln agreed, with the caveat that "he did not think himself bound to disclose his official transactions while acting as Secretary of State." He then added: "If, in the course of his official duty, these commissions should have come into his hands, and that he might either by error or intention have done wrong, it would not be expected that he should give evidence to incriminate himself." After the attorney general's remarkable admission, Marshall agreed to both conditions, but noted "that the fact whether such commissions had been in the office or not, could not be a confidential fact; it is a fact which all the world have a right to know."

Lee presented his questions to the court. They were then passed to Lincoln, who examined them and informed Marshall that he would have his responses the following morning. Of the four, the most pertinent was the last, an inquiry as to what had become of the commissions, the key to the plaintiffs' case.[16]

Lincoln returned to the witness stand the following morning. In response to Lee's first three questions, Lincoln testified that he had indeed seen a stack of commissions for justice of the peace that had been signed by Adams and affixed with the great seal, although he could not be sure that those for any of the three plaintiffs were among them. He was vague about what had happened next, but did not believe that any of the commissions that he had come across were sent to specific appointees.

The only question Lincoln refused to answer in full was the fourth. He claimed that "he had no hesitation in saying that he did not know that they ever came to the possession of Mr. Madison, nor did he know that they were in the office when Mr. Madison took possession of it. He prayed the opinion of the court whether he was obliged to disclose what had been done with the commissions."

Marshall was once again faced with the choice of how hard to press. Lincoln's response was, at best, evasive. After indicating in his final comment that he did, in fact, know what had become of the commissions, he had not elaborated on whether he was declining to answer further because the question related to his official duties or that a reply would be self-incriminating.

The chief justice chose not to pursue the matter. "The court were of opinion that [Lincoln] was not bound to say what had become of [the commissions]; if they never came to the possession of Mr. Madison, it is immaterial to the present cause what had been done with them by others."

Lee's final piece of evidence was an affidavit by James Marshall. The younger Marshall affirmed that "on the 4th of March, 1801, having been informed by some person from Alexandria that there was reason to apprehend riotous proceedings in that town on that night, he was induced to return immediately home, and to call at the office of the Secretary of State, for the commissions of the justices of the peace; that as many as 12, he believed, commissions of justices for that county were delivered to him, for which he gave a receipt, which he left in the office. That finding he could not conveniently carry the whole, he returned several of them, and struck a pen through the names of those, in the receipt, which he returned. Among the commissions he returned, according to the best of his knowledge and belief was one for Col. Hooe, and one for William Harper."

With that, Lee claimed that he had proved the existence of the commissions and he moved on to his argument. The case, he asserted, hinged on three questions: "1st. Whether the Supreme Court can award the writ of mandamus in any case? 2d. Whether it will lie to a Secretary of State in any case whatever? 3d. Whether, in the present case, the court may award a mandamus to James Madison, Secretary of State?"

Lee then spoke "at some length," making the case for an affirmative response to all three questions, especially the third. In support of the first, he drew heavily from Blackstone and the *Federalist*, but particularly from the Judiciary Act of 1789, from which he quoted Article 13. He cited other instances in which the Court had been asked to issue a *mandamus*.[17] In support of the second, Lee once more made his distinction between the secretary of state as public minister and as executive surrogate. Lee admitted that a *mandamus* could not be issued to the latter but asserted, once again citing the Judiciary Act of 1789, that the prohibition did not apply to a public minister.

At that point, Justice Paterson, a coauthor of the Judiciary Act of 1789, interrupted to ask Lee "whether he understood it to be the duty of the secretary to deliver a commission, unless ordered to do so by the president?" The question may have been innocuous, but Lee's response was to form the backbone of Marshall's opinion.

"After the president has signed a commission for an office not held at his will," Lee replied, "and it comes to the Secretary to be sealed, the president has done with it, and nothing remains, but that the secretary perform those ministerial acts which the law imposes upon him. It immediately becomes his duty to seal, record, and deliver it on demand. In such a case the appointment becomes complete by the signing and sealing; and the secretary does wrong if he withholds the commission."

Lee then moved on to the final point, whether or not the court could issue a *mandamus* against Madison. Lee spoke for hours on this question. The crux of his argument was that the president lacks authority to interfere with the process after nomination and ratification.

"The justices of the peace in the District of Columbia are judicial officers . . . they hold their offices independent of the will of the president. The appointment of such an officer is complete when the president has nominated him to the senate, and the senate having advised and consented, and the president has signed the commission, and delivered it to the secretary to be sealed. The president has then done with it; it becomes irrevocable. An appointment of a judge once completed, is made forever. He holds under the constitution. The requisites to be performed by the secretary are ministerial, ascertained by law, and he has no discretion, but must perform them; there is no dispensing power."

Since the president had no authority to instruct Madison to interfere with the delivery process, it followed, the secretary of state could act in this matter only in his public ministerial capacity, which in turn meant that Madison could indeed be served with a *mandamus*.

In summation, Lee said that a *mandamus* "is said to be a writ of discretion. But the discretion of a court always means a sound, legal discretion, not an arbitrary will. If the applicant makes out a proper case, the courts are bound to grant it. They can refuse justice to no man."

Lee took his seat. During the entire trial phase, Marshall and the court had been scrambling mightily to maintain at least the air that this was a genuine legal proceeding, but Madison's insistence on treating both the show-cause order and the Court itself as if they did not exist had made things extremely uncomfortable for the chief justice. So sensitive was Marshall to the fact that the presence of only one side was making a sham of the trial, that even the *Aurora* thought to report it. A Marshall biographer, understating the issue, remarked that lack of a defendant "gave the proceedings an especially eerie quality."[18]

The absurdity reached its zenith after Lee had completed his remarks. Marshall urgently cast about for someone to present the opposing view. Lincoln, still insisting that he was not present in his official capacity, once more declined to reply. Marshall then offered the floor to *anyone* who wished to make arguments for the defense. No one stepped forward. Of course, Madison's continued absence spoke louder than his presence would have. If he was prepared to ignore the Supreme Court of the United States in trial, he was certainly equally prepared to ignore an adverse decision.

Thus, after the first week of the most important trial in his two-year tenure as chief justice, Marshall was facing disaster. He could have certainly entered a default judgment for the plaintiff; Madison seemed to be almost daring him to do so.[19] On the other side, Lee's assertion notwithstanding, the very evidence fundamental to the case was absent, which could have easily justified a dismissal in favor of the defendant.[20] A Supreme Court that only decided narrow issues of law would not be supreme at all, but that seemed to be the role that Republicans had destined the Marshall court to play. Worse for the six Federalist justices, there seemed to be no way to avoid that unthinkable eventuality.

Marshall, of course, never admitted to anyone whether the astounding manner in which he turned this seemingly inevitable cataclysm into victory had occurred to him in advance—he did, after all, have *Talbot* as a model—or whether he came up with it by necessity after the arguments—argument—had been completed.

Whichever was the case, one conclusion is undeniable: what John Marshall achieved with his decision in *Marbury v. Madison* altered the United States as a nation, profoundly and forever, and the impact of his decision in that case is felt by every American every day.

TWENTY-ONE

Saying What the Law Is

Marshall and the court took two weeks to render a decision. During that time, Chase became ill and Court sessions were moved from the committee room in the Capitol to Stelle's Hotel, across the street.[1] Thus, the most important decision in United States Supreme Court history, that which in large part determined the Court's role in national affairs, was delivered in a hotel parlor.

Marshall's opinion has been called many things, from brilliant to deceitful, concise to tedious—sometimes all in the same breath—but whatever else *Marbury* was, it was also perhaps the most adroit exhibition of judicial legerdemain by any judge in the nation's history. So off-the-point was the bulk of the opinion that more than one commentator has asserted that it was not an opinion at all, but rather *obiter dicta*.*

Nonetheless, a masterpiece of misdirection is still a masterpiece. And it was fortunate for his fellow justices that Marshall's exposition was of Solomonic proportions—at eleven thousand words, in size as well as intellect—because nothing less would have done if the Court was to maintain relevance while avoiding Republican retribution.

Marshall began, as he had in *Talbot*, with the case itself, although in his second paragraph he signaled that this would be no ordinary decision. There he wrote of "the peculiar delicacy of this case, the novelty of some of its circumstances, and the real difficulty attending the points which occur in it."[2]

---

* *Obiter dicta* are remarks by a judge that have only incidental bearing on the case in question and are therefore not binding as precedent.

The chief justice then borrowed Lee's format of three questions, although the questions themselves had been changed. Marshall posited, "1st. Has the applicant a right to the commission he demands? 2d. If he has a right, and that right has been violated, do the laws of his country afford him a remedy? 3d. If they do afford him a remedy, is it a mandamus issuing from this court?"

As to the first, Marshall cited the District of Columbia act of February 1801, and then asserted that "a commission for William Marbury, as a justice of the peace for the county of Washington, was signed by John Adams, then President of the United States; after which the seal of the United States was affixed to it; but the commission has never reached the person for whom it was made out." (Although this had hardly been proved during the trial, if Marshall admitted as such, no need for further exposition would be necessary.)

Citing Article II of the Constitution, Marshall then divided the appointment process into three operations: 1. "nomination, the sole act of the president, and completely voluntary"; 2. "appointment . . . also the act of the president, and also a voluntary act, though it can only be performed by and with the advice and consent of the senate"; and 3. "The commission. To grant a commission to a person appointed, might, perhaps, be deemed a duty enjoined by the constitution. 'He shall,' says that instrument, 'commission all the officers of the United States.'"

Marshall proceeded to parse the distinction between "appointment" and "commissioning an appointment." "These observations are premised solely for the purpose of rendering more intelligible those which apply more directly to the particular case under consideration," Marshall noted without irony. He added, as a demonstration of intelligibility, "the commission and the appointment seem inseparable, it being almost impossible to show an appointment otherwise than by proving the existence of a commission; still the commission is not necessarily the appointment, though conclusive evidence of it."[3]

On its face, the point of all this sophistry seemed merely to demonstrate that, once the president had signed an appointment, he was removed from the commission process, which was precisely what Lee had argued. It must have been perplexing for those in attendance that Marshall had chosen to be so dense and obscure about a point that could have been made with far less effort. But, for Marshall, the style of the opinion was to be every bit as important as its substance. Like a judicial whodunit, why this was so would not be revealed until the final scene.

After the signature had been rendered, Marshall went on, the president "has then acted on the advice and consent of the senate to his own nomination. The time for deliberation has then passed. He has decided. His judgment, on the advice and consent of the senate concurring with his nomination, has been made and the officer is appointed. This appointment is evidenced by an open, unequivocal act; and being the last act required from the person making it, necessarily excludes the idea of its being so far as respects the appointment, an inchoate and incomplete transaction." Significant by its absence was any discussion of whether or not a president was *compelled* to sign a commission that had been ratified by the Senate, a clear extension of the separation of powers that he had elucidated upon, but one that was nigh unto unenforceable in real-world politics.

As Marshall had defined the process, however, once signed and sealed, the appointment was made, as least as far as the president was concerned, even if the president happened to be Jefferson and the signer Adams. Further, "The signature is a warrant for affixing the great seal to the commission: and the great seal is only to be affixed to an instrument which is complete. It attests, by an act supposed to be of public notoriety, the verity of the presidential signature." Thus, only a signed commission could be sealed—the order could not be reversed.* Nor was this act discretionary. "The commission being signed, the subsequent duty of the secretary of state is prescribed by law, and not to be guided by the will of the president."

Once again, Marshall had limited the power of the president to intrude into the commission process once it had begun. The secretary of state, again as Lee had asserted, was thus acting not as an agent for the executive, but as a public minister, accountable not to his boss but rather to "the people." "It is the duty of the secretary of state to conform to the law, and in this he is an officer of the United States, bound to obey the laws," Marshall insisted. "He acts, in this respect, as has been very properly stated at the bar, under the authority of law, and not by the instructions of the president. It is a ministerial act which the law enjoins on a particular officer for a particular purpose."

---

* Another example of Marshall's excess. No Republican or Federalist had ever suggested that an unsigned commission could be embossed with the Great Seal.

In order to demonstrate impartiality, Marshall here interjected that he had sought "anxiously for the principles on which a contrary opinion may be supported," but had found none, a two-handed swipe at Madison and the absent defense. On the one hand, Madison's boycott had forced the chief justice to undertake—or at least attempt—an adversarial role himself, while on the other hand the absence of a defense had not really mattered because there was no alternative construction that would have held.

Finally, after a lengthy discourse on why a commission differed from a deed—where delivery was an integral part of the transfer process—Marshall was finally ready to make his point. "It is, therefore, decidedly the opinion of the court, that when a commission has been signed by the President the appointment is made; and that the commission is complete when the seal of the United States has been affixed to it by the Secretary of State . . . when the officer is not removable at the will of the executive, the appointment is not revocable, and cannot be annulled. It has conferred legal rights which cannot be resumed . . . Mr. Marbury, then, since his commission was signed by the President, and sealed by the Secretary of State, was appointed . . . To withhold his commission, therefore, is an act deemed by the court not warranted by law, but violative of a vested legal right."

So, after what seemed to be an exhaustive lecture on the meaning of law and the Constitution—the object of that lecture unnamed but no mystery—Marshall had answered the key question in the affirmative. Marbury must receive his commission.

Marshall was not finished, of course, moving immediately to the second question of whether the laws of the United States afforded Marbury any remedy. Unlike the first, there was almost no suspense involving this issue. After all, if a wrong had been done, there had to be a remedy in the law. It only remained for the Court to spell out what that remedy might be. Those in the audience at Stelle's must have been aghast—the constitutional crisis that many had anticipated and Federalists had desperately wanted seemed to be at hand.

Using the same elaboration as before, Marshall waxed philosophic for over an hour, often repeating the very same arguments he had just expounded in his previous remarks, all the while without ever saying anything more necessary than his first utterance on the question: "The very essence of civil liberty certainly consists in the right of every individual to claim the protection of the laws, whenever he receives an injury." So, not surprisingly,

he concluded "That, having this legal title to the office, he has a consequent right to the commission; a refusal to deliver which is a plain violation
of that right, for which the laws of his country afford him a remedy."

All that was left, it seemed, was to determine whether Marbury was "entitled to the remedy for which he applies." This question was, by all accounts, the easiest to answer. Marbury had applied for a *mandamus* from the
Supreme Court, according to the law of the land as set down in the Judiciary Act of 1789.

The chief justice divided this final question into two parts, "1st. The nature of the writ applied for; and, 2d. The power of this court." As to the first,
Marshall read into the record Blackstone's definition of a writ of *mandamus*,
cited more support from the English judicial system, and then plunged once
more into a repetition of the minutiae of his previous arguments, all to
demonstrate once more that since the secretary of state was acting in a ministerial capacity, he could be served with a *mandamus*. "This, then, is a plain
case for a mandamus either to deliver the commission, or a copy of it from
the record," Marshall concluded. "It only remains to be inquired," he went
on, "whether it can issue from this court."

Finally, after hours of prelude, Marshall had reached bone. "If this court is
not authorized to issue a writ of mandamus to [the secretary of state], it must
be because [the act to establish the judicial courts of the United States] is unconstitutional, and therefore absolutely incapable of conferring the authority,
and assigning the duties which its words purport to confer and assign."

The constitutionality of the Judiciary Act of 1789 had never been at issue, of course, unchallenged since its passage, with the judiciary—including
the Marshall court—functioning quite readily under its precepts for more
than a decade. One of its authors was sitting with the chief justice on the
panel; another had preceded him in the job. There must, therefore, have
been no shortage of head-scratching at Stelle's at the introduction of such a
lofty question in a show-cause hearing. Marshall went on to quote from Article III, particularly the section, "the Supreme Court shall have original jurisdiction in all cases affecting ambassadors, other public ministers and
consuls, and those in which a state shall be a party. In all other cases, the
Supreme Court shall have appellate jurisdiction."

In Aristotelian fashion, Marshall first stated the argument that he intended to refute. "It has been insisted, at the bar, that if the original grant of

jurisdiction, to the Supreme and inferior courts, is general, and the clause, assigning original jurisdiction to the Supreme Court, contains no negative or restrictive words, the power remains to the legislature, to assign original jurisdiction to that court in other cases than those specified in the article which has been recited; provided those cases belong to the judicial power of the United States."

But Marshall had set up this counterargument with an obvious flaw, since the passage from Article III had clearly stated that "In *all* other cases, the Supreme Court shall have appellate jurisdiction." The chief justice leapt on that phrase. The time had come for Marshall's rabbit to emerge from his hat. "If congress remains at liberty to give this court appellate jurisdiction," he announced, "where the constitution has declared their jurisdiction shall be original, and original jurisdiction where the constitution has declared it shall be appellate; the distribution of jurisdiction, made in the constitution, is form without substance."

John Marshall in 1802

A telling point, to be sure, or at least it would have been if the Constitution had actually said what Marshall claimed it said. The chief justice had conveniently left some things out. The full sentence in Article III, Section 2 read: "In all Cases affecting Ambassadors, other public Ministers and Consuls, and those in which a State shall be Party, the supreme Court shall have original Jurisdiction. In all the other Cases before mentioned, the supreme Court shall have appellate Jurisdiction, both as to Law and Fact, *with such Exceptions, and under such Regulations as the Congress shall make.*"[4]

So, having spent all this time setting up his argument, Marshall was forced to resort to a half-truth to make it stick. One wonders how Justice Paterson, sitting next to the chief justice in undoubted stoicism, felt about this turn in the argument. Paterson, who had read Marshall's treatise in advance, had certainly been asked to fall on the sword, since he not only had been a delegate in Philadelphia when Article III was drafted, but was also a coauthor of Article 13 of the Judiciary Act of 1789. He was now being asked to support an assertion that he and his fellow authors, Caleb Strong and Oliver Ellsworth, were guilty of misreading the Constitution they had helped to draft when it was patently untrue.[*]

Having built this much of his house on a rotten foundation, however, Marshall had no choice but to finish the thing and hope it would not collapse. He explained in copious detail how the drafters of the Constitution would certainly have given the Supreme Court original jurisdiction in all instances that they thought it appropriate, proceeding as if the modifying clause that he had omitted did not exist.

In prose that could have just as easily come from Ionesco, Marshall expounded on his reasoning. "When an instrument organizing fundamentally a judicial system, divides it into one supreme and so many inferior courts as the legislature may ordain and establish; then enumerates its powers, and proceeds so far to distribute them, as to define the jurisdiction of the Supreme Court by declaring the cases in which it shall take original jurisdiction, and that in others it shall take appellate jurisdiction; the plain import of the words seems to be, that in one class of cases its jurisdiction is original, and not appellate; in the other it is appellate, and not original. If any other construction would render the clause inoperative, that is an additional

---

[*] Ellsworth, in his tenure as chief justice, had never seen fit to find fault with his own work as a senator.

reason for rejecting such other construction and for adhering to their obvious meaning."

Of course, another clause *did* render the clause inoperative—Marshall simply chose to ignore it. Based on this utterly false premise, Marshall was able to conclude, "To enable this court, then, to issue a mandamus, it must be shown to be an exercise of appellate jurisdiction, or to be necessary to enable them to exercise appellate jurisdiction."

Marshall's conclusion was hardly surprising. "The authority, therefore, given to the Supreme Court, by the act establishing the judicial courts of the United States, to issue writs of mandamus to public officers, appears not to be warranted by the constitution," he wrote. From here, a simple leap—if anything the chief justice wrote could be described as "simple"—took Marshall to the undisputed assertion that the Constitution was not law on a par with other laws, but a paramount law—a "super law," as Justice Scalia has written—and therefore when the normal collides with the super, the normal must give way.

In support of this, Marshall penned his great passage, one to which justices of all stripes have retreated in support of judicial activism ever since. "It is emphatically the province and duty of the judicial department to say what the law is. Those who apply the rule to particular cases, must of necessity expound and interpret that rule. If two laws conflict with each other the courts must decide on the operation of each."

Marshall could have ended there, but chose to drone on for an additional thousand words or so in order to support his final, simple conclusion that "a law repugnant to the constitution is void; and that courts, as well as other departments, are bound by that instrument," and "the rule [Article 13] must be discharged."

So: Marbury had been appointed; he deserved his commission; Jefferson and Madison had wantonly and willfully overstepped their authority by denying it (implying that Republicans put no value in the Constitution or the rule of law); the court system was the proper venue in which to redress this grievance; *mandamus* was precisely the right instrument to achieve that end; the justices would have loved to have been of help; but their hands were tied since they must strictly adhere to the rule of law; politics played no part in the decision, because the courts are not a political branch of government.

Q.E.D.

TWENTY-TWO

MARGINALIZATION: *STUART*, PICKERING, AND CHASE

THE *MARBURY* DECISION has been described as "a coup as bold in design and as daring in execution as that by which the Constitution had been framed."[1] This is no overstatement. The *Marbury* decision was a constitutional amendment by fiat, a *de facto* addition to Article III itself. But, unlike the amendments created under Article V, this fundamental alteration of the Constitution required no two-thirds majority in Congress or ratification by three quarters of the states. Marshall had succeeded in enunciating an immense show of power in a branch of government appointed rather than elected, whose members served for life unless they resigned or were impeached.

Although the effect of the *Marbury* decision has certainly been as profound as any single act of government in the American experience, in the immediate wake of the decision, no one seemed to notice its most crucial feature. While almost every major newspaper in the nation either printed the decision or expressed a point of view, the commentary was almost exclusively confined to the putative rebuke issued by the Court to the president. Federalists considered the slap justified and long overdue, while Republicans characterized Marshall's verbiage as mere carping, a desperate and pernicious effort by a dying party to hang on to power. On both sides, the notion of judicial review as a constitutional principle was almost entirely lost in the uproar.

There was little doubt in early 1803 which side thought itself the winner. Given their ferocious antipathy to Marshall, Jefferson and his followers were largely quiescent. "Republican newspapers, until then so alert to attack every judicial 'usurpation,' had almost nothing to say of Marshall's daring assertion of judicial supremacy which was later execrated as the very parent of Constitutional evil."[2] Their very willingness to report extensively on the decision without the almost-obligatory excoriation of the chief justice bespeaks how little attention the Republicans were paying to the underlying issue.[3] One scholar noted, "The Republican press was so delighted by the Jeffersonian victories in the two cases that it did not recognize that William Marbury had been used as a tool to plant the seeds of judicial review."[4]

Given their general acuity to Federalist intrigues, the lack of Republican reaction might seem surprising. But there seemed to be little reason to join in a battle that had already been won. By whatever artifice, through whatever machinations, in no matter how many thousands of words, Marshall seemed clearly to have surrendered. He had refused to precipitate a national crisis by pitting his branch of government against Jefferson's. Regardless of whether history would judge the Republicans short-sighted, there seemed to be no reason at the time to respond to a toothless enemy. A Supreme Court whose most potent weapon was chiding language did not seem worth the effort.*

The Federalist press, fully aware that the party had gained no real advantage in *Marbury*, was far less sanguine. The *Connecticut Courant*, for example, printed a letter that said, "Rejoice, ye democrats, at the firmness of your chieftain who dares withhold from the Justices of Columbia their commissions in violation, as the Court declared, of their vested rights." The *New York Evening Post* upbraided Jefferson in an editorial titled "Constitution Violated by President." "Behold a subtle and smooth-faced hypocrisy concealing an ambition the most criminal, the most erroneous, the most unprincipled." Another Federalist newspaper observed that "it has been solemnly decided in the Supreme Court that Mr. Jefferson, the idol of democracy, the friend of the people has trampled on the charter of their liberties."[5] The *Washington Federalist* tried to salvage shreds of victory by praising the decision as a "monument of the wisdom, impartiality, and independence of the Supreme Court," but, even here, Marshall's decision had generated only hollow enthusiasm, seeming more impressed by length than content.[6] The *Federalist* did let on that the success might be less than complete. "Let such men [Republican congressmen] read this opinion and blush, if the power of blushing still remains within them."

For all the bitterness, a surprising lack of criticism came Marshall's way for his unwillingness to fully engage the enemy. Even Hamilton's *New York*

---

* Although four years later, Samuel Chase would press this principle sufficiently to get himself impeached.

Evening Post held its fire on the chief justice, preferring to content itself
with spewing vitriol at the president. From the disproportion in the reac-
tions of the adversaries, it seems apparent that both sides knew the Federalists had lost, that nothing Marshall might have done would have changed
anything, and that the once-noble party of Washington and Adams had
been reduced to a band of fist-shakers.*

With *realpolitik* at the fore, that judicial review did not even rate a mention
is hardly shocking. Why should Republicans have cared if the Supreme Court
claimed for itself the power to declare a law against the Constitution if, as
they believed, the Court would never have the courage to use that power in
any practical matter against them?† Moreover, if it ever did so in disagreement
with a Republican executive or legislature, the decision could have merely
been ignored. Let Marshall spout principles all he wants then, Republicans
must have thought. Jefferson himself later wrote that Marshall had indeed exceeded his mandate, not by claiming the right to oversee the Constitution,
but by sticking his nose into presidential function.[7] Like Jefferson, Republicans might be piqued that Marshall seemed determined to use his office to insult the president but, in the end, talk was a currency worth very little.

The absence of discussion of judicial review in the *Marbury* postmortems
is not, then, because the principle was universally accepted, but rather because it wasn't seen as making any difference. What was seen by both sides
as the immediate issue—the conflict between Jefferson and Marshall, president and chief justice—once so inflammatory, had seemed to have finally
been resolved. The winners basked in victory, the losers groused. Philosophy seemed irrelevant.

The bulk of these periodical accounts were not published until March,
however, after the Court handed down another key decision. *Marbury* was,
after all, not the only case on the 1803 docket with the potential to incite
partisan passion and government crisis. There was still the incendiary issue
of Jefferson's court reform in *Stuart v. Laird*. Immediately after Marshall had
completed his *Marbury* decision at 2 P.M., the justices moved to the contin-
uation of arguments in *Stuart*, which had begun the previous day.

---

* Nor was there any criticism of the decision in Congress. The decision in the case that had so dom-
inated the proceedings in the previous weeks was received with nary a whisper in the House or the
Senate.
† As they did not. The Marshall court never again invoked the power of judicial review.

For constitutional questions like those posed in *Stuart*—whether the repeal of the Judiciary Act of 1801 and its replacement by the Judiciary Act of 1802 was lawful—the *Marbury* decision had, in theory, changed everything. Before *Marbury*, the question of whether or not the Court was even empowered to rule on Adams's ephemeral circuit court appointments was open to argument. Once Marshall's decision was read, however, that question, at least in the eyes of the justices, had been resolved. With precedent now on the books for the Court to strike down an act of Congress as repugnant to the Constitution, the Judiciary Acts of 1802 were as much in play as had been the Judiciary Act of 1789. *Stuart* would be the test to see if Marshall had been serious in asserting that the Court was to have final authority "to say what the law is," or had merely been pontificating.

If it were the former, a direct challenge to the constitutionality of Jefferson's court-reform act took on increased significance. *Stuart*, not *Marbury*, would then become the hinge on which the role of the judiciary in American government would swing. In *Marbury*, after all, unconstitutionality had been used to justify a result pleasing to Republicans. If the same power was extended to *Stuart*, Republicans would not be pleased at all. In that eventuality, Jefferson and the Republican Congress might choose to simply ignore the Court and, in effect, run the judiciary by decree. *Stuart* might well become the case that determined whether or not what the justices said mattered at all.

As soon as arguments began, Charles Lee, once again proving himself to be a clever and resourceful advocate, altered his remarks to incorporate the *Marbury* decision.[8] With Marshall's opinion on the record, an established precedent, Lee reasoned quite correctly that what held for *Marbury* should now hold for *Stuart*. If Section 13 of the Judiciary Act of 1789 was unconstitutional, Jefferson's court reform must be as well and must therefore be set aside.

But Lee was no longer addressing himself to Marshall. The chief justice, with a sense of propriety that had been lacking in *Marbury*, recused himself from sitting on *Stuart*. He had served on the circuit court that was at the center of the dispute, he noted, and felt it inappropriate to participate as a justice in the appeal. The irony that this sort of overlapping jurisdiction was at the heart of the plaintiff's case apparently went unremarked upon. With the senior associate, Justice Cushing, also absent due to illness, Lee therefore directed his remarks to Justice Paterson, next in seniority.

So why did Marshall cede control of the court in such a vital affair, after he had previously made such effort to control it, even dictatorially? Justices regularly sat on cases that they had heard previously on circuit.[9] "It wasn't," according to Bruce Ackerman, "an attack of judicial ethics." Rather, he notes, "Marshall withdrew in *Stuart* because he didn't want to write an opinion explaining why the commissions of Supreme Court justices were not as sacrosanct as the commissions of lowly justices of the peace. He didn't want to write an opinion explaining why it was unconstitutional for Congress to expand original jurisdiction of the Supreme Court, but it was perfectly okay for Congress to force the justices to hold trials throughout the United States. And he certainly didn't want to announce an opinion ignoring *Marbury* entirely, and thereby suggest that the Court didn't take its own pretensions seriously. Let Paterson do it."[10]

Paterson deserved better than to have been placed in this humiliating position. Just a short time before, he had been forced to sit silently at Marshall's side and acquiesce in a declaration that the authors of Article 13 of the Judiciary Act of 1789 had blundered in creating a law that went counter to the Constitution. Paterson absorbed the slight, although he was perhaps more aware than anyone else in the room of how laughable was Marshall's reasoning.

But Paterson's role takes on even greater pathos since he, not Marshall, had been the overwhelming choice among Federalists for chief justice after Ellsworth resigned, and he had coveted the position fiercely. To have been passed over for the universally respected Jay had been one thing, but when the New Yorker declined, Paterson had every reason to believe the plum would be his. But instead, it was handed to Marshall by a president many thought was irrational.[11] As Hamilton and other High Federalists saw things, the conniving Marshall had only been able to turn the trick by using his position as secretary of state to insinuate himself into Adams's fragile confidence. Marshall had, after all, been standing with the president when Jay's communication arrived and the snap decision for his replacement had been made. Paterson was too loyal a Federalist and too loyal an American to make his bitterness public, but most other Federalists had been furious with the choice.

Now Paterson had finally become chief justice, albeit for this one case only. Still, with Marshall excusing himself, at least officially, the New Jerseyan could, if he wished, grasp the reins on this most vital question instead of meekly carrying Marshall's water. Lee's arguments certainly gave him ample room to do so. High Federalists had been waiting for an opportunity to confront Jefferson for two years, and Paterson had been placed in a position to do so.

The *Stuart* opinion was delivered on March 2, 1803. The Court was back in chambers, Chase now recovered, but Cushing was still absent. The room was full, waiting to see whether Paterson would fire the shot that Marshall had declined. The spectators were braced for a long, suspense-filled day. Marshall's decision in *Marbury* had taken almost five hours to read, and it was not until the final few minutes that his intentions had been made clear.

But there would be no suspense that day. Paterson's decision was only four short paragraphs. When he had completed his reading, Federalism, for all intents and purposes, had ceased to be a political force in the United States.

The decision, such as it was, responded to only two points. The first was whether or not a court other than the midnight-judge fourth circuit— namely Marshall's fifth circuit—could hear the case, whether "as the bond was given for the delivery of property levied on by virtue of an execution issuing out of, and returnable to a court for the fourth circuit, no other court could legally proceed upon the said bond."[12] To this, Paterson gave short shrift. "Congress has constitutional authority to establish from time to time such inferior tribunals as they may think proper, and to transfer a cause from one such tribunal to another. In this last particular, there are no words in the constitution to prohibit or restrain the exercise of legislative power."[13]

Remarkably, Paterson here referred to the very passage in Article III, Section 1 that Marshall had conveniently omitted to justify striking down Article 13 in his *Marbury* opinion. The selectivity was hardly a coincidence. The last thing Marshall had wanted was to acknowledge that the legislature had the right to "transfer a cause from one such tribunal to another"—the power to issue a *mandamus*, for instance—but Paterson needed the clause as a basis for what followed.

"The present is a case of this kind," Paterson continued. "It is nothing more than the removal of the suit brought by Stuart against Laird from the court of the fourth circuit to the court of the fifth circuit, which is authorised to proceed upon and carry it into full effect. This is apparent from the ninth section of the act entitled 'an act to amend the judicial system of the United States,' passed the 29th of April 1802. The forthcoming bond is an appendage to the cause, or rather a component part of the proceedings."[14]

The first question had thus been answered. *Marbury* or no, the Court would not declare the Judiciary Act of 1802 unconstitutional. Even worse

for Federalist ideology, the five justices (Marshall might be abstaining, but
he was hardly absent) would use the despised legislation as the basis of its
ruling. In this, and in taking a simple, declarative position, and declining to
expound on the constitutional issues raised by repeal of the Judiciary Act of
1801, Paterson signaled full retreat. The justices would opt to keep their
jobs rather than make a point.

All that remained was the question of circuit-riding, and so the second
argument that Paterson addressed was the contention "that the judges of
the supreme court have no right to sit as circuit judges, not being appointed
as such, or in other words, that they ought to have distinct commissions for
that purpose."

He responded with an astonishing passage. "To this objection, which is of
recent date, it is sufficient to observe, that practice, and acquiescence under it,
for a period of several years, commencing with the organization of the judicial
system, affords an irresistible answer, and has indeed fixed the construction. It
is a contemporary interpretation of the most forcible nature. This practical
exposition is too strong and obstinate to be shaken or controlled. Of course,
the question is at rest, and ought not now to be disturbed."[15]

With this pronouncement, Paterson had completely abdicated the
Court's role to "say what the law is," the centerpiece of Marshall's *Marbury*
opinion. Instead, if one follows this reasoning, the law was simply what it
had been for twelve years, whether or not it ran counter to the Constitution.[16] Put slightly differently, part of "saying what the law is" was deciding
on a case-by-case basis whether or not the Court would use legal precedent,
constitutional interpretation, or political expediency as the basis for its ruling. That this degree of rule by whim was what the Convention delegates
had in mind is hard to swallow.*

As confounding as this abandonment of principles is to constitutional
law, it further illuminates Marshall's decision to absent himself from the
case. Even for one with Marshall's talents, the difficulties of, in effect, overruling oneself just one week after a watershed pronouncement was a bit
much. As it was, Marshall had made the grand pronouncement and Paterson had been left to snivel around it. Marshall's sense of history was too
acute for him to be unaware of which decision would be remembered.

---

* Criticism by current-day strict constructionists of activist judges follows quite closely along these
very lines.

TWENTY-THREE

WHAT THE LAW ISN'T

L ITTLE DOUBT EXISTS that Marshall believed firmly in the principles he espoused in *Marbury*. His commitment to the notion of constitutional supremacy was unwavering, from his actions on the Executive Council in Virginia to his work as an attorney to his three-decades-long tenure as chief justice. But little doubt also exists that Marshall's decision in *Marbury* was not simply an exposition of those principles, but also an exercise in practical politics, to which his commitment was unwavering as well. Time and again throughout his career, Marshall exhibited a willingness to bend, mold, and even contort both his beliefs and the law to the exigencies of the day. The decision, like the man, was an amalgam.

As to which of these two masters Marshall demonstrated a greater loyalty—in *Talbot v. Seeman*, and *United States v. Schooner Peggy*, and again in *Marbury*—he was more than willing to subordinate law to politics. But rarely if ever did he subordinate politics to law.

Thus, to determine the case's potential use to succeeding generations of jurists, it is necessary to separate the written opinion in *Marbury* from whatever underlying ideology Marshall evokes in the decision. Only Marshall's actual words, after all, can be used as legal precedent. Justice Scalia would rightly scoff at any judge who claimed a right to go beyond the page and use as a basis for argument what he or she was certain another judge *meant* in an opinion.

Yet, according to Leonard Levy, the written opinion in *Marbury* was not only "poorly reasoned," but of "slight merit, distorted reasoning, and galloping activism."[1] And as to whether the opinion should stand as precedent: "Though the Court's technical competence was not evident, its judicial

politics—egregious partisanship and calculated expediency—was excep-
tionally adroit."[2] Levy added, "Marshall grossly misinterpreted the statute
[the Judiciary Act of 1789] and Article III [of the Constitution], as well as
the nature of the writ, in order to find that the statute conflicted with Article III so that he could avoid issuing the writ without appearing to buckle
before political enemies." He might have added that, by keeping Marbury's
claim before the Supreme Court and not redirecting it to whatever court
should have had jurisdiction, Marshall ensured that nobody else would issue
the writ either.

Despite its undeniable flaws, however, the Marbury decision is far more
often heaped with praise than skewered with criticism. The characteriza-
tion "brilliant" is used in too many sources to cite. And the view that Marshall overreached is also not universal. "Far from constituting an innovative
decision, each important aspect of the opinion is grounded on familiar principles of legal interpretation," one scholar noted.[3] Former chief justice
Rehnquist called the decision "a remarkable example of judicial statesmanship" that "turned what otherwise would have been an obscure case into the
fountainhead of all of our present-day constitutional law."[4]

Yet the view that the Marbury opinion is unsound and cynical remains
widespread as well. Even Marshall's best-known biographer characterized it as
"perfectly calculated audacity."[5] Another respected commentator called Marbury "a masterwork of indirection, a brilliant example of Marshall's ability to
sidestep danger while seeming to court it, to advance in one direction while
his opponents are looking in another."[6] High praise certainly, but more for political acuity than legal acumen. The description is hardly that of a man who
refused to compromise his public trust to advance a political agenda.

Even Chief Justice Rehnquist, after his flattering description of his predecessor, added this remarkable observation: Marshall ruled, according to
the chief justice, that "there is nothing that the Supreme Court can do
about [Marbury's claim] because Congress tried to give the Supreme Court
more authority than the Constitution would permit. The doctrine of judicial review is established, but in such a self-denying way that it is the judiciary's authority which is cut back." In the multitude of Marbury analyses,
"restraint" is rarely a term used to describe the opinion. Claiming for the
Court the right of final say in constitutional interpretation hardly cuts back
its authority. But then, a chief justice would be unlikely to cast aspersions
on the very decision that was the basis for his greatest power.

What Marshall seemed to demonstrate in his *Marbury* opinion was that, when the power "to say what the law is" is unchecked, it is as prone to abuse as any other unchecked power. Marshall did not so much "say what the law was" as "say what he wanted the law to be." And further, Marshall claimed the right in the future to impose his view of what the law should be at any time he chose.

When the Marshall court's record is viewed not simply as a string of disembodied renderings of judgment, but rather as part of the overall political landscape, that the Court was as partisan a branch of government as the executive or the legislative is difficult to deny. Marshall's rulings, *Marbury* chief among them, carved out a role for the Court that expanded its power, both legal and political. Two centuries later, little evidence is to be found that the Court has become less of a political entity and more the impartial arbiter that the framers envisioned. If one backs away from legal analysis, then, and takes the view that many Supreme Court decisions are, in fact, instruments of policy—a view widespread in the public at large—then for originalists to adopt one of the most egregious examples of legislating from the bench as the basis for their one deviation from literal adherence to the Constitution is questionable at best.

Even a complete repudiation of *Marbury* does not, however, mean that the doctrine of judicial review should necessarily be scrapped, and that a movement should begin to relegate the Supreme Court to the position of weakness that Hamilton anticipated when he penned *Federalist 78*. For those who believe in a "living" Constitution, those who are today considered broad constructionists, the document evolved with the times. Judicial review, regardless of how it was initiated, has become an integral facet of our system of laws, for which history and precedent has rendered its genesis irrelevant. As Justice Paterson observed in *Stuart*, "practice and acquiescence under it for a period of several years, commencing with the organization of the judicial system . . . have indeed fixed the construction . . . This practical exposition is too strong and obstinate to be shaken or controlled."[7]

If, however, one subscribes to Justice Scalia's philosophy, it is difficult to see how a continuing defense of the right of judicial review can be maintained. The *Marbury* decision seems to meet every test of an originalist's view of bad law, certainly as corrupt as *Roe v. Wade*. In fact, with their continued insistence that judicial review as enunciated in *Marbury* is a legitimate facet of textualist doctrine, originalists have instead demonstrated that the Court is every bit the political institution now that it was in 1803. When textualists cite *Marbury* as a justification for an expansion of the Court's power, while, in the same breath, decrying "activist" judges who use the Constitution to expand civil liberties, they are engaging in their political rather than their judicial function.

If the judiciary is a political branch of government, no different in that regard from the legislative or the executive, that the Court's power should be subject to the same rigorous checks as the other two branches surely follows. If the Supreme Court is the final arbiter of constitutionality, the rarely used and unwieldy threat of impeachment as its only check is disproportionately small. If the founders had meant for the Court to actually have such power, it seems highly probable that additional checks—a three-fourths vote of Congress to override a decision, or finite terms for the justices rather than lifetime appointments—would have been almost certainly included as a restraint.

Nor does the argument hold that, in restricting the Court to appellate jurisdiction, the Constitution has provided a check, since the Court cannot choose which laws to examine but must wait for a case to come before it. In fact, once the Court's immense unchecked power was established, advocates of any position, on any law, could manufacture a challenge, knowing that the Court could choose to hear it.*

That the activist Marshall is so embraced by originalists, then, should come as no surprise. He is, after all, one of their own.

---

* In *Bush v. Gore*, the Court chose, in effect, to arbitrate a presidential election.

Appendix I

Marbury v. Madison 5 US (1 Cranch) 137

Mr. Chief Justice MARSHALL delivered the opinion of the Court.

At the last term, on the affidavits then read and filed with the clerk, a rule was granted in this case requiring the Secretary of State to show cause why a mandamus should not issue directing him to deliver to William Marbury his commission as a justice of the peace for the county of Washington, in the District of Columbia.

No cause has been shown, and the present motion is for a mandamus. The peculiar delicacy of this case, the novelty of some of its circumstances, and the real difficulty attending the points which occur in it require a complete exposition of the principles on which the opinion to be given by the Court is founded. These principles have been, on the side of the applicant, very ably argued at the bar. In rendering the opinion of the Court, there will be some departure in form, though not in substance, from the points stated in that argument.

In the order in which the Court has viewed this subject, the following questions have been considered and decided.

1. Has the applicant a right to the commission he demands?

2. If he has a right, and that right has been violated, do the laws of his country afford him a remedy?

3. If they do afford him a remedy, is it a mandamus issuing from this court?

The first object of inquiry is:

1. Has the applicant a right to the commission he demands?

His right originates in an act of Congress passed in February, 1801, concerning the District of Columbia.

After dividing the district into two counties, the eleventh section of this
law enacts, "that there shall be appointed in and for each of the said counties such number of discreet [sic] persons to be justices of the peace as the
President of the United States shall, from time to time, think expedient, to
continue in office for five years."

It appears from the affidavits that, in compliance with this law, a commission for William Marbury as a justice of peace for the County of Washington was signed by John Adams, then President of the United States,
after which the seal of the United States was affixed to it, but the commission has never reached the person for whom it was made out.

In order to determine whether he is entitled to this commission, it becomes necessary to inquire whether he has been appointed to the office. For
if he has been appointed, the law continues him in office for five years, and
he is entitled to the possession of those evidences of office, which, being
completed, became his property.

The second section of the second article of the Constitution declares,
"The President shall nominate, and, by and with the advice and consent of
the Senate, shall appoint ambassadors, other public ministers and consuls,
and all other officers of the United States, whose appointments are not otherwise provided for."

The third section declares, that "He shall commission all the officers of
the United States."

An act of Congress directs the Secretary of State to keep the seal of the
United States, "to make out and record, and affix the said seal to all civil
commissions to officers of the United States to be appointed by the President, by and with the consent of the Senate, or by the President alone; provided that the said seal shall not be affixed to any commission before the
same shall have been signed by the President of the United States."

These are the clauses of the Constitution and laws of the United States
which affect this part of the case. They seem to contemplate three distinct
operations:

1. The nomination. This is the sole act of the President, and is completely voluntary.

2. The appointment. This is also the act of the President, and is also

a voluntary act, though it can only be performed by and with the advice and consent of the Senate.

3. The commission. To grant a commission to a person appointed might perhaps be deemed a duty enjoined by the Constitution. "He shall," says that instrument, "commission all the officers of the United States."

The acts of appointing to office and commissioning the person appointed can scarcely be considered as one and the same, since the power to perform them is given in two separate and distinct sections of the Constitution. The distinction between the appointment and the commission will be rendered more apparent by adverting to that provision in the second section of the second article of the Constitution which authorises Congress "to vest by law the appointment of such inferior officers as they think proper in the President alone, in the Courts of law, or in the heads of departments"; thus contemplating cases where the law may direct the President to commission an officer appointed by the Courts or by the heads of departments. In such a case, to issue a commission would be apparently a duty distinct from the appointment, the performance of which perhaps could not legally be refused.

Although that clause of the Constitution which requires the President to commission all the officers of the United States may never have been applied to officers appointed otherwise than by himself, yet it would be difficult to deny the legislative power to apply it to such cases. Of consequence, the constitutional distinction between the appointment to an office and the commission of an officer who has been appointed remains the same as if in practice the President had commissioned officers appointed by an authority other than his own.

It follows too from the existence of this distinction that, if an appointment was to be evidenced by any public act other than the commission, the performance of such public act would create the officer, and if he was not removable at the will of the President, would either give him a right to his commission or enable him to perform the duties without it.

These observations are premised solely for the purpose of rendering more intelligible those which apply more directly to the particular case under consideration.

This is an appointment made by the President, by and with the advice and consent of the Senate, and is evidenced by no act but the commission itself. In such a case, therefore, the commission and the appointment seem inseparable, it being almost impossible to show an appointment otherwise than by proving the existence of a commission; still, the commission is not necessarily the appointment; though conclusive evidence of it.

But at what stage does it amount to this conclusive evidence?

The answer to this question seems an obvious one. The appointment, being the sole act of the President, must be completely evidenced when it is shown that he has done everything to be performed by him.

Should the commission, instead of being evidence of an appointment, even be considered as constituting the appointment itself, still it would be made when the last act to be done by the President was performed, or, at furthest, when the commission was complete.

The last act to be done by the President is the signature of the commission. He has then acted on the advice and consent of the Senate to his own nomination. The time for deliberation has then passed. He has decided. His judgment, on the advice and consent of the Senate concurring with his nomination, has been made, and the officer is appointed. This appointment is evidenced by an open, unequivocal act, and, being the last act required from the person making it, necessarily excludes the idea of its being, so far as it respects the appointment, an inchoate and incomplete transaction.

Some point of time must be taken when the power of the Executive over an officer, not removable at his will, must cease. That point of time must be when the constitutional power of appointment has been exercised. And this power has been exercised when the last act required from the person possessing the power has been performed. This last act is the signature of the commission. This idea seems to have prevailed with the Legislature when the act passed converting the Department of Foreign Affairs into the Department of State. By that act, it is enacted that the Secretary of State shall keep the seal of the United States, "and shall make out and record, and shall affix the said seal to all civil commissions to officers of the United States, to be appointed by the President: . . . provided that the said seal shall not be affixed to any commission before the same shall have been signed by the President of the United States, nor to any other instrument or act without the special warrant of the President therefor."

The signature is a warrant for affixing the great seal to the commission, and the great seal is only to be affixed to an instrument which is complete. It attests, by an act supposed to be of public notoriety, the verity of the Presidential signature.

It is never to be affixed till the commission is signed, because the signature, which gives force and effect to the commission, is conclusive evidence that the appointment is made.

The commission being signed, the subsequent duty of the Secretary of State is prescribed by law, and not to be guided by the will of the President. He is to affix the seal of the United States to the commission, and is to record it.

This is not a proceeding which may be varied if the judgment of the Executive shall suggest one more eligible, but is a precise course accurately marked out by law, and is to be strictly pursued. It is the duty of the Secretary of State to conform to the law, and in this he is an officer of the United States, bound to obey the laws. He acts, in this respect, as has been very properly stated at the bar, under the authority of law, and not by the instructions of the President. It is a ministerial act which the law enjoins on a particular officer for a particular purpose.

If it should be supposed that the solemnity of affixing the seal is necessary not only to the validity of the commission, but even to the completion of an appointment, still, when the seal is affixed, the appointment is made, and the commission is valid. No other solemnity is required by law; no other act is to be performed on the part of government. All that the Executive can do to invest the person with his office is done, and unless the appointment be then made, the Executive cannot make one without the cooperation of others.

After searching anxiously for the principles on which a contrary opinion may be supported, none has been found which appear of sufficient force to maintain the opposite doctrine.

Such as the imagination of the Court could suggest have been very deliberately examined, and after allowing them all the weight which it appears possible to give them, they do not shake the opinion which has been formed.

In considering this question, it has been conjectured that the commission may have been assimilated to a deed to the validity of which delivery is essential.

This idea is founded on the supposition that the commission is not merely evidence of an appointment, but is itself the actual appointment—a supposition by no means unquestionable. But, for the purpose of examining this objection fairly, let it be conceded that the principle claimed for its support is established.

The appointment being, under the Constitution, to be made by the President personally, the delivery of the deed of appointment, if necessary to its completion, must be made by the President also. It is not necessary that the livery should be made personally to the grantee of the office; it never is so made. The law would seem to contemplate that it should be made to the Secretary of State, since it directs the secretary to affix the seal to the commission after it shall have been signed by the President. If then the act of livery be necessary to give validity to the commission, it has been delivered when executed and given to the Secretary for the purpose of being sealed, recorded, and transmitted to the party.

But in all cases of letters patent, certain solemnities are required by law, which solemnities are the evidences of the validity of the instrument. A formal delivery to the person is not among them. In cases of commissions, the sign manual of the President and the seal of the United States are those solemnities. This objection therefore does not touch the case.

It has also occurred as possible, and barely possible, that the transmission of the commission and the acceptance thereof might be deemed necessary to complete the right of the plaintiff.

The transmission of the commission is a practice directed by convenience, but not by law. It cannot therefore be necessary to constitute the appointment, which must precede it and which is the mere act of the President. If the Executive required that every person appointed to an office should himself take means to procure his commission, the appointment would not be the less valid on that account. The appointment is the sole act of the President; the transmission of the commission is the sole act of the officer to whom that duty is assigned, and may be accelerated or retarded by circumstances which can have no influence on the appointment. A commission is transmitted to a person already appointed, not to a person to be appointed or not, as the letter enclosing the commission should happen to get into the post office and reach him in safety, or to miscarry.

It may have some tendency to elucidate this point to inquire whether the possession of the original commission be indispensably necessary to authorize a person appointed to any office to perform the duties of that office. If it was necessary, then a loss of the commission would lose the office. Not only negligence, but accident or fraud, fire or theft might deprive an individual of his office. In such a case, I presume it could not be doubted but that a copy from the record of the Office of the Secretary of State would be, to every intent and purpose, equal to the original. The act of Congress has expressly made it so. To give that copy validity, it would not be necessary to prove that the original had been transmitted and afterwards lost. The copy would be complete evidence that the original had existed, and that the appointment had been made, but not that the original had been transmitted. If indeed it should appear that the original had been mislaid in the Office of State, that circumstance would not affect the operation of the copy. When all the requisites have been performed which authorize a recording officer to record any instrument whatever, and the order for that purpose has been given, the instrument is in law considered as recorded, although the manual labour of inserting it in a book kept for that purpose may not have been performed.

In the case of commissions, the law orders the Secretary of State to record them. When, therefore, they are signed and sealed, the order for their being recorded is given, and, whether inserted in the book or not, they are in law recorded.

A copy of this record is declared equal to the original, and the fees to be paid by a person requiring a copy are ascertained by law. Can a keeper of a public record erase therefrom a commission which has been recorded? Or can he refuse a copy thereof to a person demanding it on the terms prescribed by law?

Such a copy would, equally with the original, authorize the justice of peace to proceed in the performance of his duty, because it would, equally with the original, attest his appointment.

If the transmission of a commission be not considered as necessary to give validity to an appointment, still less is its acceptance. The appointment is the sole act of the President; the acceptance is the sole act of the officer, and is, in plain common sense, posterior to the appointment. As he may resign, so may he refuse to accept; but neither the one nor the other is capable of rendering the appointment a nonentity.

That this is the understanding of the government is apparent from the whole tenor of its conduct.

A commission bears date, and the salary of the officer commences from his appointment, not from the transmission or acceptance of his commission. When a person appointed to any office refuses to accept that office, the successor is nominated in the place of the person who has declined to accept, and not in the place of the person who had been previously in office and had created the original vacancy.

It is therefore decidedly the opinion of the Court that, when a commission has been signed by the President, the appointment is made, and that the commission is complete when the seal of the United States has been affixed to it by the Secretary of State.

Where an officer is removable at the will of the Executive, the circumstance which completes his appointment is of no concern, because the act is at any time revocable, and the commission may be arrested if still in the office. But when the officer is not removable at the will of the Executive, the appointment is not revocable, and cannot be annulled. It has conferred legal rights which cannot be resumed.

The discretion of the Executive is to be exercised until the appointment has been made. But having once made the appointment, his power over the office is terminated in all cases, where by law the officer is not removable by him. The right to the office is then in the person appointed, and he has the absolute, unconditional power of accepting or rejecting it.

Mr. Marbury, then, since his commission was signed by the President and sealed by the Secretary of State, was appointed, and as the law creating the office gave the officer a right to hold for five years independent of the Executive, the appointment was not revocable, but vested in the officer legal rights which are protected by the laws of his country.

To withhold the commission, therefore, is an act deemed by the Court not warranted by law, but violative of a vested legal right.

This brings us to the second inquiry, which is:

2. If he has a right, and that right has been violated, do the laws of his country afford him a remedy?

The very essence of civil liberty certainly consists in the right of every individual to claim the protection of the laws whenever he receives an injury. One of the first duties of government is to afford that protection. In Great Britain, the King himself is sued in the respectful form of a petition, and he never fails to comply with the judgment of his court.

In the third volume of his Commentaries, page 23, Blackstone states two cases in which a remedy is afforded by mere operation of law.

"In all other cases," he says, "it is a general and indisputable rule that where there is a legal right, there is also a legal remedy by suit or action at law whenever that right is invaded."

And afterwards, page 109 of the same volume, he says, "I am next to consider such injuries as are cognizable by the Courts of common law. And

herein I shall for the present only remark that all possible injuries whatso-
ever that did not fall within the exclusive cognizance of either the ecclesi-
astical, military, or maritime tribunals are, for that very reason, within the
cognizance of the common law courts of justice, for it is a settled and invariable principle in the laws of England that every right, when withheld,
must have a remedy, and every injury its proper redress."

The Government of the United States has been emphatically termed a
government of laws, and not of men. It will certainly cease to deserve this
high appellation if the laws furnish no remedy for the violation of a vested
legal right.

If this obloquy is to be cast on the jurisprudence of our country, it must
arise from the peculiar character of the case.

It behooves us, then, to inquire whether there be in its composition any in-
gredient which shall exempt from legal investigation or exclude the injured
party from legal redress. In pursuing this inquiry, the first question which pre-
sents itself is whether this can be arranged with that class of cases which come
under the description of *damnum absque injuria*—a loss without an injury.

This description of cases never has been considered, and, it is believed,
never can be considered, as comprehending offices of trust, of honour or of
profit. The office of justice of peace in the District of Columbia is such an
office; it is therefore worthy of the attention and guardianship of the laws. It
has received that attention and guardianship. It has been created by special
act of Congress, and has been secured, so far as the laws can give security to
the person appointed to fill it, for five years. It is not then on account of the
worthlessness of the thing pursued that the injured party can be alleged to
be without remedy.

Is it in the nature of the transaction? Is the act of delivering or withholding a commission to be considered as a mere political act belonging to the
Executive department alone, for the performance of which entire confidence is placed by our Constitution in the Supreme Executive, and for any
misconduct respecting which the injured individual has no remedy?

That there may be such cases is not to be questioned. but that every act
of duty to be performed in any of the great departments of government con-
stitutes such a case is not to be admitted.

By the act concerning invalids, passed in June, 1794, the Secretary at
War is ordered to place on the pension list all persons whose names are contained in a report previously made by him to Congress. If he should refuse to

do so, would the wounded veteran be without remedy? Is it to be contended that where the law, in precise terms, directs the performance of an act in which an individual is interested, the law is incapable of securing obedience to its mandate? Is it on account of the character of the person against whom the complaint is made? Is it to be contended that the heads of departments are not amenable to the laws of their country?

Whatever the practice on particular occasions may be, the theory of this principle will certainly never be maintained. No act of the Legislature confers so extraordinary a privilege, nor can it derive countenance from the doctrines of the common law. After stating that personal injury from the King to a subject is presumed to be impossible, Blackstone, Vol. III. p. 255, says, "but injuries to the rights of property can scarcely be committed by the Crown without the intervention of its officers, for whom, the law, in matters of right, entertains no respect or delicacy, but furnishes various methods of detecting the errors and misconduct of those agents by whom the King has been deceived and induced to do a temporary injustice."

By the act passed in 1796, authorizing the sale of the lands above the mouth of Kentucky river, the purchaser, on paying his purchase money, becomes completely entitled to the property purchased, and, on producing to the Secretary of State the receipt of the treasurer upon a certificate required by the law, the President of the United States is authorized to grant him a patent. It is further enacted that all patents shall be countersigned by the Secretary of State, and recorded in his office. If the Secretary of State should choose to withhold this patent, or, the patent being lost, should refuse a copy of it, can it be imagined that the law furnishes to the injured person no remedy?

It is not believed that any person whatever would attempt to maintain such a proposition.

It follows, then, that the question whether the legality of an act of the head of a department be examinable in a court of justice or not must always depend on the nature of that act.

If some acts be examinable and others not, there must be some rule of law to guide the Court in the exercise of its jurisdiction.

In some instances, there may be difficulty in applying the rule to particular cases; but there cannot, it is believed, be much difficulty in laying down the rule.

By the Constitution of the United States, the President is invested with certain important political powers, in the exercise of which he is to use his own discretion, and is accountable only to his country in his political character and to his own conscience. To aid him in the performance of these duties, he is authorized to appoint certain officers, who act by his authority and in conformity with his orders.

In such cases, their acts are his acts; and whatever opinion may be entertained of the manner in which executive discretion may be used, still there exists, and can exist, no power to control that discretion. The subjects are political. They respect the nation, not individual rights, and, being entrusted to the Executive, the decision of the Executive is conclusive. The application of this remark will be perceived by adverting to the act of Congress for establishing the Department of Foreign Affairs. This officer, as his duties were prescribed by that act, is to conform precisely to the will of the President. He is the mere organ by whom that will is communicated. The acts of such an officer, as an officer, can never be examinable by the Courts.

But when the Legislature proceeds to impose on that officer other duties; when he is directed peremptorily to perform certain acts; when the rights of individuals are dependent on the performance of those acts; he is so far the officer of the law, is amenable to the laws for his conduct, and cannot at his discretion, sport away the vested rights of others.

The conclusion from this reasoning is that, where the heads of departments are the political or confidential agents of the Executive, merely to execute the will of the President, or rather to act in cases in which the Executive possesses a constitutional or legal discretion, nothing can be more perfectly clear than that their acts are only politically examinable. But where a specific duty is assigned by law, and individual rights depend upon the performance of that duty, it seems equally clear that the individual who considers himself injured has a right to resort to the laws of his country for a remedy.

If this be the rule, let us inquire how it applies to the case under the consideration of the Court.

The power of nominating to the Senate, and the power of appointing the person nominated, are political powers, to be exercised by the President according to his own discretion. When he has made an appointment, he has exercised his whole power, and his discretion has been completely applied to the case. If, by law, the officer be removable at the will of the President, then a new appointment may be immediately made, and the rights of the officer are terminated. But as a fact which has existed cannot be made never to have existed, the appointment cannot be annihilated, and consequently, if the officer is by law not removable at the will of the President, the rights he has acquired are protected by the law, and are not resumable by the President. They cannot be extinguished by Executive authority, and he has the privilege of asserting them in like manner as if they had been derived from any other source.

The question whether a right has vested or not is, in its nature, judicial, and must be tried by the judicial authority. If, for example, Mr. Marbury had taken the oaths of a magistrate and proceeded to act as one, in consequence of which a suit had been instituted against him in which his defence had depended on his being a magistrate; the validity of his appointment must have been determined by judicial authority.

So, if he conceives that, by virtue of his appointment, he has a legal right either to the commission which has been made out for him or to a copy of that commission, it is equally a question examinable in a court, and the decision of the Court upon it must depend on the opinion entertained of his appointment.

That question has been discussed, and the opinion is that the latest point of time which can be taken as that at which the appointment was complete and evidenced was when, after the signature of the President, the seal of the United States was affixed to the commission.

It is then the opinion of the Court:

1. That, by signing the commission of Mr. Marbury, the President of the United States appointed him a justice of peace for the County of Washington in the District of Columbia, and that the seal of the United States, affixed thereto by the Secretary of State, is conclusive testimony of the verity of the signature, and of the completion of the appointment, and that the appointment conferred on him a legal right to the office for the space of five years.

2. That, having this legal title to the office, he has a consequent right to the commission, a refusal to deliver which is a plain violation of that right, for which the laws of his country afford him a remedy.

It remains to be inquired whether,

3. He is entitled to the remedy for which he applies. This depends on:

1. The nature of the writ applied for, and
2. The power of this court.
1. The nature of the writ.

Blackstone, in the third volume of his Commentaries, page 110, defines a mandamus to be "a command issuing in the King's name from the Court of King's Bench, and directed to any person, corporation, or inferior court of judicature within the King's dominions requiring them to do some particular thing therein specified which appertains to their office and duty, and which the Court of King's Bench has previously determined, or at least supposes, to be consonant to right and justice."

Lord Mansfield, in 3 Burrows, 1266, in the case of *The King v. Baker et al.*, states with much precision and explicitness the cases in which this writ may be used.

"Whenever," says that very able judge, "there is a right to execute an office, perform a service, or exercise a franchise (more especially if it be in a matter of public concern or attended with profit), and a person is kept out of possession, or dispossessed of such right, and has no other specific legal remedy, this court ought to assist by mandamus, upon reasons of justice, as the writ expresses, and upon reasons of public policy, to preserve peace, order and good government."

In the same case, he says, "this writ ought to be used upon all occasions where the law has established no specific remedy, and where in justice and good government there ought to be one."

In addition to the authorities now particularly cited, many others were relied on at the bar which show how far the practice has conformed to the general doctrines that have been just quoted.

This writ, if awarded, would be directed to an officer of government, and its mandate to him would be, to use the words of Blackstone, "to do a particular thing therein specified, which appertains to his office and duty and which the Court has previously determined or at least supposes to be consonant to right and justice."

Or, in the words of Lord Mansfield, the applicant, in this case, has a right to execute an office of public concern, and is kept out of possession of that right.

These circumstances certainly concur in this case.

Still, to render the mandamus a proper remedy, the officer to whom it is to be directed must be one to whom, on legal principles, such writ may be directed, and the person applying for it must be without any other specific and legal remedy.

1. With respect to the officer to whom it would be directed. The intimate political relation, subsisting between the President of the United States and the heads of departments, necessarily renders any legal investigation of the acts of one of those high officers peculiarly irksome, as well as delicate, and excites some hesitation with respect to the propriety of entering into such investigation. Impressions are often received without much reflection or examination, and it is not wonderful that, in such a case as this, the assertion by an individual of his legal claims in a court of justice, to which claims it is the duty of that court to attend, should, at first view, be considered by some as an attempt to intrude into the cabinet and to intermeddle with the prerogatives of the Executive.

It is scarcely necessary for the Court to disclaim all pretensions to such a jurisdiction. An extravagance so absurd and excessive could not have been entertained for a moment. The province of the Court is solely to decide on the rights of individuals, not to inquire how the Executive or Executive officers perform duties in which they have a discretion. Questions, in their nature political or which are, by the Constitution and laws, submitted to the Executive, can never be made in this court.

But, if this be not such a question; if so far from being an intrusion into the secrets of the cabinet, it respects a paper which, according to law, is upon record, and to a copy of which the law gives a right, on the payment of ten cents; if it be no intermeddling with a subject over which the Executive can be considered as having exercised any control; what is there in the exalted station of the officer which shall bar a citizen from asserting in a court of justice his legal rights, or shall forbid a court to listen to the claim or to issue a mandamus directing the performance of a duty not depending on Executive discretion, but on particular acts of Congress and the general principles of law?

If one of the heads of departments commits any illegal act under colour of his office by which an individual sustains an injury, it cannot be pretended that his office alone exempts him from being sued in the ordinary mode of proceeding, and being compelled to obey the judgment of the law. How then can his office exempt him from this particular mode of deciding on the legality of his conduct if the case be such a case as would, were any other individual the party complained of, authorize the process?

It is not by the office of the person to whom the writ is directed, but the nature of the thing to be done, that the propriety or impropriety of issuing a mandamus is to be determined. Where the head of a department acts in a case in which Executive discretion is to be exercised, in which he is the mere organ of Executive will, it is again repeated, that any application to a court to control, in any respect, his conduct, would be rejected without hesitation.

But where he is directed by law to do a certain act affecting the absolute rights of individuals, in the performance of which he is not placed under the particular direction of the President, and the performance of which the President cannot lawfully forbid, and therefore is never presumed to have forbidden—as for example, to record a commission, or a patent for land, which has received all the legal solemnities; or to give a copy of such record—in such cases, it is not perceived on what ground the Courts of the country are further excused from the duty of giving judgment that right to be done to an injured individual than if the same services were to be performed by a person not the head of a department.

This opinion seems not now for the first time to be taken up in this country.

It must be well recollected that, in 1792, an act passed, directing the secretary at war to place on the pension list such disabled officers and soldiers as should be reported to him by the Circuit Courts, which act, so far as the duty was imposed on the Courts, was deemed unconstitutional; but some of the judges, thinking that the law might be executed by them in the character of commissioners, proceeded to act and to report in that character.

This law being deemed unconstitutional at the circuits, was repealed, and a different system was established; but the question whether those persons who had been reported by the judges, as commissioners, were entitled, in consequence of that report, to be placed on the pension list was a legal question, properly determinable in the Courts, although the act of placing such persons on the list was to be performed by the head of a department.

That this question might be properly settled, Congress passed an act in February, 1793, making it the duty of the Secretary of War, in conjunction with the Attorney General, to take such measures as might be necessary to obtain an adjudication of the Supreme Court of the United States on the validity of any such rights, claimed under the act aforesaid.

After the passage of this act, a mandamus was moved for, to be directed to the Secretary of War, commanding him to place on the pension list a person stating himself to be on the report of the judges.

There is, therefore, much reason to believe that this mode of trying the legal right of the complainant was deemed by the head of a department, and by the highest law officer of the United States, the most proper which could be selected for the purpose.

When the subject was brought before the Court, the decision was not that a mandamus would not lie to the head of a department directing him to perform an act enjoined by law, in the performance of which an individual had a vested interest, but that a mandamus ought not to issue in that case— the decision necessarily to be made if the report of the commissioners did not confer on the applicant a legal right.

The judgment in that case is understood to have decided the merits of all claims of that description, and the persons, on the report of the commissioners, found it necessary to pursue the mode prescribed by the law subsequent to that which had been deemed unconstitutional in order to place themselves on the pension list.

The doctrine, therefore, now advanced is by no means a novel one.

It is true that the mandamus now moved for is not for the performance of an act expressly enjoined by statute.

It is to deliver a commission, on which subjects the acts of Congress are silent. This difference is not considered as affecting the case. It has already been stated that the applicant has, to that commission, a vested legal right of which the Executive cannot deprive him. He has been appointed to an office from which he is not removable at the will of the Executive, and, being so appointed, he has a right to the commission which the Secretary has received from the President for his use. The act of Congress does not, indeed, order the Secretary of State to send it to him, but it is placed in his hands for the person entitled to it, and cannot be more lawfully withheld by him than by another person.

It was at first doubted whether the action of detinue was not a specific legal remedy for the commission which has been withheld from Mr. Marbury, in which case a mandamus would be improper. But this doubt has yielded to the consideration that the judgment in detinue is for the thing itself, or its value. The value of a public office not to be sold is incapable of being ascertained, and the applicant has a right to the office itself, or to nothing. He will obtain the office by obtaining the commission or a copy of it from the record.

This, then, is a plain case of a mandamus, either to deliver the commission or a copy of it from the record, and it only remains to be inquired:

Whether it can issue from this Court.

The act to establish the judicial courts of the United States authorizes the Supreme Court "to issue writs of mandamus, in cases warranted by the principles and usages of law, to any courts appointed, or persons holding office, under the authority of the United States."

The Secretary of State, being a person, holding an office under the authority of the United States, is precisely within the letter of the description, and if this Court is not authorized to issue a writ of mandamus to such an officer, it must be because the law is unconstitutional, and therefore absolutely incapable of conferring the authority and assigning the duties which its words purport to confer and assign.

The Constitution vests the whole judicial power of the United States in one Supreme Court, and such inferior courts as Congress shall, from time to time, ordain and establish. This power is expressly extended to all cases arising under the laws of the United States; and consequently, in some form, may be exercised over the present case, because the right claimed is given by a law of the United States.

In the distribution of this power, it is declared that "The Supreme Court shall have original jurisdiction in all cases affecting ambassadors, other public ministers and consuls, and those in which a state shall be a party. In all other cases, the Supreme Court shall have appellate jurisdiction."

It has been insisted at the bar, that, as the original grant of jurisdiction to the Supreme and inferior courts is general, and the clause assigning original jurisdiction to the Supreme Court contains no negative or restrictive words, the power remains to the Legislature to assign original jurisdiction to that Court in other cases than those specified in the article which has been recited, provided those cases belong to the judicial power of the United States.

If it had been intended to leave it in the discretion of the Legislature to apportion the judicial power between the Supreme and inferior courts according to the will of that body, it would certainly have been useless to have proceeded further than to have defined the judicial power and the tribunals in which it should be vested. The subsequent part of the section is mere surplusage—is entirely without meaning—if such is to be the construction. If

Congress remains at liberty to give this court appellate jurisdiction where the Constitution has declared their jurisdiction shall be original, and original jurisdiction where the Constitution has declared it shall be appellate, the distribution of jurisdiction made in the Constitution, is form without substance.

Affirmative words are often, in their operation, negative of other objects than those affirmed, and, in this case, a negative or exclusive sense must be given to them or they have no operation at all.

It cannot be presumed that any clause in the Constitution is intended to be without effect, and therefore such construction is inadmissible unless the words require it.

If the solicitude of the Convention respecting our peace with foreign powers induced a provision that the Supreme Court should take original jurisdiction in cases which might be supposed to affect them, yet the clause would have proceeded no further than to provide for such cases if no further restriction on the powers of Congress had been intended. That they should have appellate jurisdiction in all other cases, with such exceptions as Congress might make, is no restriction unless the words be deemed exclusive of original jurisdiction.

When an instrument organizing fundamentally a judicial system divides it into one Supreme and so many inferior courts as the Legislature may ordain and establish, then enumerates its powers, and proceeds so far to distribute them as to define the jurisdiction of the Supreme Court by declaring the cases in which it shall take original jurisdiction, and that in others it shall take appellate jurisdiction, the plain import of the words seems to be that, in one class of cases, its jurisdiction is original, and not appellate; in the other, it is appellate, and not original. If any other construction would render the clause inoperative, that is an additional reason for rejecting such other construction, and for adhering to the obvious meaning.

To enable this court then to issue a mandamus, it must be shown to be an exercise of appellate jurisdiction, or to be necessary to enable them to exercise appellate jurisdiction.

It has been stated at the bar that the appellate jurisdiction may be exercised in a variety of forms, and that, if it be the will of the Legislature that a mandamus should be used for that purpose, that will must be obeyed. This is true; yet the jurisdiction must be appellate, not original.

It is the essential criterion of appellate jurisdiction that it revises and corrects the proceedings in a cause already instituted, and does not create that case. Although, therefore, a mandamus may be directed to courts, yet to issue such a writ to an officer for the delivery of a paper is, in effect, the same as to sustain an original action for that paper, and therefore seems not to belong to appellate, but to original jurisdiction. Neither is it necessary in such a case as this to enable the Court to exercise its appellate jurisdiction.

The authority, therefore, given to the Supreme Court by the act establishing the judicial courts of the United States to issue writs of mandamus to public officers appears not to be warranted by the Constitution, and it becomes necessary to inquire whether a jurisdiction so conferred can be exercised.

The question whether an act repugnant to the Constitution can become the law of the land is a question deeply interesting to the United States, but, happily, not of an intricacy proportioned to its interest. It seems only necessary to recognise certain principles, supposed to have been long and well established, to decide it.

That the people have an original right to establish for their future government such principles as, in their opinion, shall most conduce to their own happiness is the basis on which the whole American fabric has been erected. The exercise of this original right is a very great exertion; nor can it nor ought it to be frequently repeated. The principles, therefore, so established are deemed fundamental. And as the authority from which they proceed, is supreme, and can seldom act, they are designed to be permanent.

This original and supreme will organizes the government and assigns to different departments their respective powers. It may either stop here or establish certain limits not to be transcended by those departments.

The Government of the United States is of the latter description. The powers of the Legislature are defined and limited; and that those limits may not be mistaken or forgotten, the Constitution is written. To what purpose are powers limited, and to what purpose is that limitation committed to writing, if these limits may at any time be passed by those intended to be restrained? The distinction between a government with limited and unlimited powers is abolished if those limits do not confine the persons on whom they are imposed, and if acts prohibited and acts allowed are of equal obligation. It is a proposition too plain to be contested that the Constitution controls any legislative act repugnant to it, or that the Legislature may alter the Constitution by an ordinary act.

Between these alternatives there is no middle ground. The Constitution is either a superior, paramount law, unchangeable by ordinary means, or it is on a level with ordinary legislative acts, and, like other acts, is alterable when the legislature shall please to alter it.

If the former part of the alternative be true, then a legislative act contrary to the Constitution is not law; if the latter part be true, then written Constitutions are absurd attempts on the part of the people to limit a power in its own nature illimitable.

Certainly all those who have framed written Constitutions contemplate them as forming the fundamental and paramount law of the nation, and consequently the theory of every such government must be that an act of the Legislature repugnant to the Constitution is void.

This theory is essentially attached to a written Constitution, and is consequently to be considered by this Court as one of the fundamental principles of our society. It is not, therefore, to be lost sight of in the further consideration of this subject.

If an act of the Legislature repugnant to the Constitution is void, does it, notwithstanding its invalidity, bind the Courts and oblige them to give it effect? Or, in other words, though it be not law, does it constitute a rule as operative as if it was a law? This would be to overthrow in fact what was established in theory, and would seem, at first view, an absurdity too gross to be insisted on. It shall, however, receive a more attentive consideration.

It is emphatically the province and duty of the Judicial Department to say what the law is. Those who apply the rule to particular cases must, of necessity, expound and interpret that rule. If two laws conflict with each other, the Courts must decide on the operation of each.

So, if a law be in opposition to the Constitution, if both the law and the Constitution apply to a particular case, so that the Court must either decide that case conformably to the law, disregarding the Constitution, or conformably to the Constitution, disregarding the law, the Court must determine which of these conflicting rules governs the case. This is of the very essence of judicial duty.

If, then, the Courts are to regard the Constitution, and the Constitution is superior to any ordinary act of the Legislature, the Constitution, and not such ordinary act, must govern the case to which they both apply.

Those, then, who controvert the principle that the Constitution is to be considered in court as a paramount law are reduced to the necessity of maintaining that courts must close their eyes on the Constitution, and see only the law.

This doctrine would subvert the very foundation of all written Constitutions. It would declare that an act which, according to the principles and theory of our government, is entirely void, is yet, in practice, completely obligatory. It would declare that, if the Legislature shall do what is expressly forbidden, such act, notwithstanding the express prohibition, is in reality effectual. It would be giving to the Legislature a practical and real omnipotence with the same breath which professes to restrict their powers within narrow limits. It is prescribing limits, and declaring that those limits may be passed at pleasure.

That it thus reduces to nothing what we have deemed the greatest improvement on political institutions—a written Constitution, would of itself be sufficient, in America where written Constitutions have been viewed with so much reverence, for rejecting the construction. But the peculiar expressions of the Constitution of the United States furnish additional arguments in favour of its rejection.

The judicial power of the United States is extended to all cases arising under the Constitution.

Could it be the intention of those who gave this power to say that, in using it, the Constitution should not be looked into? That a case arising under the Constitution should be decided without examining the instrument under which it arises?

This is too extravagant to be maintained.

In some cases then, the Constitution must be looked into by the judges. And if they can open it at all, what part of it are they forbidden to read or to obey?

There are many other parts of the Constitution which serve to illustrate this subject.

It is declared that "no tax or duty shall be laid on articles exported from any State." Suppose a duty on the export of cotton, of tobacco, or of flour, and a suit instituted to recover it. Ought judgment to be rendered in such a case? ought the judges to close their eyes on the Constitution, and only see the law?

The Constitution declares that "no bill of attainder or *ex post facto* law shall be passed."

If, however, such a bill should be passed and a person should be prosecuted under it, must the Court condemn to death those victims whom the Constitution endeavours to preserve?

"No person," says the Constitution, "shall be convicted of treason unless on the testimony of two witnesses to the same overt act, or on confession in open court."

Here, the language of the Constitution is addressed especially to the Courts. It prescribes, directly for them, a rule of evidence not to be departed from. If the Legislature should change that rule, and declare one witness, or a confession out of court, sufficient for conviction, must the constitutional principle yield to the legislative act?

From these and many other selections which might be made, it is apparent that the framers of the Constitution contemplated that instrument as a rule for the government of courts, as well as of the Legislature.

Why otherwise does it direct the judges to take an oath to support it? This oath certainly applies in an especial manner to their conduct in their official character. How immoral to impose it on them if they were to be used as the instruments, and the knowing instruments, for violating what they swear to support!

The oath of office, too, imposed by the Legislature, is completely demonstrative of the legislative opinion on this subject. It is in these words:

"I do solemnly swear that I will administer justice without respect to persons, and do equal right to the poor and to the rich; and that I will faithfully and impartially discharge all the duties incumbent on me as according to the best of my abilities and understanding, agreeably to the Constitution and laws of the United States."

Why does a judge swear to discharge his duties agreeably to the Constitution of the United States if that Constitution forms no rule for his government? if it is closed upon him and cannot be inspected by him?

If such be the real state of things, this is worse than solemn mockery. To prescribe or to take this oath becomes equally a crime.

It is also not entirely unworthy of observation that, in declaring what shall be the supreme law of the land, the Constitution itself is first mentioned, and not the laws of the United States generally, but those only which shall be made in pursuance of the Constitution, have that rank.

Thus, the particular phraseology of the Constitution of the United States confirms and strengthens the principle, supposed to be essential to all written Constitutions, that a law repugnant to the Constitution is void, and that courts, as well as other departments, are bound by that instrument.

The rule must be discharged.

Appendix II

Stuart v. Laird 5 U.S. (1 Cranch) 299

ERROR TO THE FIFTH CIRCUIT OF THE VIRGINIA DISTRICT

MR. CHIEF JUSTICE Marshall having tried the cause in the court below, declined giving an opinion.

MR. JUSTICE PATERSON delivered the opinion of the Court.

On an action instituted by John Laird against Hugh Stuart, a judgment was entered in a Court for the Fourth Circuit in the Eastern District of Virginia, in December term, 1801. On this judgment, an execution was issued, returnable to April term, 1802, in the same court. In the term of December, 1802, John Laird obtained judgment at a Court for the Fifth Circuit in the Virginia District against Hugh Stuart and Charles L. Carter upon their bond for the forthcoming and delivery of certain property therein mentioned, which had been levied upon by virtue of the above execution against the said Hugh Stuart.

Two reasons have been assigned by counsel for reversing the judgment on the forthcoming bond. 1. That as the bond was given for the delivery of property levied on by virtue of an execution issuing out of, and returnable to a court for the Fourth Circuit, no other court could legally proceed upon the said bond. This is true if there be no statutable provision to direct and authorize such proceeding. Congress has constitutional authority to establish from time to time such inferior tribunals as they may think proper and to transfer a cause from one such tribunal to another. In this last particular, there are no words in the Constitution to prohibit or restrain the exercise of legislative power.

The present is a case of this kind. It is nothing more than the removal of the suit brought by Stuart against Laird from the Court of the Fourth Circuit to the Court of the Fifth Circuit, which is authorized to proceed upon and carry it into full effect. This is apparent from the ninth section of the act entitled "An act to amend the judicial system of the United States," passed 29 April, 1802. The forthcoming bond is an appendage to the cause, or rather a component part of the proceedings.

2. Another reason for reversal is that the judges of the Supreme Court have no right to sit as circuit judges, not being appointed as such, or in other words, that they ought to have distinct commissions for that purpose. To this objection, which is of recent date, it is sufficient to observe that practice and acquiescence under it for a period of several years, commencing with the organization of the judicial system, afford an irresistible answer and have indeed fixed the construction. It is a contemporary interpretation of the most forcible nature. This practical exposition is too strong and obstinate to be shaken or controlled. Of course the question is at rest, and ought not now to be disturbed.

Judgment affirmed.

NOTES

ONE: LAW AND POLITICS

1 Scalia speech quoted at http://www.courttv.com/archive/legaldocs/rights/scalia.html.

2 Functionally, there was no difficulty, as the Court was not in session at the time.

3 Letter to John Dickinson, December 19, 1801, found at http://memory.loc.gov/master/mss/mtj/mtj1/025/0200/0291.jpg.

4 The three others were Dennis Ramsay, Robert Townsend Hooe, and William Harper.

5 There has also been widespread speculation that the suit was a put-up job by Federalists, as part of a strategy to use the courts to thwart Jefferson.

6 The final sentence of Section 13 reads: "The Supreme Court shall also have appellate jurisdiction from the circuit courts and courts of the several states, in the cases hereinafter specially provided for; and shall have power to issue writs of prohibition to the district courts, when proceeding as courts of admiralty and maritime jurisdiction, and writs of *mandamus*, in cases warranted by the principles and usages of law, to any courts appointed, or persons holding office, under the authority of the United States."

7 Yale law professor Bruce Ackerman has claimed that Marshall's decision created a "new" Constitution.

8 He should have declined even to sit on the case, as he had been a party to it. Marshall did in fact recuse himself from a companion case, *Stuart v. Laird*, which had promised to be far more incendiary.

9 "The man who made the Court supreme" was coined by Marshall biographer Albert Beveridge.

10 The Court was far less confrontational in *Stuart*, but in that case it acted without the chief justice.

11 Elkins and McKitrick, *Age of Federalism*, p. 234.

TWO: CONVENTION: A FEW GOOD MEN

1 The convention had been called for May 14, but only representatives from Pennsylvania and Virginia were present, so the meeting was adjourned.

2 http://www.archives.gov/national-archives-experience/charters/constitution_founding_fathers_overview.html.

3 The only provision in the Articles for national courts was in adjudicating prize cases—ownership, and disposition of ships taken on the high seas.

4 Not every state had an executive per se.

5 Shays's Rebellion had aimed at just this.

6 Farrand, v. 1, p. 29.

7 *Ibid.*, v. 1, p. 244.

8 *Ibid.*, v. 1, p. 124; Paterson and Rutledge agreed on little else.

9 *Ibid.*

10 Article III, Section 2, Clause 1 reads: "The judicial Power shall extend to all Cases, in Law and Equity, arising under this Constitution, the Laws of the United States, and Treaties made, or which shall be made, under their Authority;—to all Cases affecting Ambassadors, other public Ministers and Consuls;—to all Cases of admiralty and maritime Jurisdiction;—to Controversies to which the United States shall be a Party;—to Controversies between two or more States;—between a State and Citizens of another State;—between Citizens of different States;—between Citizens of the same State claiming Lands under Grants of different States, and between a State, or the Citizens thereof, and foreign States, Citizens or Subjects."

11 Robert Lowry Clinton, for example, stated categorically that "the idea of limiting legislative power by judicial nonapplication of statutes in certain cases was clearly understood" (Clinton, p. 56). Forrest McDonald asserted that there was "general agreement" that the courts would "have the power to strike down legislative acts if they were in violation of the Constitution" (*Novus Ordo Seclorum*, p. 254).

12 McDonald noted that "at least delegates of widely divergent political views . . . asserted that the courts would have such power and no one argued to the contrary" (*ibid.*).

13 http://www.yale.edu/lawweb/avalon/virginia.htm.

14 *Ibid.*

15 http://www.mass.gov/legis/const.htm.

16 *Ibid.*

17 A council of revision was one of Madison's favored notions. He fought for it long and hard, but it was ultimately rejected by the delegates.

18 Beveridge is among the few who recognized the distinction. "No words in the Constitution gave the Judiciary the power to annul legislation. The subject had been discussed . . . but the brief and scattering debate had arisen upon the proposition to make the President and Justices of the Supreme Court members of a Council of

Revision with power to negative [sic; this word meant "negate" or "veto" at the time] acts of Congress. No direct resolution was ever offered to the effect that the Judiciary should be given power to declare acts of Congress unconstitutional" (Beveridge, v. III, pp. 114–15).

19 Farrand, v. 1, p. 21. Significantly, section 8 of the plan is listed after that which defines the executive (section 7) but before the judiciary (section 9), a clear indication that Madison, although the council of revision would contain judges, considered it distinct from the judiciary itself. The exact wording is: "The Executive and a convenient number of the National Judiciary, ought to compose a Council of revision with authority to examine every act of the National Legislature before it shall operate, & every act of a particular Legislature before a Negative thereon shall be final; and that the dissent of the said Council shall amount to a rejection, unless the Act of the National Legislature be again passed, or that of a particular Legislature be again negatived by [blank] of the members of each branch."

20 This debate is in Farrand, v. 1, pp. 97–103.

21 Mason claimed that he would have less concern if the executive consisted of more than one person. "If more than one had been fixed on, greater powers might have been entrusted to the Executive. He hoped the attempt to give such powers would have its weight hereafter as an argument for increasing the number of the Executive."

22 Since Virginia only had six delegates at the Convention (George Wythe had gone home due to illness), Madison and Mason, the state's two most powerful delegates, were unable to persuade a single colleague, including Edmund Randolph, the titular author of the Virginia Plan, to support a Council of Revision instead. Had even one other Virginian voted no, the state's vote would have been "divided."

23 This debate is in Farrand, v. 2, pp. 73–80.

24 Martin later served for thirty years as Maryland's attorney general and represented his state, unsuccessfully, in another of Marshall's cataclysmic decisions, *McCulloch v. Maryland.*

25 But Luther Martin left the convention in disgust at the end of August to become an opponent of the Constitution in the Maryland ratifying debates. Yet, despite the source, this statement is also cited as proof of the delegates' acceptance of judicial review (Clinton, p. 60).

26 Madison made clear the following year that he viewed a council of revision as necessarily encompassing both branches. "A revisionary power is meant as a check to precipitate, to unjust, and to unconstitutional laws. These important ends would it is conceded be more effectually secured, without disarming the Legislature of its requisite authority, by requiring bills to be separately communicated to the Exec: & Judicy depts[.] If either of these object, let ⅔, if both ¾ of each House be necessary to overrule the objection; and if either or both protest agst a bill as violating the

Constitution, let it moreover be suspended notwithstanding the overruling proportion of the Assembly, until there shall have been a subsequent election of the H. of
Ds and a re-passage of the bill by ⅔ or ¾ of both Houses, as the case may be. It sd
not be allowed the Judges or ye. Executive to pronounce a law thus enacted uncon-
stitul & invalid. In the State Constitutions & indeed in the Fedl one also, no provision is made for the case of a disagreement in expounding them; and as the
Courts are generally the last in making ye decision, it results to them by refusing or
not refusing to execute a law, to stamp it with its final character. This makes the Judiciary Dept paramount in fact to the Legislature, which was never intended
and can never be proper." Madison, October 1788: "Observations on the 'Draught
of a Constitution for Virginia'": http://memory.loc.gov/cgi-bin/query/r?ammem/
mjmtext:@FIELD(DOCID+@lit(jmo50096)).

27 Levy, *Original Intent*, p. 100.

28 Farrand, v. 2, p. 177.

29 *Ibid.*, v. 2, p. 590.

30 Morris himself never let on.

31 Quoted in Storing, v. 2, p. 39. Emphasis from the original.

32 Elliot, v. 3, p. 22.

THREE: TO THE STATES: THE STRUGGLE TO RATIFY BEGINS

1 The record of the Pennsylvania incident is extensive and detailed in McMaster and
Stone, p. 64. The authenticity of the New Hampshire lunch may be apocryphal, but
is nonetheless lavishly recounted in McDonald, *E Pluribus Unum*, pp. 353–54.

2 Except for Pennsylvania, these were all "small" states that had come to the Constitutional Convention opposed to scrapping the Articles until the Connecticut compromise ensured their support by granting by-state voting in the Senate.

3 It was also the home of ferocious opponents of the Constitution, such as Patrick
Henry, George Mason, and Richard Henry Lee.

4 Elliot, v. 3, p. 626.

5 The lunch at which Anti-Federalist delegates were allegedly given copious
amounts of spirits may or may not have enabled the Federalist victory.

6 On June 25, the record in the Virginia ratifying convention reads: "*New Hampshire*
does not approve of the Constitution as it stands . . . *North Carolina* is decidedly
against it . . . *New York*, we have every reason to believe, will reject the Constitution, unless amendments be obtained . . . *Rhode Island* is not worthy the attention
of this house. She is of no weight or importance to influence any general subject of
consequence" (Elliot, v. 3, p. 628).

7 Times change. Fauquier County, only about forty miles west of Washington, D.C.,
is now filled with upscale bedroom suburbs, populated largely by men and women
who work in the capital.

8 Marshall never produced a full autobiography but, in 1827, at age seventy-two, penned an abbreviated account of his life for his friend and fellow justice Joseph Story.

9 In the late seventeenth and early eighteenth centuries, eligible women of good breeding far outnumbered men. As a result, there were any number of opportunities for solid, hard-working men like Thomas Marshall to improve their lots.

10 J. Smith, p. 23.

11 Marshall, p. 13.

12 *Ibid.*

13 J. Smith, p. 64.

14 When Marshall was sixteen, Thomas took a newly arrived pastor into his home; this man helped tutor the boy, introducing him to Livy and Horace. Marshall, p. 13.

15 J. Smith, p. 33.

16 Marshall, p. 15.

17 J. Smith, p. 61.

18 *Ibid.*, p. 64.

19 Marshall, p. 15.

20 *Ibid.*, p. 16.

21 J. Smith, pp. 84–85.

22 *Ibid.*, p. 75.

23 The Virginia House of Burgesses was renamed in 1776 and became the lower house of the Virginia Assembly.

24 Beveridge, v. 1, p. 205.

25 Marshall, p. 16.

26 To differentiate it from Henry's "populist" faction (J. Smith, p. 90).

27 Quoted in J. Smith, p. 95. The entire affair is also from Smith, pp. 93–96. Beveridge, as Smith points out with obvious satisfaction, "apparently was unaware of the council of state's decision."

28 William Blackstone, *Commentaries*, Introduction, Sec. III, pp. 90–91; www.yale.edu/lawweb/avalon/blackstone/introa.htm#3.

29 *Ibid.*

30 *Ibid.*

31 Charles de Secondat, Baron de Montesquieu, the great eighteenth-century political philosopher.

32 Montesquieu, *Spirit*, Book XI, Section 6; www.constitution.org/cm/sol_11.htm.

33 *Ibid.*

34 J. Smith, p. 95.

35 *Ibid.*, p. 96.

36 Marshall's use of the council as a vehicle for personal advancement caused Thomas Jefferson to propose abolishing the body "so that it would no longer provide a stepping-stone for 'young and ambitious men'" (quoted in J. Smith, p. 97).

37 Beveridge, v. 1, p. 212.
38 As Jean Smith points out, this was to be his only judicial experience until his elevation to the Supreme Court (p. 105).

FOUR: MAKING A NEW NATION: RATIFICATION IN VIRGINIA

1 McDonald, *E Pluribus Unum*, p. 357.
2 Elliot, v. 3, p. 60.
3 *Ibid.*, v. 3, p. 86.
4 *Ibid.*, v. 3, p. 517.
5 *Ibid.*
6 Although he would not cite these debates in his opinion, this was precisely the reasoning that Chief Justice Marshall would employ in his *Marbury* decision.
7 Elliot, v. 3, p. 551.
8 *Ibid.*, v. 3, p. 552.
9 *Ibid.*
10 *Ibid.*
11 Many would argue that the federal judiciary has done just that.
12 Elliot, v. 3, p. 553. Emphasis added.
13 *Ibid.*, p. 554.

FIVE: UNITING A NEW NATION: RATIFICATION IN NEW YORK

1 Ford, v. 34, p. 281.
2 Yates had also cast the sole dissenting vote against the Northwest Ordinance the year before.
3 Ford, p. 282.
4 According to Forrest McDonald, Anti-Federalists held a 46–19 majority when the convention began (*E Pluribus Unum*, p. 360).
5 Elliot, v. 1, p. 480.
6 Brutus 1. October 18, 1787. http://www.liberty-page.com/foundingdocs/antifedpap/brutus/1.html.
7 *Ibid.*
8 *Ibid.*
9 It never was revealed. Although no definitive evidence has been uncovered, it is now generally assumed that Brutus was that same Robert Yates who had left Philadelphia in anger the previous July.
10 Unlike Brutus's essays, all of which appeared in the *Journal*, the Publius essays appeared in a number of different periodicals, including the *Independent Journal*, the *New York Packet*, the *Daily Advertiser*, and McLean's *Edition*.
11 Clinton Rossiter in Madison et al., *The Federalist or The New Constitution*, p. vii.

12 Chernow states, "The Federalist is so renowned as the foremost exposition of the Constitution that it is easy to forget its original aim: ratification in [New York]" (p. 261).

13 Hamilton's attribution of specific essays turned out to be somewhat inaccurate. He ascribed numbers 2–5 and 54 to Jay, when it should have been 64; but far more significantly, he took credit for fourteen essays that had almost certainly been written either entirely or in large part by Madison. The controversy as to who actually wrote what has raged for the better part of two centuries.

14 Madison et al., p. 33.

15 *Ibid.*

16 Brutus 11. January 31, 1788. http://www.liberty-page.com/foundingdocs/antifedpap/brutus/11.html.

17 Brutus 15. March 20, 1788. http://www.liberty-page.com/foundingdocs/antifedpap/brutus/15.html.

18 *Ibid.*

19 Brutus 11. January 31, 1788. http://www.liberty-page.com/foundingdocs/antifedpap/brutus/11.html.

20 *Ibid.*

21 Madison et al., p. 464.

22 *Ibid.*, pp. 465–66.

23 *Ibid.*, p. 467.

24 *Ibid.*, p. 468.

25 *Ibid.*, p. 469.

26 Elliot, v. 2, pp. 410–11. Emphasis in original.

27 *Ibid.*, p. 412.

28 *Ibid.*, pp. 413–14.

SIX: TRANSITION: CONGRESS IS TRANSFORMED AND SO IS MADISON

1 In addition, both states had submitted a bill of rights, Virginia's containing an additional twenty articles.

2 Ketcham, p. 275.

3 *Ibid.*

4 Madison to Edmund Randolph, November 23, 1788. http://memory.loc.gov/cgi-bin/query/r?ammem/mjmtext:@FIELD(DOCID+@lit(jmo50100)).

5 Madison to Madison Sr., December 18, 1788. http://memory.loc.gov/master/mss/mjm/03/0800/0871.jpg.

6 Nicholas to Madison, January 2, 1789. http://memory.loc.gov/cgi-bin/query/D?mjm:11:./temp/~ammem_kMZz::.

7 Madison to Eve, January 2, 1789. http://memory.loc.gov/cgi-bin/query/D?mjm:12:./temp/~ammem_kMZz::.

8   According to Article II, Section 1, each elector was allowed two votes, one for president and one for vice president, although he was not required to specify which office each of his votes was for. That voting scheme would result in a good deal of mischief in the election of 1800.

9   Pennsylvania's other senator was the financier Robert Morris, one of the best-known men in America, while Maclay was a virtual unknown, a surveyor, politician, and judge from the countryside. While Morris was a committed Federalist, Maclay was the opposite. Maclay would spend only two years in the Senate but, during that time, would keep a journal that has become a classic of American political history. Alternately scabrous, ironic, witty, self-righteous, and insightful, Maclay's journal provides as much a quotidian account of the First Congress as Samuel Pepys did with respect to Restoration London. Why the obscure Maclay rather than Morris was appointed to these committees is unknown, but history is richer as a result.

10 *Senate Journal*, April 7, 1789.

11 Izard, Lee, and Wingate had no legal training or experience at all. Carroll, Maclay, Few, and Bassett had either studied the law or practiced it, but none was in any way a scholar or theoretician (Goebel, p. 458).

12 Most of what we know of the committee's early progress has been gleaned from Maclay's journal and letters written by various members to friends back home, although even here information is scant (*ibid.*, pp. 459–61).

13 Maclay, p. 33. Maclay did not name the members, but there is other evidence of their appointment, not the least of which is that the bill that emerged was in the handwriting of the three men.

14 *Ibid.*, p. 75.

15 Goebel called it "a playbill."

16 The bill was lengthy, consisting of thirty-five sections, and contained numerous ambiguities and controversial provisions. Entire books have been written analyzing this piece of legislation. This study, however, will confine itself to those portions of the bill that will bear on the events of 1801–1803.

17 Quoted in Goebel, pp. 472 f.

18 Baker, Supreme Court Historical Society, 1977 Yearbook. http://www .supremecourthistory.org/myweb/77journal/baker77.htm.

19 Maclay, p. 85.

20 *Ibid.*

21 *Ibid.*

22 *Ibid.*, p. 95.

23 *Ibid.*, p. 91.

24 Quoted in Goebel, p. 504.

25 The national debate over amendments and the eventual passage of the Bill of Rights are fascinating, but are beyond the purview of this book. For a good

narrative history, see Labunski; or, for a deeper, more scholarly take, see Amar, *Bill of Rights*.

26 Hamilton's attempt in 1804 to deny Madison's authorship of many of the *Federalist* essays is completely understandable in this light.

27 These amendments involved a good deal more than individual liberties. Some were structural and some related to issues of federalism. Before the amendment debate was finished, virtually every article of the Constitution was reexamined. In some respects, the amendment debate was the *de facto* second convention that Anti-Federalists had been clamoring for.

28 *Annals*, v. 1, p. 441.

29 *Ibid.*, v. 1, p. 447.

30 *Ibid.*, p. 448.

31 *Ibid.*, v. 1, pp. 685–86.

32 During this debate, Roger Sherman proposed that any amendments be included as a supplement, so that the original wording of the Constitution would remain for posterity. His motion passed on August 19.

33 *Annals*, v. 1, p. 755.

34 The first two, one dealing with congressional size and the other with congressional compensation, failed, although the 27th Amendment reinstituted the second. Thus, the current first amendment was originally the third.

35 *Annals*, v. 1, pp. 812–15.

36 *Ibid.*, pp. 826–51.

37 *Ibid.*, p. 835.

38 *Ibid.*, p. 851.

39 Ellsworth, Paterson, Madison, Robert Morris, Roger Sherman, Elbridge Gerry, Rufus King, Pierce Butler. Other, less important, Philadelphia delegates were present as well, including Abraham Baldwin, Thomas Fitzsimons, Nicholas Gilman, John Langdon, George Read, George Clymer, Hugh Williamson, Richard Bassett, Daniel Carroll, William Few, William Samuel Johnson, and Caleb Strong.

40 Except for the brief period discussed in subsequent chapters, the Judiciary Act of 1789 remained in force until supplanted by the Judiciary Act of 1891. Circuit-riding was thus not permanently abolished until that year.

SEVEN: A LONG AND FRUSTRATING RIDE: JAY TAKES THE REINS

1 Quoted in Warren, v. 1, p. 34.

2 Quoted in *ibid.*, v. 1, pp. 32–33.

3 *Ibid.*, p. 32.

4 *Ibid.*, v. 1, p. 37.

5 With North Carolina joined, Washington was thus able to line up the three circuits with two resident justices for each.

6 Rutledge stewed over the slight for the next five years, even carping in letters to friends, none of which prevented Washington from nominating him for chief justice when Jay resigned in 1795.

7 Previously the Royal Exchange.

8 www.supremecourthistory.org/02_history/subs_sites/02_d.html.

9 Warren, v. 2, p. 86.

10 *Ibid.*, v. 1, p. 58.

11 The Supreme Court would take up much the same question five years later in *Ware v. Hylton*, perhaps the most important pre-Marshall case extant, if for no other reason than that Marshall, appearing for the defense, argued against supremacy of the national government.

12 Warren, v. 1, p. 66.

13 When Marshall, in another of his landmark cases, *McCulloch v. Maryland*, permanently established the primacy of the national government over the states in 1819, he pointedly avoided using any of the Jay court's decisions as precedent. Marshall was notorious about wanting to be seen as creating his sculptures from scratch, fundamental law, and logic, so perhaps he simply avoided giving Jay credit. Equally possible, however, was that he did not consider any of these precedents sufficient to buttress his argument.

14 Federal Judges Association, Tuesday, May 8, 2000. www.supremecourtus.gov/publicinfo/speeches/sp_05-08-01.html.

15 So minimal was his participation that he is not even listed as an associate on the Supreme Court Historical Society Web site.

16 There was neither a Constitutional nor statutory prohibition against his doing so.

17 *Statutes*, 2nd Congress, 1st Session, p. 253.

18 But only after some fancy legal footwork. See Casto, pp. 175–76.

19 2 US 409.

20 *Ibid.* Other circuit courts had attempted to alternately express grave doubts about the propriety of the role and dance around the issue.

21 Johnson made a sound decision, as it turned out, since he lived for another twenty-six years, dying at the age of eighty-six in 1819, Supreme Court justices continuing to ride circuit all the while.

22 *Statutes*, 2nd Congress, 2nd Session, p. 333.

23 By statute, this amount was equal to $500,000.

24 Casto notes that Iredell's "entire opinion may be plausibly explained as a determination to hold the states immune without regard to the apparent meaning of the applicable constitutional and statutory provisions" (p. 190).

25 2 US 453.

26 Casto, p. 192.

27 2 US 471.

28 *Ibid.*, p. 474.

29 Which of the three branches of government represented "the people" had been a continuing question. Almost no one used that term with respect to the indirectly elected executive. Republicans tended toward the legislative, but Federalists, particularly when advocating judicial oversight, would apply the term to the courts. Representing "the people" would thus become a prime justification for Marshall in declaring that the courts were the branch "to say what the law is."

30 *Senate Journal*, February 20, 1793.

EIGHT: ONCE AND FUTURE CHIEFS: JAY AND MARSHALL COLLIDE

1 In 1789, Marshall serviced more than three hundred clients (J. Smith, p. 145).

2 Marshall's role is ably defined in J. Smith, pp. 155–56.

3 Quoted in Stahr, p. 298.

4 *Ibid.*

5 Beveridge, v. 2, p. 188.

6 Marshall's performance was roundly praised, including a high compliment from a British aristocrat who happened to be in the audience (J. Smith, p. 157).

NINE: A QUESTION OF PRIORITIES: THE ABSENT CHIEF JUSTICE

1 Chernow, p. 434.

2 Another of the four cases concerned state sovereignty, again featuring Georgia. With the Eleventh Amendment working its way through the system, Jay this time ruled in Georgia's favor.

3 Warren, pp. 116–17.

4 *Ibid.*

5 There is ongoing disagreement as to whether Jay accepted eagerly or with reluctance. Stahr (pp. 324–25) and Warren (v. 1, p. 125) indicate the latter, but other sources, including former Chief Justice Warren Burger, suggest the former (http://www.supremecourthistory.org/04_library/subs_volumes/04_c12_e.html). Subsequent events would demonstrate that Burger was probably correct.

6 The regular Senate session had ended on March 4, but a special session, by the newly elected 4th Congress, had been called on June 8 to discuss the treaty; it ran until June 26.

7 Warren, v. 1, p. 129.

8 *Ibid.*, v. 1, pp. 130–31. Tales of Rutledge's mental state became more and more outrageous. One rumor had him eating gavels.

9 Rutledge did not resign until December 28, before which there were reports that he attempted suicide. He left public life and died five years later.

TEN: A TASTE OF THE FUTURE: MARSHALL VISITS THE COURT

1   3 US 210.
2   *Ibid.*, pp. 210–11.
3   *Ibid.*, p. 213.
4   *Ibid.*
5   *Ibid.*
6   Iredell submitted an opinion based on notes, asserting once more that the plaintiffs had no recourse to the individual, but only to Virginia.
7   3 US 244–45.
8   *Ibid.*, p. 282.
9   Marshall, p. 22.

ELEVEN: YANKEES WIN: ELLSWORTH AT THE HELM

1   Stephens Mason of Virginia was the only nay, significant because Mason, a soon-to-be Republican, demonstrated the fault lines in Washington's Federalism that would rupture in the coming years.
2   Warren, v. 1, p. 153.

TWELVE: AS SIMPLE AS XYZ: MARSHALL ASCENDANT

1   Elkins and McKitrick, p. 542.
2   Marshall, p. 23.
3   J. Smith, pp. 185–86.
4   The eccentric, idiosyncratic Gerry has been roundly vilified for his behavior in Paris, but he proved every bit as frustrating to Talleyrand as Talleyrand had been to the delegation. See Elkins and McKitrick, pp. 537–79.
5   *Ibid.*, p. 570.

THIRTEEN: FIRST IN QUASI-WAR: ADAMS ON A TIGHTROPE

1   There were other reasons for the rift as well, of course, but the Sedition Act does seem to have pushed many Republicans over the edge. As to marching on Washington, see Ackerman, Chapter 4.
2   Quoted in J. Smith, p. 245.
3   Smith, p. 242.
4   *Statutes at Large*, 5th Congress, 2nd Session, p. 572.
5   *Ibid.*, p. 574.
6   *Ibid.*, 5th Congress, 3rd Session, p. 716.
7   4 US 39. This was to be Moore's only written opinion as a member of the Court.
8   *Ibid.*, p. 40.
9   *Ibid.*, pp. 41–43.

10 Since Section 1 of the Judiciary Act of 1789 required the presence of four justices for a quorum, Chase was forced to file an opinion.

11 He didn't own up to the real reason, of course, but said instead, "The Judges agreeing unanimously in their opinion, I presumed that the sense of the Court would have been delivered by the president; and therefore, I have not prepared a formal argument on the occasion" (4 US 44).

12 *Ibid.*, p. 45.

Fourteen: Default Judgment: Marshall to the Bench

1 *Bills and Resolutions*, 6th Congress, 33:1–44.

2 *Ibid.*, 6th Congress, 53.

3 Quoted in Dewey, p. 52.

4 Chernow, p. 608.

5 For the best discussions, see Ferling and Chernow.

6 Quoted in Chernow, p. 609.

7 *Ibid.* Had Jay done so, Adams would have been reelected, as it turned out.

8 Hamilton, born in the West Indies, could not be president.

9 Elkins and McKitrick, pp. 735–36.

10 Grant, p. 424. Lack of moral principle might be subjective, but as to the second epithet there could be no doubt.

11 *Senate Executive Journal.* 1st Congress, 2nd Session, May 7, 1800.

12 *Ibid.*, May 12, 1800.

13 *Ibid.*

14 *Papers of Alexander Hamilton*, v. 24, p. 573, quoted in Chernow, p. 615.

15 Ferling, p. 137.

16 It is a testament to a simpler time that the entire store of government documents and records fit into seven packing cases (Ferling, p. 137).

17 Quoted in Ketchum, p. 408. Only the towns of Georgetown, on the Maryland side of the Potomac, and Alexandria, across the river, had been settled previously.

18 *Senate Journal*, 6th Congress, 2nd Session, November 22, 1800.

19 *Ibid.*

20 Jefferson to Madison, December 19, 1800. http://memory.loc.gov/cgi-bin/am-page?collId=mjm&fileName=25/mjm25.db&recNum=622&itemLink=D?mjm:3:./temp/~ammem_FCOh::

21 Ferling, p. 171.

22 *Ibid.*, p. 172.

23 Civil war is not an overstatement. Later in the crisis, troops actually massed to thwart any attempt by Federalists to remain in power. See Ackerman, Chapter 4.

24 Ackerman, p. 122.

25 Quoted in Stahr, p. 363.

26 Jefferson to Madison, December 19, 1800. *op cit.*

27 http://memory.loc.gov/master/mss/mjm/25/0600/0627d.jpg.

28 Stahr, p. 364.

29 Dewey, p. 51.

30 Marshall had earlier suggested Associate Justice William Paterson for the post, but Adams had categorically refused to consider a man he viewed as a political enemy.

31 Marshall, p. 29.

32 *House Journal*, January 20, 1801.

33 *Ibid.*

34 Quoted in J. Smith, p. 285. John Randolph later referred to the chamber as "the cave of Trophonius."

35 J. Smith, p. 283.

Fifteen: Two Bills: Adams's Last Stand

1 *Annals*, 6th Congress, House, January 5, 1801. The House stayed with two districts, but divided them by latitude instead of longitude.

2 *Ibid.*, January 7, 1801.

3 *Ibid.*, January 5, 1801.

4 Lewis Morris, Federalist of Vermont.

5 *Annals*, 6th Congress, House, February 10, 1801.

6 As Bruce Ackerman points out in his excellent *Failure of the Founding Fathers*, during the reading, an additional unforeseen scenario was manifested when, due to technical irregularities with the signatures, Georgia's ballot was found not to conform to constitutional standards. The ballot could—and probably should—have therefore been disallowed, thus denying Jefferson and Burr a majority and most likely the election. (If no candidate received a majority, Adams, Pinckney, and even Jay would have joined Jefferson and Burr as the top five vote-getters and been thrown back in the mix. The Federalist House could have then chosen a Federalist President.) Jefferson, however, conveniently ignoring the phrase "conflict of interest," chose to accept the ballot, thereby allowing the subsequent drama to play out (pp. 59–74).

7 *Annals*, 6th Congress, House, February 11, 1801.

8 *Ibid.*

9 *Ibid.*

10 2 *Statutes* 89–100.

11 *Annals*, 6th Congress, House, February 17, 1801.

12 For an excellent and compelling account, see Ferling, pp. 187–93, although his record of the votes does not always agree with the House record, and Ackerman, pp. 80–108.

13 Ferling, pp. 194–96. Jefferson later claimed to have turned down any quid pro quo, although recent scholarship has cast doubt on his claim of innocence.

14 Ferling reports that his fellows screamed "Traitor, traitor" (p. 191).

15 Forte, p. 353.

16 2 *Statutes* 103–8.

17 James Madison to Thomas Jefferson, February 28, 1801. Library of Congress, James Madison Papers.

18 As Dewey pointed out, there were only 15,265 residents of the District, about one fifth of whom were slaves, so "President Adams was thoughtfully providing these counties with a justice of the peace for every 363–½ persons, irrespective of age, sex, color, or condition of servitude" (p. 76).

19 Thus, for all the mischief that the Judiciary Act of 1801 was to engender, it was not, contrary to popular conception, in any way responsible for judicial review. William Marbury had no connection with that piece of legislation. He received his appointment under the District of Columbia Act.

20 Stoddert was considered one of the most able men in Adams's administration, and his presence on the list of appointees belies the accepted myth that Adams had appointed a bunch of nonentities to the posts. Laird would later figure in a crucial constitutional case of his own.

21 Forte, p. 353.

SIXTEEN: SUNSET AT MIDNIGHT

1 They were circuit court judges George Keith Taylor and William McClung and United States attorney Joseph Hamilton Daveiss.

2 The testimony was by clerks Jacob Wagner and Daniel Brent during the *Marbury* case, and there are, as will be seen, solid reasons for skepticism. Also, if Wagner and Brent were correct, there would have been a good deal of shuttling back and forth, for which no solid evidence exists.

3 Quoted in Dewey, p. 58.

4 Thomas Jefferson to Archibald Stuart, April 8, 1801. *The Works of Thomas Jefferson in Twelve Volumes.* Federal Edition. Collected and edited by Paul Leicester Ford.

5 Sharing the carriage was Adams's High Federalist nemesis, Theodore Sedgwick.

6 Quoted in Dewey, pp. 79–80.

7 Forte, pp. 357–58.

8 Standard, at least, for Federalists. Agrarian Republicans, who held little in paper assets, loathed the practice.

9 Forte, p. 363.

SEVENTEEN: THE NEW DAY

1 His conciliation was more public than private. That very day, after swearing in the new president, Marshall went home and wrote to Pinckney. Although conceding that Jefferson's inaugural was "well-judged and conciliatory," he added, "The

Democrats are divided into speculative theorists & absolute terrorists. With the latter I am disposed to class Mr. Jefferson" (Beveridge, v. 3, pp. 11, 18).

2 *Senate Journal*, 4 March 1801.

3 *Ibid.*, pp. 148–49. For a fuller analysis of Jefferson's inaugural, see Elkins and McKitrick.

4 While technically the 7th Congress, many of the new electees did not have time to make it to Washington City after Adams belatedly called a special session of the outgoing Congress to greet the new president. As a result, many of the deposed 6th congressmen sat in instead. Speculation that they would give Jefferson trouble with confirmations proved incorrect.

5 Jefferson to William B. Giles, March 23, 1801. *The Works of Thomas Jefferson in Twelve Volumes*. Federal Edition. Collected and edited by Paul Leicester Ford. Emphasis in original.

6 *Ibid.*

7 Thomas Jefferson to Archibald Stuart, April 8, 1801. Library of Congress, Thomas Jefferson Papers.

8 Thomas Jefferson to William Johnson, June 12, 1823. Library of Congress, Thomas Jefferson Papers.

9 *Ibid.*

EIGHTEEN: "BEYOND COMPARISON THE WEAKEST OF THE THREE": MARSHALL TAKES THE COURT

1 J. Smith, pp. 288–290.

2 4 US 1, p. 42.

3 4 US 1, p. 28.

4 5 US 1, p. 43.

5 For example, *Talbot* was cited in *Holtzman v. Schlesinger*, a Vietnam War case.

6 Thomas Jefferson to William Johnson, June 12, 1823. Library of Congress, Thomas Jefferson Papers.

NINETEEN: REPEAL: THE SEVENTH CONGRESS

1 Thomas Jefferson to Benjamin Rush, December 20, 1801. Library of Congress, Thomas Jefferson Papers.

2 *Senate Journal*, December 8, 1801.

3 *Ex post facto*, Latin for "from a thing done afterward," is a law that applies retroactively. The Constitution specifically bans *ex post facto* laws by Congress (Article I, Section 9) and the states (Article I, Section 10). Marshall's reasoning was, in fact, a justification of the very type of situation that the Constitution prohibited. So, once again, Marshall was not so much interpreting the Constitution as rewriting it.

4 Although Adams had signed the ratified treaty in February, Napoleon objected to the clause that seemed to promise reparations. Agreement had subsequently been reached, and Jefferson submitted the revised treaty to the Senate, where it had been ratified on December 19. Jefferson's signature on December 21 finally closed the book on the Convention of 1800.

5 J. Smith, p. 298.

6 *Senate Journal*, January 6, 1802.

7 Thomas Jefferson to Benjamin Rush, December 20, 1801. Library of Congress, Thomas Jefferson Papers.

8 Thomas Jefferson to John Dickinson, December 19, 1801. Library of Congress, Thomas Jefferson Papers.

9 *Annals*, 7th Congress, Senate, January 8, 1802, p. 28.

10 *Ibid.*, p. 30.

11 *Ibid.*, p. 39.

12 *Ibid.*

13 *Ibid.*, p. 31.

14 *Ibid.*, p. 25.

15 *Ibid.*

16 *Ibid.*, January 12, 1802, p. 55.

17 *Ibid.*, p. 56.

18 *Ibid.*, p. 57.

19 *Ibid.*, House, February 20, 1802, p. 659.

20 Quoted in Malone, p. 123.

21 *Annals*, 7th Congress, p. 145. States' Rights firebrand John C. Calhoun was Colhoun's cousin.

22 *Ibid.*

23 Colhoun's indecision is not surprising. Of all the states that had sent Republicans to the Senate for the first time in 1801, South Carolina had perhaps both the strongest Federalist tradition and the most active Federalist opposition.

24 *Annals*, 7th Congress, Senate, February 2, 1802, p. 148. Once again, congressional reporters transcribed in the third person.

25 *Ibid.*, pp. 148–49.

26 *Ibid.*, p. 150.

27 *Ibid.*, p. 160. As it turned out, Bradley's vote was unnecessary, as one Federalist senator, John Howard of Maryland, was absent. Colhoun again voted with the Federalists.

28 *Ibid.*, 178–79.

29 *Ibid.*, p. 179.

30 *Ibid.*, p. 180.

31 The importance of this exchange cannot be overstated. It is a clear rebuttal of Mc-Donald, Beveridge, and the myriad other historians who have claimed that, during the constitutional debates, judicial review was a tacitly understood power of the courts. Morris's failure to cite that fact, or even to refer to the Convention, is clear evidence that there was no such agreement in Philadelphia, but rather that judicial review was either a conscious omission by a group of delegates who expected to control the legislature in perpetuity or an issue they considered too hot to handle one way or another.

32 The District of Columbia circuit court, established under a different law, remained unaffected.

33 Beveridge claims that the entire debate was really about just this question; but, as an overt Federalist cheerleader, his opinions must be taken with many grains of salt (v. 3, pp. 102–10).

34 Hamilton had written to Bayard immediately after the repeal, suggesting that the legislation be tested in the Supreme Court as soon as possible (J. Smith, p. 305).

35 *Annals*, 7th Congress, p. 257; 2 *Statutes* 156.

36 Colhoun was absent for much of his remaining tenure, which ended prematurely on October 26, 1802, when he died at his home in South Carolina.

37 A motion in the House to add a Kentucky–Tennessee seventh circuit was defeated (*Annals*, 7th Congress, p. 1215).

38 It is impossible not to wonder how much of Bayard's passion was engendered by guilt over breaking the electoral deadlock thirteen months before.

39 *Annals*, 7th Congress, 1st Session, pp. 1235–1236.

40 He would consider circuit-riding an unconstitutional provision for the remainder of his life (Ackerman, p. 164).

41 J. Smith, p. 306.

42 As contrasted with his assertion in *Marbury* that "it is emphatically the province and duty of the judicial department to say what the law is."

43 J. Smith, p. 307. One reason for Morris's reaction was his belief that Marshall had previously voiced the exact opposite opinion, but whether Marshall had actually done so or Morris had simply been told he had is unclear.

44 According to Jean Smith, Marshall did this in a spirit of statesmanship, taking no position himself on whether the justices should effectively go on strike. Ackerman violently disagrees, citing compelling evidence that Marshall favored a refusal to ride circuit and transmitted those sentiments to his fellow Federalists, thus accounting in part for Morris's disgust with his later acquiescence (pp. 342–43). Beveridge acknowledged Marshall's desire to refuse the circuit-riding chore, calling it "heroic," but asserted that his fellows—doubtlessly excluding Chase—lacked the backbone to join him (v. 3, p. 122).

45 Warren, v. 1, p. 271.

46 Whatever sentiments Marshall had first expressed were now moot. Practical politics had, as they always would with Marshall, superseded ideology.

47 Roane, an outstanding legal theoretician and a bitter Marshall enemy, was at the time a member of the Virginia Supreme Court of Appeals. His Republican credentials had been made all the stronger by his marriage to Patrick Henry's daughter, Anne.

48 J. Smith, p. 307. The most substantial improvement in the more limited circuit-riding obligation then had existed under the 1789 act.

TWENTY: SUICIDE SQUEEZE: HAMILTON V. MARSHALL

1 A number of historians have referred to High Federalists as "irreconcilables." The word "obstructionist" has also been employed.

2 Richard Bassett, Bayard's father-in-law, penned a long and erudite protest to the new law which, if he chose, Marshall could have used as a model for a demurral on solid constitutional grounds (Ackerman, pp. 276–97). Marshall, however, was not in the least interested in raising constitutional issues that not only would be ignored by Republicans but might also cost him his job.

3 The other combatant was the arch-Republican Matthew Lyon, who had begun the battle by publicly insulting Griswold two weeks earlier. Griswold responded by calling Lyon a coward. Lyon, a notoriously disreputable character, then publicly spit in Griswold's face, earning him the sobriquet of "Spitting Lyon." On February 15, 1798, after Griswold launched his attack without warning, Lyon gathered himself at the water table, then counterattacked with a pair of fire tongs. Griswold pulled the tongs from Lyon's hands and beat him further. Lyon was later expelled from the House and jailed for violating the Sedition Act.

4 Laird sued in federal court because he was a resident of Maryland suing in Virginia.

5 *Annals*, 7th Congress, 2nd Session, p. 427.

6 *Ibid.*, p. 431.

7 *Ibid.*, p. 438.

8 *Ibid.*, p. 32. Harper seems to have dropped out.

9 *Ibid.*, p. 34.

10 *Ibid.*, p. 50.

11 *Ibid.*, pp. 52–77.

12 Of course, historians, including this one, have little choice in the matter. Compare that with, say, the O. J. Simpson case, in which virtually every American had an opportunity to evaluate the defendant, the prosecutors, the defense team, the evidence, the jury, and, therefore, the decision.

13 Since, unlike most Court cases, this was an original action and not an appeal, the justices were, in fact, trial judges. If Marshall had wished, he could have ruled summarily for the plaintiffs since the defendants had not shown up.

14   Moore may have missed either the second day or the first two days (Dewey, p. 98; J. Smith, p. 624).

15   The degree to which historians dance around this obvious contrivance by Lee and Marshall is astonishing. Jean Smith, for example, says simply "Lee chose not to call the chief justice" (p. 316), while Warren and Beveridge ignore the omission entirely.

16   Lincoln, who only became secretary of state when Marshall vacated the office, could not testify as to any other stage in the process. The only issue that mattered to Lee was proving that the commissions had existed in the first place.

17   *United States v. Judge Lawrence*; *United States v. Hopkins*.

18   J. Smith, p. 316.

19   Commenting on the decision, Jean Smith noted: "A less astute, or a more partisan, judge might have ruled for Marbury by default (p. 319).

20   Subsequent to the trial, but before Marshall issued his ruling, Lee presented an affidavit from another clerk at the Department of State, one Hazen Kimball, which stated that he had been present in the offices in March 1801 and had seen the signed and sealed commissions of Marbury and Hooe. Kimball was never formally examined, however (1 Cranch 153).

TWENTY-ONE: SAYING WHAT THE LAW IS

1   Conrad and McMunn's had burned down, and Stelle's had become the justices' new residence.

2   The opinion is in 5 US 137–80.

3   These sections of the opinion are rarely cited, since they were rendered moot when Marshall effectively annulled them when he declared Article 13 of the Judiciary Act of 1789 unconstitutional. The omission is unfortunate, since these tortuous arguments are more important to understanding Marshall's overall strategy than are the meatier sections later in the opinion. *Marbury*'s density is of particular contrast to the simple, straightforward language of *Stuart*.

4   Emphasis added.

TWENTY-TWO: MARGINALIZATION: *STUART*, PICKERING, AND CHASE

1   Beveridge, v. 2, p. 142.

2   *Ibid.*, v. 2, p. 154.

3   J. Smith, p. 325.

4   Dewey, p. 100. The second case was *Stuart v. Laird*, to be discussed below.

5   Quoted in Warren, v. 1, pp. 246–48.

6   Dewey, p. 138.

7   Jefferson wrote in a letter to George Hay in June 1807, during the Burr trial, that Marshall's decision was an "attempt" to gain "control . . . in subversion of the in-

dependence of the Executive and Senate within their peculiar department." Library of Congress, Thomas Jefferson Papers.

8 By far the most rigorous and penetrating analysis of *Stuart* is by Ackerman, who demonstrates that Lee's argument, largely reflective of Marshall's *Marbury* decision, must therefore have been made after the chief justice had finished his reading (pp. 182–88).

9 As Justice Washington had sat on *Talbot v. Seeman.*

10 Ackerman, pp. 187–88.

11 Whether or not Adams had actually become unhinged, High Federalists certainly believed he had.

12 5 US 299.

13 *Ibid.*

14 *Ibid.*, pp. 308–9.

15 *Ibid.*, p. 309.

16 Ackerman notes, "Paterson does not say that the justices could *rightfully* ride circuit, any more than he says that Congress could *rightfully* strip the circuit judges of their commissions." In other words, he adds, "*Marbury* was yesterday, and today is today" (p. 186).

Twenty-Three: What the Law Isn't

1 Levy, *Original Intent*, p. 77.

2 *Ibid.*

3 Clinton, p. 100.

4 Speech to the Federal Judges Association, May 2001. http://www.supremecourtus.gov/publicinfo/speeches/sp_05-08-01.html.

5 Beveridge, v. 3, p. 32.

6 McCloskey, p. 40.

7 5 US 299.

Select Bibliography

Annals of Congress. Washington, D.C.: Gales and Seaton, 1834–1856. http://lcweb2.loc
.gov/ammem/amlaw/lwac.html.
House and Senate Bills and Resolutions. http://lcweb2.loc.gov/ammem/amlaw/lwhbsb.html.
House Journal. Washington, D.C.: U.S. G.P.O. http://lcweb2.loc.gov/ammem/amlaw/
lwhj.html.
Senate Executive Journal. Washington, D.C.: U.S. G.P.O., 1828–. http://lcweb2.loc.gov/
ammem/amlaw/lwej.html.
Senate Journal. Washington, D.C.: U.S. G.P.O. http://lcweb2.loc.gov/ammem/amlaw/lwsj
.html.
United States Statutes at Large. http://lcweb2.loc.gov/ammem/amlaw/lwcat.html#sl.

Ackerman, Bruce. *The Failure of the Founding Fathers: Jefferson, Marshall, and the Rise of
Presidential Democracy.* Cambridge, Massachusetts: The Belknap Press of Harvard
University, 2005.
Adams, William Howard. *Gouverneur Morris: An Independent Life.* New Haven: Yale Uni-
versity Press, 2003.
Amar, Akhil Reed. *America's Constitution: A Biography.* New York: Random House, 2005.
———. *The Bill of Rights: Creation and Reconstruction.* New Haven: Yale University
Press, 1998.
Baker, Leonard. *The Circuit Riding Justices.* Washington, D.C.: Supreme Court Historical
Society, 1977 Yearbook.
Beveridge, Albert J. *The Life of John Marshall.* 4 vols. Boston: Houghton Mifflin, 1916.
Bickford, Charlene Bangs, and Kenneth R. Bowling. *Birth of the Nation: The First Federal
Congress 1789–1791.* Madison, Wisconsin: Madison House, 1989.
Blackstone, William. *Commentaries on the Laws of England.* Oxford: Clarendon Press,
1765–1769.

Bowling, Kenneth R., and Helen E. Veit (eds.). *The Diary of William Maclay and other Notes on Senate Debates: March 4, 1789–March 3, 1791*. Baltimore: Johns Hopkins University Press, 1988.

Casto, William R. *The Supreme Court in the Early Republic: The Chief Justiceships of John Jay and Oliver Ellsworth*. Columbia: University of South Carolina Press, 1995.

Chernow, Ron. *Alexander Hamilton*. New York: Penguin, 2004.

Clinton, Robert Lowry. *Marbury v. Madison and Judicial Review*. Lawrence: University of Kansas Press, 1989.

Dewey, Donald O. *Marshall versus Jefferson: The Political Background of Marbury v. Madison*. New York: Alfred A. Knopf, 1970.

Elkins, Stanley, and Eric McKitrick. *The Age of Federalism: The Early American Republic, 1788–1800*. New York: Oxford University Press, 1996.

Elliot, Jonathan. *The debates in the several state conventions on the adoption of the federal Constitution, as recommended by the general convention at Philadelphia, in 1787*. Washington, D.C.: Constitution Society, 1836.

Ellis, Richard E. *The Jeffersonian Crisis: Courts and Politics in the Young Republic*. New York: Oxford University Press, 1971.

Farrand, Max (ed.). *The Records of the Federal Convention of 1787*. 4 vols. New Haven: Yale University Press, 1937.

Ferling, John. *Adams vs. Jefferson: The Tumultuous Election of 1800*. New York: Oxford University Press, 2004.

Ford, Worthington C. et. al. (eds.). *Journals of the Continental Congress, 1774–1789*. Washington, D.C., 1904–37.

Forte, David. *Marbury's Travails: Federalist Politics and William Marbury's Appointment as Justice of the Peace*. Washington, D.C.: Catholic University Law Review, Winter, 1996.

Goebel, Julius, Jr. *The Oliver Wendell Holmes Devise History of the Supreme Court of the United States: Antecedents and Beginnings to 1801*. New York: Macmillan, 1971.

Grant, James. *John Adams: Party of One*. New York: Farrar, Straus and Giroux, 2005.

Jensen, Merrill. *The New Nation: A History of the United States During Confederation, 1781–1789*. New York: Alfred A. Knopf and Company, 1950.

Kahn, Paul W. *The Reign of Law: Marbury v. Madison and the Construction of America*. New Haven: Yale University Press, 1997.

Ketcham, Ralph. *James Madison: A Biography*. Charlottesville: University Press of Virginia, 1971.

Labunski, Richard. *James Madison and the Struggle for the Bill of Rights*. New York: Oxford University Press, 2006.

Levy, Leonard W. (ed.). *American Constitutional Law: Historical Essays*. New York: Harper and Row, 1966.

———. *Original Intent and the Framers' Constitution*. New York: Macmillan, 1988.

Madison, James; Hamilton, Alexander; Jay, John. *The Federalist or The New Constitution.* New York: The Heritage Press, 1945. Originally published in 1788.

Malone, Dumas. *Jefferson and His Time.* Boston: Little, Brown, 1951.

Marcus, Maeva (ed.). *Origins of the Federal Judiciary: Essays on the Judiciary Act of 1789.* New York: Oxford University Press, 1992.

Marshall, John. *The Events of My Life.* Ann Arbor: The William L. Clements Library, 2001.

McCloskey, Robert G. *The American Supreme Court.* Chicago: University of Chicago Press, 1960.

McDonald, Forrest. *Novus Ordo Seclorum: The Intellectual Origins of the Constitution.* Lawrence: University of Kansas Press, 1985.

———. *E Pluribus Unum: The Formation of the American Republic 1776–1790.* Indianapolis: Liberty Press, 1979.

McMaster, John Bach, and Frederick D. Stone. *Pennsylvania and the Federal Convention, 1787–1788.* Philadelphia: Historical Society of Philadelphia, 1788.

Montesquieu, Baron de (Charles de Secondat). *The Spirit of Laws.* Translated by Thomas Nugent, revised by J. V. Prichard. London: G. Bell & Sons, 1914.

Nelson, William E. *Marbury v. Madsion: The Origins and Legacy of Judicial Review.* Lawrence: University of Kansas Press, 2000.

Rakove, Jack N. *Original Meanings: Politics and Ideas in the Making of the Constitution.* New York: Alfred A. Knopf, 1996.

Ritz, Wilfred J. *Rewriting the History of the Judiciary Act of 1789: Exposing Myths, Challenging Premises, and Using New Evidence.* Norman: University of Oklahoma Press, 1989.

Rosen, Jeffrey. *The Supreme Court: The Personalities and Rivalries That Defined America.* New York: Times Books, 2006.

Rubenfeld, Jed. *Revolution by Judiciary: The Structure of American Constitutional Law.* Cambridge, Massachusetts: Harvard University Press, 2005.

Scalia, Antonin. *A Matter of Interpretation.* Princeton: Princeton University Press, 1997.

Smith, Jean Edward. *John Marshall: Definer of a Nation.* New York: Henry Holt and Company, 1996.

Smith, Paul H., et al. (eds.). *Letters of Delegates to Congress, 1774–1789.* 25 volumes. Washington, D.C.: Library of Congress, 1976–2000.

Stahr, Walter. *John Jay.* New York: Hambledon and London, 2005.

Storing, Herbert J. (ed.). *The Complete Anti-Federalist.* 7 volumes. Chicago: University of Chicago Press, 1981.

Warren, Charles. *The Supreme Court in United States History: 1789 to 1821.* Boston: Little, Brown, and Company, 1922.

INDEX

Note: Page numbers in *italics* indicate photographs.

A Note on the Author

Lawrence Goldstone holds a Ph.D. in American Constitutional Studies and is the author of several highly praised works of narrative history, including *Dark Bargain: Slavery, Profits, and the Struggle for the Constitution* and, with his wife, Nancy, *Out of the Flames* and *The Friar and the Cipher*. He is also the author of the medical mystery *The Anatomy of Deception*. He lives in Connecticut.